# The
# *Accidental*
# Influencer

# The
# *Accidental*
# Influencer

## BELLA YOUNGER

HarperCollins*Publishers*

HarperCollins*Publishers*
1 London Bridge Street
London SE1 9GF

www.harpercollins.co.uk

HarperCollins*Publishers*
1st Floor, Watermarque Building, Ringsend Road
Dublin 4, Ireland

First published by HarperCollins*Publishers* 2021

1 3 5 7 9 10 8 6 4 2

© Bella Younger 2021

Bella Younger asserts the moral right to
be identified as the author of this work

A catalogue record of this book is
available from the British Library

ISBN 978-0-00-840249-5

Printed and bound in Great Britain by
CPI Group (UK) Ltd, Croydon

MIX
Paper from
responsible sources
FSC™ C007454

This book is produced from independently certified FSC™ paper
to ensure responsible forest management.

For more information visit: www.harpercollins.co.uk/green

For Francesca, aka the men in white coats.
I owe you a life.

# Introduction

In a 2019 study* of two thousand 13- to 38-year-old Americans, over half of the respondents said they would become an influencer given the opportunity, and 86 per cent would post sponsored content (known as 'sponcon'). I was one of the lucky few who got that chance, and I'm going to tell you why I wouldn't do it again.

Although I'd never describe myself as an influencer, for the purposes of this book I think it's right to accept that I am – or at least, I was. At my peak, I had almost 150,000 followers and still I acted like the influencer version of that girl who claims they're 'not like other girls' while doing everything that 'other girls' do, including sponcon, personal appearances, gifted stays and press trips. I wanted to be the Instagram cool girl, the renegade who sat on the sidelines, satirising the people who really cared. But I really cared. I cared about Instagram a lot. And much like the cool girl who eats junk food while remaining a size eight, and who loves sports, farts essential oils and is a bit above gossiping, actually, the Instagram cool girl doesn't exist. I thought I could be an influencer without *really* being an influencer. I thought I could have lots of followers without *needing*

---

* https://morningconsult.com/form/influencer-report-engaging-gen-z-and-millennials-download/

followers. I thought I could monetise my account without selling out. I thought that I was different, that I wasn't like other girls. But I was, and that's why I had to stop.

Like a lot of women who grew up in the nineties and the noughties, I was led to believe that I needed to make myself smaller; I was too loud, too emotional, too angry, too big. I drank too much, told too many jokes, knew I was funnier than the boys.

By the time I reached my mid-twenties, I'd had enough. Enough of being presented with new ways to control myself so I could be a nice girl. Enough of being denied opportunities because I didn't fit a specific mould. I was tired of waiting for someone to tell me I was funny. I saw social media as a fast-track to success, and for a while, it was.

# The Origins of Influence

Who was the original influencer? A cursory google assures me that it was Shakespeare, but it could also be Andy Warhol, Nancy Mitford, Princess Margaret or God. It seems ridiculous to compare the people we deem 'influencers' today to people who are undoubtedly icons, but before you could fill your feed with identikit women in luxe athleisure, icons were influencers and they could make anything fly off the shelves.

The first ever #collab was in 1767 between Wedgwood and the Royal family. After Queen Charlotte gave them permission to name their tableware Queen's Ware, their family business turned into a global enterprise, causing Kardashian levels of market domination. No wonder Meghan and Harry left the Royal family. They just wanted to put their faces on their own tea towels. Is that too much to ask?

As influence has evolved, so has the type of person taking advantage of it. Michael Jordan's Nike collaboration was the Yeezy of his day. Elizabeth Hurley's contract with Estée Lauder made her a vintage Kylie Jenner. Celebrity endorsement hasn't ended, but followers are slowly starting to eclipse the value of fame.

When I was at school, there wasn't a single girl who didn't want to be Sienna Miller. She was the face that launched a thousand coin belts and she represented everything I wished I was. Naturally beautiful, effortlessly stylish, going out with actual Jude Law.

Her influence was potent. Almost overnight my all-girls boarding school looked like a Boho episode of *Black Mirror*, where the school becomes populated by blonde, back-brushed clones with bad highlights, wearing fake UGGs, ratty gilets and comically enormous belts.

We could afford to become bargain-bin versions of her with our pocket money. She was the first celebrity who to me seemed within reach. I thought if I met her, we'd definitely be friends. I made it my mission to emulate her casual *je ne sais quois*. Convinced I was only a gypsy skirt away from an 'I woke up like this' nonchalance that could be bought in Portobello Market.

'The less I look like I've tried, the better,' I told myself, before securing a gladiator belt around my pyjama bottoms and heading to the pub.

When binning said ratty gilet years later, my mother remembers that at least it was better than the Paris Hilton phase, during which I committed to a Miss Sixty mini-skirt so short it came with in-built denim knickers.

Teenage girls have always wanted to be just like their favourite celebrities, but without Instagram, we had to settle for scanning the pages of our favourite magazines. I favoured a combination of what I considered to be high and low literature in my adolescence. The high was *Tatler* and the low was *Heat*, ensuring I was drip-fed inspiration from all of my idols, American celebrities with DUIs and nineties' 'It Girls' with coke problems. At my school, girls taking politics A level were allowed a newspaper account to help them stay on top of current affairs. What they hadn't accounted for was that the newsagent didn't know the score, and along with the *FT*, we all signed ourselves up for an annual subscription to *Heat*, *Now*, *Closer* and *Tatler*.

Tara Palmer-Tomkinson, Lady Victoria Hervey, Paris Hilton and Tara Reid were, to me, the original influencers. I would have cut off my hand to go on a night out with these bottle-blonde legends. They were famous for being famous and they gave no fucks. They were privileged and problematic but nobody cared because they looked like so much fun. They told us you could be famous for being gorgeous and a laugh. When I get my braces off and stop looking like Heath Ledger, I thought, I am going to be an It Girl.

My dream encounter with a real-life It Girl came in my twenties, when my friend Liv and I had turned up at her parents' house hungover after a party. Her godfather was coming over and we were told that he had a new girlfriend. We were more than a bit surprised that the girlfriend was Tara Palmer-Tomkinson. I knew by then that when the lights go up in Chinawhite it still has a sticky floor and I was desperate to hear her tales from the tabloid trenches.

'I bet you a tenner I can get her to talk about coke,' I said.

'£20 if you can get her on to her nose.'

When we walked back into the kitchen moaning about our hangovers, it was like a red rag to a bull. Tara was the funniest, most charismatic and most indiscreet person I'd ever met. She immediately launched into tales from her party years, her nose job and the trick she used to play on Prince Charles. As a child, she would mix up a concoction of peanut butter and Nutella, pile it onto the carpet and step on it.

'Charles, look what the corgis have done,' she'd say. Then she'd pick up her shoe and lick it.

She told us that she used to throw bags of cocaine into the air and sniff, and that she always packed her passport on a night out because she never knew where she would end up. Once, she said, she had played a game where she and her friends had spun a globe while blindfolded and had to fly wherever their finger landed. She started coming down in Krakow.

Unfortunately, I was never destined to be an It Girl of Tara's calibre. In the circles I ended up moving in, everyone was far more concerned with wheatgrass than cocaine.

Unsure, insecure teenage girls are the perfect influencees, and although I like to think I've now gone my own way, my taste now still isn't really mine. Today I am wearing bootcut black jeans from Zara, cowboy boots from GANNI and a white shirt with an impossibly large collar that I saw one of the skinny French influencers wearing on Instagram. These women lurk in the background of my every sartorial choice, falsely leading me to believe that with every new Breton top or trench, I too will come closer to becoming thin and French.

Unsurprisingly, the collar doesn't make me look thin or French. Instead, I look like I'm posing for a portrait in sixteenth-century Holland or I'm the ghost of a Victorian child. Later today I will probably do an exercise class in a bid to rail against the will of nature, and because the female body type currently considered acceptable involves abs; I know I will never have abs, no matter how hard I try, but try I must, because the Instagram algorithm tells me that everybody else has them.

This probably all sounds quite depressing. Those of you familiar with my work will know that I did my absolute best to take people out of the cycle of unattainable aspiration we're bombarded with on Instagram, but I'm not immune to influence. The influencers have invaded my sovereignty, and I am cursed to like what they like because you cannot be what you cannot see, and today everyone I can see, is thin and fucking French.

The word 'influencer' in the terms that we've come to understand was added to the dictionary on 9 May 2019. This new breed of influencer fed into our desire to platform people who are 'just like us'. Celebs are no longer just in glossy magazines and on red carpets. They're in our homes, on our televisions and now in our pockets. The most valuable commodity a celebrity can have is 'relatability'. The top ten most successful influencers named in a YouGov poll were mostly 'normal people' like Joe Wicks, Joe Sugg and Mrs Hinch. We're happier to be sold to by people with whom we believe we share common ground.

The efficacy of influencers comes from their ability to make you feel like you could be just like them. You will likely never be as rich or successful as Zoella, but she still wears jumpers from Topshop and uses Rimmel eyeliner. Her success isn't intimidating, but tangible.

I often wonder if I should be resisting influence. To admit to being influenced is to give up the attractive idea that, as individuals or societies, we are entirely self-contained. I've thought about who I might be and what I'd look like without external influence, and I would probably be an agoraphobic swamp demon with a dangerously large collection of fleeces. I'm inherently drawn to things that feel soft. My love of fleece, I assure you, is sovereign.

In Oscar Wilde's *The Picture of Dorian Gray*, Lord Henry says, 'all influence is immoral ... to influence a person is to give him one's own soul. He does not think his natural thoughts, or burn with his natural passions. His virtues are not real to him. His sins, if there are such things as sins, are borrowed.'

When I look at influencers, knowing what I do, I can't help but think that Instagram has sucked the soul out of being sold to. My idols of old were messy, hilarious and iconic. I devoured Tara's satirical, *Sunday Times* column, 'Yah'. I got hammered in the nightclubs they frequented. Tara Palmer-Tomkinson and Darren Day in *I'm a Celebrity Get Me Out of Here* were my Romeo and Juliet. The lives of the influencers I follow now are curated to the point of being mundane. Posey couple shots lead to black-and-white weddings in tasteful gowns made by designer friends. TPT just wanted to be loved. She reminded me of me.

# 200 Followers

It's 2015, and I'm comparing myself to Lena Dunham. Again. It's a Monday morning and I'm hungover and self-flagellating. Lena has become my measuring stick for success or lack thereof, and checking up on her has become a ritual. No matter that she lives in a New York brownstone with her rock star boyfriend while I live in a basement in Hackney with my best friend, Liv.

We're the same age and we're in similar(ish) industries, so I'm using Lena's Instagram account to remind myself of what could have been in another life. I am twenty-seven and slowly accepting that I've left the age where staggering success will see me labelled as an ingénue.

Why does success look so much sweeter before you're twenty-five? I wonder as I shovel Nutella toast into my mouth. People never call you a genius when you make it in your thirties.

I land on a post that Lena's written about her mental health, and how annoying it is when people tell you to exercise. 'It ain't about the ass, it's about the brain. Thank you,' she writes sassily while posing in a sports bra and leggings.

'Another thing we have in common,' I think. We're both scriptwriters in our twenties with depression and anxiety, only difference is Lena's scripts get made and I'm still hanging round television execs hoping my ubiquitous presence is all that's needed for a producer to crack and give me a shot.

It's comforting that she talks so openly about her mental health. I rarely mention mine, except to Liv. She's been through similar issues and she gets it. We are in agreement that Sertraline makes you look and feel like an owl on crack.

'Do I still have red-wine fangs?' I ask her, rubbing my top lip.

'No, but you have Nutella in your hair.'

Starting your week at your lowest ebb doesn't bode well.

'What I wouldn't give for a 3.2-million-dollar book deal,' I daydream while attempting to dry hump my way onto a packed tube. 'I'd probably need millions of Instagram followers first. Or to be family friends with Meryl Streep.'

YouTuber Zoella has just signed a two-book deal with Penguin, in spite of not having shown any previous literary ambitions. I'd tried putting out a couple of vlogs, but I found that it made me feel old and technologically inept. It was also pretty difficult finding time to film with a full-time job.

I was working in television, as a development researcher for the company that makes *MasterChef*. My foot in the door had come unexpectedly, after I'd been made redundant from a job writing product descriptions in a basement below a shop. It was so badly run they kept forgetting to pay me and I once took out a Wonga loan to pay my rent. The day they let me go, the CEO accidentally transferred me £500 that was meant for his wife, sacked me, then asked for it back.

By the time I turned up at a friend's wedding, unemployed and convinced my degree had been a total waste of time, I found myself sat next to a Scot. Meeting another Scot in the wild can go one of two ways for me. I sound distinctly English and my parents are Tories, which tend to be two things that rub Scots up the wrong way. This man and I, however, had history. Derek was from Ayrshire and was the head of

Entertainment Development at the BBC. He told me that my grandfather had been his MP when he was a child, during a teacher's strike. 'You're the reason I can't read or count,' he said, narrowing his eyes before erupting into laughter. 'I'm going to get you a job.' True to his word, Derek called me a couple of days later to ask if I had any experience as a runner on my CV.

'I did a couple of days on shoots when I first graduated,' I lied. I started that week.

When I arrived at the BBC, everyone was aware that I was the boss's pet. I tried to hold my privilege close to my chest but I hadn't a hope. On my first day, Derek announced to the office that his new assistant was 'so posh her grandfather signs the banknotes in Scotland'. I didn't take the job very seriously because I didn't take myself very seriously. And how could I when a producer asked me one Friday afternoon if I could shoot that weekend and I said, 'Yes, my father has an estate in Scotland.' He said, 'I meant, can you use a camera?'

The novelty of working at Television Centre never wore off. Its donut shape meant I could rollerblade from my office to where they used to film *Top of the Pops*. My immediate superior was the glorious Nickie from Birkenhead, a vegetarian who rarely ate vegetables and subsisted on a diet of chips and pink wine. She was perpetually furious, smoked like a chimney and, like me, was going to be a writer. 'I was once asked to write an episode of *Miranda*,' she said.

I was immediately obsessed with her. Together, it was our job to read unsolicited TV ideas sent in from the public and reply with why they were never going to get made. Someone had once written in with the idea for *The Weakest Link*, so we considered each idea seriously, even *Dale's Bales*, a show where Dale Winton rated the nation's haybales out of ten, and *The Only Way is Gareth*, a show in which Gareth Gates and Gareth

Southgate were chained together in a room until one of them either surrendered or died.

I wasn't expected to do any writing, so instead I spent most of my time with Nickie, smoking in the *Blue Peter* garden by Shep's grave. I leaned into my role as office jester, beginning a relentless campaign to be put on the TV. As soon as I got my hands on a BBC email address, I got to spamming. I would email casting teams, comedy commissioners and well-placed co-ordinators asking to buy them coffee and pick their brains. I had written two sitcom pilots. One was called *Totty*, based on the bad behaviour of myself and my schoolfriends, and the other was called *Me and My Housemate, Sue*, which was based on a period where my friend's mum moved into our flatshare after a divorce, so she could get herself back on the dating scene.

I showed them to anyone who would read them, even getting as far as a meeting with someone at BBC Glasgow. I cold-emailed agents, tapped up every contact I could fathom, but everyone was saying the same thing: perform your material first; take a show to Edinburgh; show us what you can do. I was terrified at that thought, so instead I auditioned for reality TV shows, once carrying a plastic shotgun across Hampstead Heath for a show called *Kookyville*. I even appeared in the pilot for a BBC version of what would become *Gogglebox*. I consider it my luckiest break that none of these shows worked out.

I left the BBC when Derek did, no doubt to the relief of everybody there. I was now a development researcher for factual shows, but I couldn't shake the feeling that I was half-way up a ladder I didn't want to climb.

This was how I found myself, one Friday afternoon, secretly writing a comedy show at work that I was planning to take to the Edinburgh Festival.

'Bella,' said my boss, Faye, over the top of her computer. 'Are you busy?'

She knew I wasn't busy. We'd been auditioning potential *MasterChef* contestants in the office and I'd elected myself as taster. I made a habit of electing myself as anything to do with being on telly, just in case I was 'discovered' by one of the office execs, and had spent the last twenty minutes loudly parlaying my inexpert opinion on a contestant's biryani. Last week the head of the company asked Faye if she'd hired me solely as her personal entertainer. I would like to point out that I entertained everyone; I was a job-lot jester that everyone could enjoy. And I wasn't terrible at my job, just easily distracted.

I paused for ten seconds so it looked like I was finishing something important.

'Can you do some research on wellness please? Some girl called Deliciously Ella's got the fastest-selling cookbook in the country and I want to know if we should put her on the telly.'

I had been blissfully unaware of wellness up until that point. As far as I was concerned, wellness was just the opposite of illness, like not having a hangover or a cold. The idea that you could be more well than well had never crossed my mind.

Sure, I knew about diets. I knew that cutting carbs was the fastest way to lose weight and that I should be eating my 5 a day. I'd noticed a recent uptick in my friends going to yoga and buying NutriBullets, but chia seeds and bee pollen were as far from my wheelhouse as barbecued guinea pig. Until that afternoon, I simply did not know they existed.

It soon became clear that middle-class consumers worshipped at wellness's altar, and when wellness is a religion, everyone needs a priest. If Gwyneth Paltrow is wellness's Pope, Deliciously Ella is the Archbishop of Canterbury. Ella had used her new 'lifestyle not diet' to manage a chronic condition called PoTS, which affects the central nervous system. She had written a popular blog about her condition, claiming to be a reformed sugar monster. You can never be too rich or too thin, as the old adage goes, and nobody embodied that ethos to me more than Deliciously Ella. Ella Woodward was model-beautiful, her mother was a Sainsbury and they had a live-in butler and a house on Mustique.

Her blog promised that if you ate like her you could be like her, and her Instagram made her life look pretty amazing. No one ever mentioned that becoming a wellness influencer takes time, effort and funds. No one seemed to care that you can't post a picture of you doing a headstand on a tropical beach without a trip to the tropics. Her feed was full of gushing women admiring her perfect life and thanking her for saving them from their disgusting, sugar-filled lives.

'I'm not going to let some rich stick insect tell me what I can and cannot eat!' I barked at Faye.

'Why, Bella? Does it remind you of school?' Faye loved joking about me being posh. At my boarding school eating disorders were so rife we could have been a feeder school for the Priory. I'd have put money on my peers being into this.

Sure enough, I got stuck into my research and found that Deliciously Ella was not alone. There were reams of these 'wellness warriors' looking to turn me onto their 'lifestyle not diet'. Some claimed to have cured everything from IBS to eczema. One even claimed to have cured her cancer. They were all beautiful, slim and upper-middle class. They reminded me of the popular girls at uni who we called 'the pretty but borings'. I didn't see a huge amount of potential for a TV show. If we gave them a show, we'd be legitimising them.

'I've got an idea for a show,' I said. 'It's called debunk the junk and we'll get them to cook their food for actual doctors and dieticians and tell them it's all a bunch of NutriBullshit.'

Faye rolled her eyes.

'Are you aware that all of these women have eating disorders?' I said.

'You can't be sure of that, just ask yourself whether they'd make good telly.'

I was certain that none of them would make good telly. They might have the enthusiasm of children's television presenters but their food looked revolting, and it didn't contain enough calories to sustain a gnat. They talked about glowing through wan smiles while arranging ingredients in bowls and calling it cooking. They chastised foods they deemed to be 'processed'. All food is processed, I thought to myself. Even stirring is a process.

I'll admit, I am clearly not a doctor and it isn't often I'm one to make armchair diagnoses, but I know what controlled eating looks like. What these women were doing might not have been as damaging as the girls at my school eating cotton wool and drinking bleach, but the mental arithmetic behind it is the same. They legitimised a problematic relationship with food and carried on the toxic message that thinness is aspirational.

My lifestyle kept me reasonably slim, although in less abstemious ways. I'd been living my life as a sufficiently functioning swamp demon for some time powered by wine, fags, Diet Coke and junk. I spent most of my weekend chasing a party, waking for long enough each day to eat a solitary pizza or an entire pot of hummus with a packet of pitta.

The only one of my 5 a day I regularly ingested was the grapes in wine. I was a mess and I knew I had to sort it out before my mother saw me and screamed, but I was living in East London in my twenties and my biggest motivation was fun.

At work I ate the same packed lunch every day, chucking in an obligatory salad leaf and an occasional Calippo to ward off scurvy. Liv couldn't cook and I couldn't be bothered so dinner was often liquid, or made up of two to three components from the M&S party food aisle. Pork in pastry hadn't failed me yet and in the right light I could almost pull off a crop top. Life was good, and it would be all the better when I was a famous comedian.

Motivated more by fun than anything else, I started reading out the wellness witches' Instagram captions to Faye in an exaggerated posh voice. There was a lot of talk about nourishing your body and being blessed. There were also a huge amount of 'puddings' made from vegetables: 'avocado chocolate mousse', 'beetroot and sweet potato brownies'.

'This is ludicrous!' I harrumphed at Faye. 'You should check their porridge against the price of gold.'

'Just think about turning all those followers into viewers,' she replied. My thoughts turned back to Lena, then I fell down a wellness hole.

'What the fuck do they mean by "eat clean"?' I carried on grumbling. 'As if vegetables pulled from the literal mud are cleaner than a Snickers that comes out of a wrapper.'

'Alright, Deliciously Bella, why don't you start your own blog about the merits of drinking for three days straight before nourishing your body with eleven Domino's and a vat of Ben & Jerry's?'

I laughed it off. I already had a personal Instagram account. I'd only posted about seven times. Usually photos of dogs or beaches or my vast collection of Harry Potter socks. I had a couple of hundred followers and averaged around three likes per post. Posting made me feel anxious. I couldn't bring myself to believe that anyone was really interested in my unremarkable life. As a distraction from reading yet another blog post about the benefits of nut butter, I started looking for online wellness parodies. I found a satirical yoga instructor called 'Awaken with JP', but I couldn't find any evidence of women making a joke about wellness.

Maybe it could be funny. I thought. If people liked it, maybe I could persuade them to come and see my Edinburgh show. My only guaranteed audience thus far was my parents and their friends. It might be nice to see some people who weren't wearing red trousers.

I searched the name Deliciously Bella and found the account already existed. A lady in Australia was busy documenting badly lit puddings, so I settled on Deliciously Stella instead. I uploaded a sweaty gym selfie and various photos of me lying prostrate on the sofa. I found a picture where I was covered head to toe in Domino's boxes and smoking a fag. I captioned the photos as if I was a premier wellness guru using all of the wellness warriors' hashtags. That should spice up their explore page, I thought. Then I got back to work.

# Steamed Vaginas and Spiralisers

Well, well, wellness. Where do I start with this matcha-fuelled juggernaut of an industry? When I first found out about it, I thought it had to be a prank, or something for Americans. Why, in a country like the UK, where healthcare is free at the point of service, would you want to be more than well?

Who decided that you could be weller, or the wellest, or that wellness was anything more than not being ill?

I don't want to lay all of the blame at Gwyneth Paltrow's door but when I typed 'wellness' into Google for the first time, her name was everywhere, embedded in the hundreds of thousands of search results like a beautiful Hollywood computer virus. The contents of her website, goop, read like that of a mad aunt who you stopped seeing because she drank her own piss and looked like she'd got lost in a Swedish concept store.

The article titles are so bizarre, it feels like performance art:

'How to cleanse your body with sacred herbs.'

'Can planetary gongs heal your astrological wounds?'

At the time of writing you can buy a 'marine collagen super-powder' for £85 or a tablecloth for $650.

Goop promises to 'nourish the inner aspect'. She claimed to 'just want to find the balance between Tofu and cigarettes', but I was unsure where colonic irrigation fell in that Venn diagram.

On her quest to peddle miracle cures to the white middle-classes, Gwyneth waged war on the vagina, suggesting everything from steaming it with mugwort to shoving an overpriced egg up there to 'balance hormones, regulate menstrual cycles, prevent uterine prolapse and increase bladder control.'

In the end, the egg got her sued and gynaecologists everywhere reminded us that the vagina is nature's self-cleaning oven. As if to prove just how much her yoni appreciated all her unnecessary interventions, Gwyneth went ahead and released a candle that smelled like her vagina. It sold out immediately. Who's laughing now?

In short, wellness is bats, but it's now a one-trillion-dollar industry and has trickled down from La La Land into our everyday lexicon. Its earning power has even outstripped that of Big Pharma. Apparently we're now listening to the most popular girl in the class instead of the teacher.

It appears that wellness is a reaction to some sort of levelled playing field. With most people having ready access to clean water, affordable food and free healthcare, rich people have committed to shelling out huge sums of money to try to cheat death.

The question 'Are you well?' is now as long as a piece of string. Sure, you feel well, but could you be weller? Would you be more well if you'd eaten more chia seeds this morning, or slept in a hyperbaric chamber? Would you be more well if you did more yoga, ate less gluten and bought $1,000 towels from goop?

Wellness is now measured by which multivitamin you take, which gym cult you subscribe to and how willing you are to pretend that spiralised courgettes are a suitable alternative to pasta. Wellness means not eating gluten or dairy. It means mindfulness, headspace, crystals, goop. It means grass-fed, vegan, avocado, seeds. It means spend money, cheat death.

Of course, goop and Gwyneth Paltrow are leading the charge. Gwyneth's abs could sell ice to the Eskimos, which she was almost doing by selling water bottles 'infused with crystals' for $80.

The optimisation of water has got to be one of capitalism's most shocking acts of charlatanism. Smartwater, charcoal water, vitamin water, alkaline water. Now you can be a water connoisseur, you could open a restaurant that serves bliss bowls and mung beans with a lululemon-clad water sommelier. Come to think of it I'm surprised that hasn't happened. Maybe it has in LA.

Alkaline water claims to be able to alter the pH of our bodies, which, if successful, would literally kill us. Our bodies are made up of 87 per cent water. We need it like we need oxygen. It has been here for longer than anything that has lived on this planet, and we, the people of 2020, think it can somehow be improved upon. This is arrogant delusion at its most magnificent. The only thing it is capable of alkalising is our urine. It's the literal definition of flushing money down the drain.

This type of wellness stole yoga from the Indians and gave it to white women with arses like ten-year-old boys. It is powered by consumerism and promises delivery from ageing through £200 face tonic. It is full of empty promises, stretching our gullibility like elastic.

Clean eating was an early off-shoot of the wellness craze that exploded in 2015. Nowhere was this more evident than on Instagram.

I watched friends put their new lifestyle on their credit card, bulk-buy yoga classes they would likely never complete, raid Holland & Barrett for tinctures that would gather dust in neglected bathroom cabinets.

The lists of foods to avoid seemed endless. Healthy food was described as 'clean' and 'guilt free'. I chuckled at the thought of them doing Hail Marys after 'cheat day', when they allowed themselves to eat 'sugar-free' crumble that was packed with maple syrup and fruit. One of which is full of sugar and the other, well, the other just is sugar, so that makes a lot of sense.

Apparently dairy was demonic and poor gluten was the devil himself. Gluten was described as 'toxic', and 'sandpaper for the gut'. As far as I could tell, nobody had a scientific or medical reason for the gluten-hate. There was even something called 'gluten face', which presumably leads to you being deformed by your addiction to toast.

My granny was a coeliac. She literally couldn't eat gluten and it was awful because she loved high tea. Gluten is a protein that holds bread together and makes it spongy, springy and delicious. Granny had to eat bread prescribed to her on the NHS, which was as dense as clay. Why would anyone lucky enough to eat a scone without gastric failure demonise nature's glue?

'She also wasn't small,' I said matter-of-factly to no one in particular. 'Plus, gluten-free produce is often expensive and full of sugar.'

I looked at the recipes on these clean-eaters' websites and added up the cost of the ingredients for a bowl of porridge. The bee pollen alone cost £15.

I watched hours of footage of thin, white, posh women who claimed that spiralised courgette was an excellent alternative to pasta. I tried to imagine who would spend £1,000 on goop towels or drink out of a water bottle charged with crystals. Did I know these people? Did they walk among us? I started to feel concerned that I couldn't do a handstand, and jealous that all these women's lives resembled one long beach holiday.

Since embracing wellness, they all said, they had more energy, their hair was stronger and their eyes were brighter. What I'm sure they really meant is that wellness makes you thin. The nineties and the noughties had been a difficult time to be a woman who struggled with her weight. It was the era of heroin chic, of Diet Coke and fags, of nothing tastes as good as skinny feels. While not healthy in any way, this approach to making yourself smaller was at least honest. Clean eating managed to repackage self-loathing as self-love. By 'counting goodness not calories', the emphasis was on making your body a temple not a nightclub, and losing weight was rarely flat-out mentioned, just implied.

They were walking, talking, breathing examples of society's conflation of beauty and goodness.

'They're gorgeous so they must be right,' was the message being conveyed, and lo and behold we lapped it up, convinced this was not only the best aesthetic choice to be made, but the moral one, too. Clean eating was touted as an act of self-care. The message was that you'll only eat well if you think you're worth it. Like the choice to eat chicken nuggets was a reflection of your low self-esteem.

I would hazard a guess that in 2015 there was not a middle-class white woman in Britain who did not own, or know someone who owned, a spiraliser. Hell, even I owned a spiraliser, a stocking-filler from my mother who'd panic-bought in Lakeland. Carbs without the calories is what it professed to offer, while making food as filling as a bowl of ice. Brownies were filled with sweet potato, flaxseeds were the new flour.

'Eat enough beetroot brownies,' they claimed, 'and you'll forget you even liked real brownies at all!'

You should leave them alone, I thought to myself. They aren't bothering you and if you don't buy into it, that's fine. It isn't harming anyone.

But that wasn't strictly true. It was harming people by ascribing moral value to food. The terms 'guilt free', 'cheat day' and, most irritatingly, 'clean' were everywhere, suggesting that people who weren't subscribing to this 'lifestyle not diet' were eating 'dirty'.

Moralistic language has seeped into the lexicon of gym instructors everywhere, most notably at SoulCycle, where they tell you that 'in a single moment, you can reset your entire life.' It's a scientifically proven fact that exercise is important for maintaining good physical and mental health, but it does not possess divine qualities. Having a toned arse and a frequent endorphin buzz does not make you a better person, even if you did 'show up for yourself today'.

My biggest qualm with clean eating and wellness was that it is expensive and time-consuming. Life is hard enough without having to labour over the virtue of everything you eat. But the point was that these women's lives were not hard. Like myself, they were privately educated and well-off, a lot of them were bankrolled by a parent or spouse. Most importantly, these people had time to boil their bones and soak their oats, and money to buy their spurious dusts. It's all very well to claim that porridge is a simple food, but when it has twenty toppings and they all cost at least six quid each you're looking at a mighty boujee breakfast.

I developed a taste for a very niche type of schadenfreude. I delighted in news that a wellness blogger had been pictured eating sticky toffee pudding in a restaurant or that someone with their own range of spiralisers was hiding a secret, sordid coke problem. I didn't need to look far to find the stories, people were all too thrilled to snitch on these perfect princesses. A man once approached me on a train, claiming to be Deliciously Ella's former private chef. He told me that the whole family ate sweets by the bucket load. Another time a friend sent me a video of her eating cake in a restaurant. I don't know what they thought I would do with the information. I had decided it would be classier not to talk about Ella in the press. She had liked a couple of my photos, which I screenshotted so that I had my receipts and continued to say as little as possible. I had heard from mutual friends that she wasn't a fan of the account, and that she categorically did not find it funny. I was surprised by this. The account could hardly be described as cruel, and every time I did an interview I wanged on about how much I respected her as a businesswoman. I do respect her as a businesswoman, but as a person with a sense of humour, she needed some work.

At its worst, wellness can give people false confidence that they are above illness, or even that they can cure it. In 2015 a blogger known as the Food Babe was found to have fabricated a cancer diagnosis so that she could claim to have 'cured' herself through wellness.

When the coronavirus pandemic hit, a friend (who I love and respect very much) said that he didn't think he would get it because he takes so many vitamins. I subsequently gave it to him, a fact of which I am not proud but could not have been avoided after he gave me a much-needed hug. The arrival of an untreatable virus we knew nothing about brought wellness into sharp perspective. No amount of yoga, tinctures or immune-boosting Mylk could stop it in its tracks. Fit and healthy people lost their lives, but the wellness illusion only gathered steam.

Elle Macpherson recommended taking 'immune boosting' powdered plum (£85), a US website called The Beet suggested eating red peppers to 'pump up skin and boost immunity', because god knows you'll want good skin on your deathbed. The same site suggests that the optimum amount of garlic to eat in a day is 'more than most of us can fathom'.

In 2019, a gynaecologist's tweets went viral after she pleaded with women to please not put garlic into their vaginas to treat yeast infections, after a YouTube video suggesting it was watched 2.5 million times.

Here lies the crux of my real issue with wellness. It is completely and entirely unregulated and anyone with a following can say anything. This is especially dangerous if the person suggesting whatever woeful remedy they've dreamed up is conventionally beautiful, or rich, or has an aspirational lifestyle. We as humans are desperate to better ourselves, to bring meaning to our lives, to live our best lives.

It's tempting to believe that if you eat, drink, sleep and vaginal steam like a movie star or a millionaire maybe you could live like one. But mung beans won't get you a butler or better bone structure.

From where I was sitting, wellness was so much more about how you look than how you feel. Looking well means looking slim. It means glowing. It means looking like you spend a lot of money on supplements, when nine times out of ten it's Botox. It means spend more, feel smug, post about it, repeat.

# 10,000 Followers

People always ask me if I bought followers, and I'm aware that it seems inconceivable that the account grew so quickly, but within a couple of months I had 10,000 followers, interest from newspapers and was about to head up to Edinburgh to perform my first show.

I'd showed Faye my new Instagram account after a couple of days.

'This,' she said, 'is hilarious.'

I'd already got some strangers following me, and I'd seen that a friend of a friend had posted about me on Facebook.

'That,' I said smugly, pointing at my phone, 'is someone I don't know.'

'But I thought you knew everyone?' she teased. The office seemed to think I was like a public-school Kevin Bacon and could be traced to anyone with a double-barrelled surname. In reality, my brain functions like an address book. I'm brilliant with faces and names and, somewhat disconcertingly, could tell you the dating history of most people I've met.

'Who else have you shown?' she asked with glee.

The truth was that I hadn't shown anyone yet. I'd been using all the same hashtags as the wellness gurus and people must have been accidentally directed to my page. The photos all had over ten likes and someone had left a cry laughing emoji under the Domino's picture.

'Bella! You have a real-life fan!'

Bolstered by Faye's reaction and intrigued by how simple it had been to get my content in front of an audience, I screenshotted the account and sent it to some friends to gauge whether or not it was funny.

My friend Archie was the quickest to reply: 'You will never get a boyfriend again.'

I can't pretend that being openly vile on Instagram wasn't nerve-wracking. I wasn't so self-assured that looking disgusting didn't matter to me. It was a classic case of fake it till you make it. One of my favourite quotes to reference at speaking events was from Amy Poehler, who said that 'vanity is the death of comedy'. I realise now that I was interpreting it the wrong way: I was using comedy to kill my vanity, and it was working.

The name change proved to be unexpectedly fortuitous. A different name meant that the account belonged to a different person. I may have been embarrassed to smear barbecue sauce on my face for a gag, but Stella wasn't. Stella didn't care about her weight or what other people thought. All she cared about was eating snacks, drinking beers and having a laugh. She had no shame and I had so much. Being her was incredible.

I quickly worked out that the best way to get noticed on Instagram was to comment on other people's photos. For professionals, this is known as community management, for me it was cyber social climbing. Every time I commented on a famous person's picture they would see my handle. The beauty of the name Deliciously Stella was that as Deliciously Ella's career continued to skyrocket, my career began to slowly gather pace. You are only as good as your last picture, and I realised people reacted best to images that directly parodied other people's content. A packet of strawberry laces – unremarkable. A packet of strawberry laces coming out of a spiraliser while I smiled manically in a Breton top? Gold.

Because I was playing a character I felt no shame in commenting on every account I could. I was gaining roughly 100 followers a day. Faye banned me from looking at my phone in office hours. I greedily watched the number go up. I thought less and less about what the account could do for my Edinburgh show and more about what it could do for me. The account started growing through word of mouth and I researched each follower meticulously. Every day I edged closer to fame.

'A journalist is following me!'

'Prince George's godfather!'

'A fucking celebrity chef!'

Faye alerted me to the last one.

'Bella. She's been into the office. She's actually a big deal.'

I was pulled into a meeting with the company CEO to make sure I wasn't going to upset any potential talent. Faye encouraged me to keep going. After all, it had been her idea.

'I can't believe people love it this much. Is it even that funny?'

Within five weeks I had almost 1,000 followers. A week later, it was confirmed that people very much thought that it was that funny.

A friend forwarded me a message from her mum: 'You didn't tell me Bella was going to be in *Grazia*?!'

I screamed and dropped my phone. 'Faye! Stella's in bloody *Grazia*!'

'Go and buy it now!' she replied.

I pelted out of the door and into Sainsbury's, shaking as I rifled through *Grazia* in the queue. There it was, clear as day, a tiny corner in an article on fad diets that described me as hilarious. They had printed a quote that I had stolen from somewhere else, but that didn't matter. They had cited @deliciouslystella. I was famous.

For the rest of the day I was ecstatic. This was the most exciting thing that had ever happened to me.

'Do you think I'll get recognised on the tube?' I asked Faye, who had rightly confiscated and hidden the copy of *Grazia* to try to encourage me to do some work.

'Bella, there isn't even a picture of you in the magazine. Please get back to work. We're interviewing a ten-year-old with a column in *Tatler* about eating out in Soho.'

Of course, how could I forget? I may have had two lines written about me in *Grazia* but this girl had a column and she was only a third of my age. Her father was a famous DJ and she lived above the smoking area of the Groucho. I thought about asking her to mention me to *Tatler* but knew that Faye would kill me.

We were developing a show called *Dinky Diners* where we sent child food critics to review Michelin-starred restaurants. My job was to go to their houses with adult foods and see if they did indeed have sophisticated palates and not just pushy parents. Most of our applications came from stage schools and more than one child had gagged their way through a spoonful of olive tapenade while their parents shot daggers at them across the room.

Since the *Grazia* article, I'd jumped by almost a thousand followers and had entered into a passionate relationship with my mobile phone. I was head over heels. The more followers I got, the better I felt. I couldn't stand to be apart from my phone. Every notification made my heart soar. I stroked it maniacally, refreshing constantly. Faye threatened to lock it in a box.

I arrived at work early to assist on my next *Dinky Diners* shoot. The director and I were testing a potential child food critic with a pot of gentleman's relish.

Faye stared me down with an already cocked eyebrow.

'I need your phone to be on aeroplane mode for the whole shoot today. Bex needs your full attention, so no Instagram.'

I reluctantly agreed to turn it off as soon as we got there. Then as I was leaving the office, Davina McCall tweeted about my account. Faye's head was in her hands.

'I'll turn it off, I promise!' I squealed, hyperventilating while I piled kit into the car. When we got to the house Bex gave me five minutes to compose myself before I went in. I turned my phone on silent so I could feel the notifications in my back pocket. Validation buzzed in my buttocks and after two agonising hours with a child who refused to eat anything bar a packet of Pom-Bears I exploded onto the street outside to check my phone.

'SHE'S TWEETED ABOUT MY EDINBURGH SHOW!' I screamed at the director. It was true. Davina McCall had tweeted my Edinburgh poster. Fuck, I thought. This show had better be good. After Davina came Gizzi Erskine, and after Gizzi came Jamie Oliver. Actual celebrities were tweeting about me.

Thus far in life my only encounters with celebrities had been at work, when I'd been making them cups of tea, or with Lizo from *Newsround*, who spent a lot of the noughties hanging out in bars on the King's Road.

A columnist from the *Independent* asked for an interview and the debrief commissioned me to write my first ever published article.

I spent a whole afternoon deliberating over what to write. I could tell that Faye was exasperated.

'What do you think they want me to write? Should I write it as Bella or Stella?'

I was in two minds. Part of me yearned to write a think piece about the dangers of clean eating and the unrealistic expectations wellness witches were setting for normal women, the other part of me wanted to make people laugh.

'Bella,' said Faye. 'I thought you wanted to be a comedian, not an activist.'

'I do.'

'Then don't sign up to be a role model.'

I was finally going to be a writer. I couldn't believe it. It was all I'd ever wanted and it suddenly seemed so easy. I had previously thought my failure to be published was due to a lack of talent or a lack of access to nepotism. Now I knew it was down to a lack of followers. Who needs internships when you have Instagram?

I spent the weekend writing a wellness guide as Deliciously Stella. If this is the best thing to come out of this experience, I thought. It's been worth it.

Determined to take my brush with fame as far as it could go, I set to work growing the account. I made sure to post every day, carefully researching popular hashtags and strategically following and engaging with people with proximity to celebrities. I worked out that if a celeb saw me interacting with one of their friends, they'd likely look at my account. I had become skilled in the art of the Instagram booby trap.

Occasionally I would strike gold, pleasing the algorithm so much with my combination of keywords that I'd end up on the discover page (joining a specially curated selection of what Instagram thought its users might want to see each day), a sure-fire way to snap up followers. People always ask me if I bought followers, but I wouldn't have known how to.

Instead, I owe it all to my picture of avocado toast. For 2015 was the year avocado toast went mainstream. Of course, it remains a cultural cipher. How, when and where we consume avotoast says something about where the world is headed. That's just the way it is. First it became a cliché of hipsterdom, then the talisman for millennial malaise. To some it was the perfect way to load up on 'good fats', for others it was the reason young people couldn't buy houses, and for bloggers that green and yellow just popped under a crema filter. On any given day in 2015, 70 per cent of Instagram squares were filled with avocado on toast. On one day so was mine: a picture of Haribo eggs on avocado toast is what brought me to the masses. I repeated it in various guises again and again. On the tenth anniversary of Deliciously Stella's birth I will photograph Kinder eggs on avocado toast and wait for the crowd to go wild.

I was careful to make sure that my content was satirical, but also silly enough never to be unkind. I started gaining a following from the very wellness women I was poking fun at. They were desperate to prove that you can make brownies out of vegetables and dust and still have a sense of humour. Knowing they found something funny that wasn't salad made me more confident. Finally, I was offered a proper olive branch. A leading clean-eater invited me to her book launch in Fortnum & Mason. She had 40,000 followers, looked like a supermodel and was about to publish a book. Three things that made the situation quite intimidating. I begged Faye to come with me.

'What if it's a trap?' I said. 'What if Deliciously Ella's there and they just want to tell me I'm a mean bitch who's jealous because she's shit at yoga?'

'Are you jealous because you're shit at yoga?'

'No. I mean, I wouldn't say no to being able to do a head-stand, but I don't want to go to a party where I don't know anyone like a fame-hungry loon.'

'You are a fame-hungry loon. You have a comedy show to promote. How is that going, by the way?'

The Edinburgh show was going OK. I'd performed a couple of previews for friends in pub function rooms and I was pretty sure it would be ready for August. My only concern was that I'd been writing the show for months and it had absolutely noth-ing to do with Deliciously Stella.

'Stop being a baby. Go to the party and talk about yourself, you love that. I'm sure someone will think you're funny. And if nobody knows who you are you can just eat some free food and leave.'

I was convinced that nobody would know who I was. I arrived and gave my name to the PR apologetically. To my great surprise I was immediately swept through the party in the direction of the clean-eater. I paused to grab a canapé on the way over and arrived with my mouth full and twisted into a grimace.

'Aren't they good?' she said. 'They're made out of prunes and cashew foam.'

Grateful that my mouth was too full to reply, I tried not to gag while she told me how funny she thought my account was. I was surprised to find that I really liked her. She was funny and down to earth. I thought that in a world where I wasn't parodying her, perhaps we could have been friends. We were joined by an American yogi who starred in the reality show *Ladies of London*. Her daughter was starting at Edinburgh University and she said she'd come and see my comedy show.

'What are you gonna do? Are you gonna cook food on stage?'

'Oh no,' I said. 'The show isn't about Deliciously Stella.'

She gently grabbed my arm.

'Honey,' she said. 'You need to give the people what they want.'

I rolled into work the next day, anxious and hungover. 'I have to rewrite my Edinburgh show,' I said with my head in my hands. 'I have to give the people what they want.'

Faye rolled an exercise ball around to sit next to me at my desk. 'Listen,' she said. 'You have written a brilliant, political, clever show that is true to what you want to say about yourself. You don't owe anyone anything. You're also not that famous, so you need to calm down.'

I don't know what I was more nervous about, doing a show as Bella, or not doing a show as Stella.

Having 10,000 followers felt very famous to me. That was 10,000 people who might come to the show and be bitterly disappointed. I'd been planning it for months, before Stella was even a twinkle in my eye. It was about working in left-wing media when you come from a Scottish Tory dynasty. The poster read: 'from the school that brought you Miranda Hart, Clare Balding and Kate Middleton.' My press release promised stories about Prince Harry's arse. Whether or not I could deliver on those without being super-injunctioned, I was yet to find out.

'Do you think there's at least a bit of crossover between the show and Stella? I talk about food a bit, mainly because nobody at boarding school really ate any, but that's kind of on-brand.'

Faye could see I was clutching at straws.

'You don't know that any of your followers are going to Edinburgh. Plus your show is free, so they're hardly going to ask for their money back.'

She was right. I was performing a show on the Free Fringe, which I thought would mean little-to-no financial risk. What I hadn't taken into account was that I had written a show entirely dependent on the use of a projector, which I would have to buy, and that flyers, accommodation and PR could all potentially bankrupt me.

Faye seemed to read my mind.

'You know if you get enough followers you can make money from Instagram. Lots of people are working with brands. They make a killing.'

As far as I could tell, brands only worked with singers, actors and Kardashians. Why would they want to work with me? I wasn't anyone important.

'Not true,' said Faye. 'I met a chef last week who was sponsored by Le Creuset. You should at least be able to get some free Haribo.'

I did not get any free Haribo, but I was happy to live on the attention alone. My account was growing steadily and my posts were getting funnier. Coming up with post ideas turned into a sort of party piece. I started crowdsourcing jokes from friends and acquaintances, building up a reserve in case I woke up one day with nothing amusing to say.

I had always been nervous about going to Edinburgh. In many ways it was an insane thing to do. I had only ever performed comedy before for five minutes, and I'd done that a total of seven times. Now I'd written an hour-long show that I had to perform every night for the whole month of August.

I'd done it because I wanted to be remembered for something more than being fun at parties. And because a man I dated who wore leggings to festivals said he wasn't sure I was funny. Now I'd managed to prove that I was funny just by being witty on Instagram, doing a real-life stand-up comedy show felt like a lot of unnecessary hard work.

'Why don't I wait until next year and just do a Stella show?' I asked my mum. I was planning to live with her and my dad while I did the show, in the countryside outside Edinburgh.

'Haven't you paid the deposit? And written the show? And bought a projector and all of your posters? Also don't forget you've already agreed to sublet your room in London to that hippie.'

'Yes, but you know what the Fringe is like. Nobody will notice if I'm not there.'

'I shall notice you're not there. I've told all my friends and they're very excited. Plus I've already started thinking about what I'm going to feed you.'

My mum, a feeder with a deep freeze that could comfortably hide six bodies, has never made a disappointing meal. Moving home for the month meant never eating the same meal twice, and a window of opportunity for my mother to try to fatten me up.

Mum had bought Deliciously Ella's book and insisted it wasn't all bad, once you 'adapted' the recipes to include lashings of butter and cream.

'The problem is she's afraid of seasoning,' she said.

'The problem is that she cannot cook.'

'Listen, if you're worried you're not going to be very good just think of that penis-y puppet thing you went to. That show completely sold out and it damn near scarred you for life.'

I had attended the Fringe in some capacity every year since I could remember. It was my mum's preferred time of year for me to have friends to stay in the holidays as we'd always be out of the house. She'd book back-to-back shows, drop us off in town and come and pick us up, tipsy on cider we'd smuggled into performances. Once, when I was fourteen, she treated me to something more 'adult'. It was called 'puppetry of the penis' and as far as my mum could tell from the show description it involved people making penis shapes out of objects behind a screen. Stranger things have happened at the Fringe. Once we'd settled into our seats, two naked men walked onto the stage and, just like the title had promised, started to make puppets, out of their penises. The show's crescendo came when one man stood on a skateboard with his scrotum stretched into a sail, while the other helicoptered his own cock to create a breeze to wheel his comrade off stage. Mum received our news with a deadpan: 'fuck'. Then she booked us tickets to see the Lady Boys of Bangkok.

'Yes,' I say. 'If in doubt I'll just strip.'

'Lovely, darling. For your packed lunch in August, do you like orzo?'

'The Greek liqueur?'

'No, the pasta.'

'Whatever you want, Mum. Let's work it out closer to the time.'

I decided to approach Edinburgh like someone would a marathon. It would be hard. I would have to train, but at the end everybody would congratulate me and I'd get to bring it up at dinner parties forever more. If the people wanted Stella, I wasn't ready to give her to them. For now, Bella was all I had.

The week before the show I felt like I had snakes for guts. There was no way I was going to pull this off. I had managed to secure only one feeble bit of press about the show, in the Diary section of *The Herald* newspaper. It had been written by a contemporary of my politician grandfather. I didn't see it appealing to my target demographic.

I spent most of the lead-up fantasising about natural disasters that would cause the festival to be cancelled. Where was coronavirus in 2015? If I'd known all I had to do was eat a bat I'd have headed straight to Wuhan. In all honesty, I wouldn't have been able to eat a bat. I was so nervous the only thing I could get down me was Mum's homemade granola bars, which she made me keep in my pockets at all times.

Sensing an oncoming meltdown, Mum sent me to go and see her friend Susannah, a cranial osteopath whom my siblings call 'the witch' because she decorates her house with a lot of drapes and once claimed to have moved my womb. She hovered her fingers over me for an hour and charged me £60, before telling me that my happy place was the sea and it might be a good idea to go to the beach.

I sat on the sand with my sister and stared at the swirling foam.

'Do you think I should get in?'

'Nah.'

'Would it be funny for Deliciously Stella?'

She paused for thought as a biting gust of wind almost blew us off the dunes.

'I don't think Stella likes the sea.'

My sister Francesca was on her university summer holidays and had agreed to help me distribute flyers, running up to strangers on the Royal Mile and begging people to make the twenty-minute trek to see my show. The day before my first show we ran around Edinburgh armed with Blu-Tack, covering other posters with our own. A journalist sent me a direct message on Instagram.

'Urgent. What's your phone number?' She called me straight away and said she wanted to speak to me for the *Evening Standard* but we'd need to do the interview via email within the hour.

'Francesca. How far away are we from the car?' It was a forty-minute drive back to my parents' house. We'd never make it. My phone was low on battery and every internet café was heaving with Fringe tourists. I called my dad.

'Dad. It's an emergency. I need to borrow a meeting room in your office.'

'Um. OK. Does this really constitute an emergency?'

'I need somewhere quiet with a computer to do an interview for THE *EVENING STANDARD*. My show depends on it!'

Dad was miffed because I wouldn't let him come and see the show. I thought it would make me unnecessarily nervous and I wasn't sure he'd love all of the material. I'd already had to run one of the jokes by my sister, Beana.

Beana, who was working as a management consultant in London, hadn't had the good fortune of hearing the whole show before it started. So she phoned and pleaded with me to tell her what was in it. She was bringing her boyfriend and some friends to Edinburgh for moral support and she needed to know if there was anything that might cause him to run a mile.

'I might mention that you fancy Dad,' I confessed.

'For fuck's sake!' She screamed. 'Anything but that. Anything but that stupid joke.'

My sister and I annoy each other a lot, but nothing tickles me more than suggesting that she's flirting with my father. I know it's revolting and you're probably thinking I'm truly fucked up, but when your sister walks downstairs in her pyjama shorts, there's really nothing funnier than shouting: 'For God's sake, Beana! Dad is a married man. Mum is right here!'

'Ugh,' she conceded. 'Fine. At least I don't have to flyer for you. But if Dom dumps me I will set you on fire.'

I decided it was best that Dad didn't know about this particular joke. Especially now that I needed his office.

'Any chance you could set me up with a meeting room in about fifteen minutes? And could you also get me a coffee and a sandwich from Pret?'

I arrived at my father's office with a bag full of posters and was ushered past his colleagues into a conference room.

'I need the room back in forty-five minutes,' he said, handing me a flat white and a *jambon beurre*. I opened up the questions from the journalist and got to work on selling myself as a woman of the people. The filthy antidote to the cult of 'eat clean'.

'Most of us can't squeeze in a delicious organic breakfast in Neal's Yard at 11am,' I said. 'Some of us are having a packet of Hula Hoops and a Sprite on the morning commute because we drank too much the night before and are going to be chained to our desks for the next twelve hours.'

I defended myself against the accusation that I was a troll: 'I don't think Stella would be as popular if all I did was comment things like "Get in a bloody salad spinner you wet lettuce and have a bloody Snickers while you're in there".'

I remembered to include a concessionary line about how much I admired wellness's support for female entrepreneurship, but, most importantly, I absolutely hammered the details of my completely unrelated Edinburgh show.

The day before the show we arranged my flyers over my naked body and posted about the show on Instagram. Combined with what turned out to be a very successful puff piece in the *Evening Standard*, I managed to draw in an audience.

'If I told you three months ago that the *Evening Standard* would write about your Edinburgh show, would you have believed me?' asked my friend Emily, who I had roped in to help set up alongside my sister Francesca.

'Absolutely not.'

'What if I told you you'd have almost 10,000 Instagram followers?'

'Definitely not.'

'What if …'

Emily was interrupted when a girl who'd been staring at me walked straight over. I frantically racked my brain, reaching for her name. How did I know her? Were we at primary school together? What was her fucking name?!

'Excuse me,' she said. 'Are you Deliciously Stella?'

Emily roared from across the street, terrifying a nearby mime group. 'I'm sorry. But did you just celebrity spot my friend?!'

The girl looked mortified. I looked mortified. 'Thank you?' I said.

My sister looked on in horror. 'You know you've just created a monster.'

I spent the rest of the day on cloud nine. I loved Instagram. Social media was the future. It didn't matter how my show went, I was Deliciously Stella. An official celebrity. Sure, nobody knew my real name, or anything about me other than that I loved junk food and hated yoga. In my head I was basically Jennifer Aniston. I felt an immediate urge to go to Pret and see if I could get a free coffee. Instead we went and ate the packed lunch my mum had made us in a park. I was terrified that I was starting to come down with a cold and Mum had reminded me that you feed a cold and starve a fever. My packed lunch included pâté, vegetarian terrine, some sort of chicken dish, a packet of Wotsits and two Tunnock's Caramel Wafers.

People say that the Fringe is like summer camp, and it's true. In Edinburgh in August there are a lot of comedians away from home, together in one place. They were all drinking together, sleeping together, celebrating and commiserating together and I was somewhere else. I could say that I felt distant because I was staying with my parents, because I couldn't go out drinking, because I had to drive to the countryside, that I wasn't meeting people because I hadn't spent enough time on the open-mic circuit. But the truth is that I spent the entire month on Instagram.

After the *Standard* piece came out, the narrative around me shifted. I wasn't just a comedian who was good at puns, I was standing up to the unrealistic standards set by 'perfect' women on Instagram.

Suddenly, I was 'the next big thing'. A journalist from the *Daily Mail* announced that I was 'the new Lena Dunham': 'You're exactly what women need right now. You just say it like it is,' they said.

I'd be lying if I said that I didn't find these comparisons extremely flattering. I was reminded of the opening scene of Lena Dunham's sitcom, *Girls*, where she tells her parents that she thinks she might be 'the voice of her generation', or at least a voice of a generation.

Was I sure of what I stood for at twenty-seven? Were all my political opinions fully formed? I got the impression that when I spoke, it wouldn't just be for myself, it would be for 'millennial women'. I didn't want to misrepresent myself or say the wrong thing or, worse, completely scupper my chances of being 'the next big thing'.

'Just try not to be too political,' said Emily, knowing full well this was an impossibility.

I am by nature utterly non-confrontational on a micro scale. If you borrow my top and return it covered in fag burns you'll probably get away with it. I just don't like an argument. But when it comes to injustice on a bigger scale, I am a tyrant.

My family are very traditional and I grew up in Scotland surrounded by golf courses with all-male memberships. When I was sixteen I begged my father to smuggle me into Muirfield, where they host the Open, so I could rip open my t-shirt like the hulk and show all the members my tits. I love nothing more than debating a posh old man, and at my all-girls school I was taught politics separately from my classmates because my passion for feminism was considered disruptive.

I told my friends, 'These people are setting unrealistic standards for normal women, making us buy shit we don't need and damaging our mental health. I am not going to use this platform to only make jokes about sweets.'

I finally had the platform I'd always craved, and I was going to use it to make a difference.

By the time an agent got in touch to say she was coming to see the show, I was worried she wouldn't be able to get in. I reserved her a seat in the front row, but it was a Saturday, so my feeble 'reserved' sign was trampled onto the beer-soaked carpet. I peeked outside before heading off to change and saw what looked like a Countryside Alliance march queueing to get into the pub. My parents' friends had finally made it.

'I hope the bar stocks some half-decent wine,' I said to my sister.

'I'll go upstairs and tell them to order gin.'

My venue was packed with people who were so surprised to
see me on a stage I could have farted and got a standing ovation.
It was one of the best performances of my life. Halfway through
the show I took off a tweed waistcoat to reveal a frontless
swimming costume. My dad's best friend turned puce and
almost fell off his chair.

There were so many people there that the agent – denied
her 'reserved' seat – was standing at the back, and when I finally
delivered my closing line, everyone was on their feet. The dads
were braying and hurling twenties into my bucket. For the first
time I thought a comedy career might not be that strange an
idea.

The agent's name was Caroline and we were the same age.
We'd met a couple of years earlier when I'd come to Edinburgh
as a comedy scout for the BBC. She asked to meet me in a
Turkish café where we drank tea and caught up on how our
festivals were going. Maybe she really did just want to catch up.

I prepared myself for rejection, then she asked if she could
represent me. I had been told under no circumstances to go
with the first person who asks, so I oohed and ahhed awkwardly
while I texted my sister under the table:

'SHE WANTS TO BE MY AGENT!'

I have a tendency to get over-excited and say yes to things
without much thought, so I emailed my only friend who had
experience with agents. He said: 'It doesn't matter what agency
you go with, as long as you get on with the person who's repre-
senting you.' I instinctively knew that going with Caroline was
the right choice. I was three weeks into my first comedy run
and I had an agent. Things were definitely on the right track.

My new agent invited me to a showbiz party thrown by the
cable channel Dave in a church in Leith. The end of the Fringe
run starts to bleed into the Edinburgh Television Festival, so the
city is filled with TV's decision makers and 50 per cent more

cocaine. You could have got high on the air in that church. Agents wheeled around their new signings with rictus gurns and for the first time I felt like I could finally relax. The TV execs felt more like my people than the comedians had all month.

'You know,' they said, 'next year you've got to do a show as Stella.'

# Bella vs Stella

'What young girls don't realise is that somebody beaming
at you on a book is not beautiful, thin and rich because
she eats organically farmed seeds. She's beautiful, thin
and rich because her parents are beautiful, thin and rich.
It's called genetics, and the class system.
– Me, *Suitcase* magazine

It only took a couple of months to do exactly what Faye warned
me not to. I self-styled myself as an activist, decided to be a role
model, and I made it political.

'You are aware that you also possess good genes and benefit
from the class system, aren't you, darling?' asked my mum.

'Of course. But I'm not saying my privilege has anything to
do with how many lentils I eat, so I'm being honest.'

'You don't honestly eat Liquorice Allsorts for breakfast like
you do on your account either.'

'I know. But everybody knows I'm playing a character.'

She wasn't convinced. It wasn't my intention to paint myself
as an everywoman. I knew you could only be an everywoman
for as long as they'd let you. Lena Dunham had been an everywoman until people changed their minds and started talking
about her artist parents. Phoebe Waller-Bridge was an everywoman until people worked out she was related to a baronet.

Like me, these women's privileges were hiding in plain sight. They just had to wait until somebody was ready to deploy them against them.

I decided that the best way forward was to be completely honest about who I was. Jack Whitehall is very successful because of his poshness. Why couldn't it be the same for me? What I had failed to realise was that all platformed women must represent every woman, and with Instagram only showing people my face in silent squares, people were able to project their own fantasy about who I really was.

In the pursuit of 'keeping it real', in interviews I readily offered my back story, but it was hardly ever mentioned. A woman from the *Hackney Gazette* almost screamed when I picked up the phone, before stuttering: 'I read that you were from Edinburgh and you lived in Hackney?! This isn't what I was expecting at all.'

At best it felt like my background didn't fit who people wanted me to be, at worst it felt like they were disappointed. One article defected from the norm, mentioning the school I went to and that my grandfather had been an eighties' politician. A prominent *Guardian* food writer who up until that point had been my champion, tweeted that she was disappointed. She could no longer in good faith support me knowing who he was.

After that, I decided it was better to hide it. My friends suggested that I might have developed 'a podcast voice'. I hadn't even noticed the de-clipping of my vowels and the dropping of my Ts. Listening back, I can hear myself desperately performing damage control.

'Just one more thing,' a producer would always ask, at the end of an exciting meeting. 'Does your voice always sound like this?' I'd let out a deep, frustrated sigh and reply with a deadpan, 'Of course not. This is just the voice I put on in meetings to put off commissioners and alienate the British public.'

'We'll send you her podcast,' my agent always said. 'She sounds much less posh on that.'

I did sound much less posh on it, or more accurately I didn't sound like myself. I sounded like a drunk *Mary Poppins*-era Dick Van Dyke or a public-school GCSE drama student trying to play Fagin, which I was, or at least had been at some point.

My friends, like my mum, thought I should just be myself, with everything that entails.

'I don't understand why it's suddenly a secret. Your whole first Edinburgh show was about being posh.'

'It isn't a secret. It just isn't something I'm leading with right now.'

Mark Zuckerberg once said that 'having two identities for yourself is an example of a lack of integrity', but people never seemed to doubt the integrity of Deliciously Stella. I was Bella at home and Stella online and everyone knew the difference, or so I thought.

As I started getting more followers, it became increasingly apparent that while I was still Bella, most people thought I was Stella. The first time I realised that my online and offline self had become one was in a meeting with a production company. Two ecstatic producers had ushered me into a meeting room, giggling like schoolgirls.

'We've got a surprise for you!' they squealed. 'We've put on a Deliciously Stella spread!'

An anxious runner tottered in with a tray. It was overflowing with confectionery. Haribo fried eggs, fizzy laces and Sprite. A diabetic death at 9am.

'Would you like a coffee or a green juice?' they asked with a nudge and a wink. I reached for the Sprite and laughed.

'You know me so well!'

The Sprite soured as it hit the dregs of that morning's toothpaste.

'We just love you here at *** Pictures because you're so real. You're not like other influencers, you're really authentic.' I washed down an early-morning Haribo egg with another gulp of Sprite.

'Yeah, well, I do love sweets.'

I wasn't lying. I do love sweets. I just don't favour them at 9am, or on toast, on my face, strapped to my abs or forced through a spiraliser. I thought I was making jokes, not providing a commentary on my actual diet or how I lived my life.

'Do you think they really think you eat Haribo eggs on your avocado toast?' my sister asked when I told her.

'I don't know. Yesterday I posted a picture of myself wearing a lasagne sheet I'd poked eye holes in as a face mask. They must think I'm insane.'

She tutted.

'Maybe it's like when you told Mum you loved hippos when you were eight and now every time you go home there's something weird and hippo-themed waiting on your bed.'

'Maybe. I'm at risk of becoming a hippo if this carries on. Last week a male model DM'd me on Instagram while I was on the cross trainer.'

'Yikes.'

'He said: Busted you in the gym. Don't worry. Your secret's safe with me.'

'How fit was he?'

'Very.'

'And you?'

'Looked like a beetroot with gout.'

'Of course. I'll never understand that statistic that claims that one in three couples meet in the gym.'

The blurring line between Stella and Bella was becoming increasingly problematic. I'd noticed myself modifying my behaviour to better fit the habits of my alter ego. It seemed that the world would prefer it if Stella was my true self. It was, after all, her not I who was accruing my current fame.

We had a fair bit of crossover. Stella was anarchic, loved junk food and was done with insufferable women performing beach yoga. So was I, only this wasn't all I was and I was fearing that what made me Bella too was starting to get a bit lost.

Something that will inevitably happen if you become an accidental influencer is that everyone will become obsessed with how 'authentic' or 'real' you are. 'Do you really put Mars Bars in spiralisers/drink wine in the gym/put ketchup on your face?' they will ask.

You will diplomatically say, 'Yes, I have eaten everything that I've posted on my account,' because it's true, you do eat Peperamis sometimes. And people prefer to be sold stuff by people they could be friends with, so it's in your interest not to come across as a faker. Somewhat naively I thought that people took my content with a pinch of salt because it was all jokes, but it turned out a lot of people thought I woke up on a normal day, walked outside and did a dance while shaking a ham which I captioned 'protein shake'.

What people really want to know is how much you live and breathe your 'personal brand'. Your personal brand as an influencer is basically the things that you like, and it can really be anything. The very best influencers have streamlined their personal brands to very specific things, like bird-watching or burgers. They then become very good at selling that specific thing and can make a lot of money. If you're beautiful and thin, congratulations! You can sell anything. Even if it looks like you'd rather die than put it in your mouth.

Stella's personal brand was loving junk food and hating exercise, so I was a very good ambassador for fast-food joints and a not very good one for gyms. The problem with this for me was that I actually moderately liked both junk food and exercise.

'The thing about Deliciously Stella,' people said, 'is that she just doesn't care.'

'She makes me feel so much better about myself.'

I was able to 'satirise the body beautiful', as claimed by the *Daily Mail*, because it was universally accepted that I didn't have or want it. The media painted me as an anti-hero, the only woman brave enough to stick two fingers up to the bloated corpse of diet culture, but I was no stranger to a diet and diet culture was not dead. Clean eating had not killed it by dressing it up as a lifestyle. No number of beautiful, successful plus-size women were going to stop it. Body positivity couldn't stop it, body neutrality couldn't stop it, Dove campaigns couldn't stop it, and I definitely couldn't stop it.

My own history with diets had been a long and torrid affair. Every time I failed at a diet, either through a lack of willpower or having momentarily reached my 'goal', I'd return to my default position, which is that I want to taste everything. My mother thinks it's a delayed reaction to having been a fussy child. I made my friends' parents peel my fish fingers and insisted that I didn't like pasta. Now I love food. I will eat anything apart from something that comes from goats. Goats eat out of bins.

I love trying new food, I love decadent food. I like food that is oozy, tart, rich, crunchy, sloppy, sweet and smooth. I would eat everything all the time if I could, but I've been programmed to deny myself. I know what I have to do to 'pass' as naturally slim. That's what diet culture does.

I've been on a diet since I was ten years old and my matron lined us up outside the san for a weigh-in before sending us out to compare notes. I was a slim, active and unusually heavy child. I don't mean heavy in the way you politely try to describe someone who's fat. I mean heavy. My mother will always claim that I have 'heavy bones', but the truth is that I am an absolute unit. My BMI is in the obese range, my doctors are befuddled. I am 5ft 4 and a size 10 and yet I never weigh less than 12 stone.

When at times I get sad and thin, my body looks like the framework of a marquee. None of the rest of me is big. I have small feet, small hands, incredibly wispy hair and yet, I am convinced that in a car wreck, it would be I who would receive a magical rush of adrenalin, enabling me to lift the car and save my friends.

I was very lucky to go to a school where girls were allowed to bring their pony. I didn't have a pony so I had to borrow one if I wanted to skip games by going for a hack. Asking for permission was incredibly nerve-wracking. I was shy and worried that I wouldn't be considered a good-enough rider for these girls who were so equestrian some resembled horses themselves. On the day of the weigh-in, I awkwardly requested an opportunity to sit on some flea-bitten barrel of a steed and was told, with deadpan delivery, that I was too big.

My mother was also always on a diet. She tried Atkins, Dukan and SlimFast and myriad pyramid schemes. Our larder often stank of cabbage soup and she still pours cream into her coffee, a habit that she picked up from a book called *From Pig to Twig*.

When I asked for endless boxes of Special K to be sent to school to eat instead of meals, she complied. I thought that by summer I'd be laughing in a bright red swimsuit, but I ate them alongside meals and I ballooned. Just because I was always on a diet doesn't mean I was ever any good at them. For me, the Dukan has always been an excuse to eat nothing but cheese.

Of course, now I couldn't care less what number I see on a scale. I'll never be needed on the top of a cheerleading pyramid and I'm far too scarred from Hotdog the pony to become a jockey. The legacy of these years, however, is that I know the absolute bare minimum of effort I need to make if I want to keep my body how I like it. That's how I became the acceptable face of excess.

'How come you're so slim when you eat all this junk?' asked a journalist from the Russian *Metro*.

'You know it wouldn't be funny if you were fat,' stated the *New York Daily News*.

Naively I'd assumed my weight would be left out of this conversation. Of course, it was *de rigueur* for other women in the public eye to be asked about their diets. I want to know what Jennifer Aniston eats because I want to look like her. Hearing that it's mostly apples and almond butter is comforting. It soothes me to know that she suffers. I couldn't imagine that anyone wanted to be like Deliciously Stella, so I was genuinely surprised when people asked for my health and fitness routine.

I had assumed that my deliberate attempts to de-glamourise myself might have made my body invisible, but I appeared to have found a media sweet spot – one where I was neither intimidatingly slim nor accused of encouraging obesity. God forbid a woman who eats junk food should look like she does. Society loves to glamourise the unhealthy and small. We did, after all, name an epidemic of eating disorders 'heroin chic'.

As time passed and the account became more popular, my DMs started to fill with women thanking me for helping them with their body image issues. If I could love myself, they could too. It felt good to help, but I was confused. Was I cheating the system by promoting junk food while maintaining an accepted body type, or was I so #brave for existing in my body that I'd helped women with disordered eating?

I am a cisgender white woman who oscillates between a size 10 and a size 12. A poster girl for the disenfranchised I am not. It's a damning indictment of the perfection required from women on Instagram at the time that my untoned arms were considered revolutionary at all. Now, the slim woman being praised for their 'body confidence' is a recognisable trope. Models hunch in unflattering positions to show off their (skin) rolls, and one need only look at the popularity of Jameela Jamil or Chessie King to see how #inspiring it can be to be a size 12. I was praised for being #brave for revealing my ab-less torso and 'crazy' for putting ketchup on my face. On reflection, maybe the ketchup was crazy. The smell of vinegar didn't leave my hair for days.

Soon enough I was asked to speak about body confidence at events. People asked me for advice on how they could love their bodies, too. It occurred to me for the first time that I might have some sort of influence. This was why so many people were buying into wellness. We had regressed to become a world where influencers had replaced experts and followers are more important than knowledge.

The more requests that flooded in, the less idea I had of how to say no. Was my body shape really so radical? Was it wild that I was openly fraternising with sweets? I wasn't even eating them in my posts. I wondered if it was a problem that I didn't always feel as body confident as Stella. Did I want to be the face of junk food? Should I fake it till I make it?

It soon became clear I wasn't going to be given time to choose. The people had decided. I was the patron saint of Haribo and everyone knows the best way to please the people is to give them what they want.

I needed likes; likes led to money and exposure, which led to more work. What I wanted and what the people wanted had become intertwined. I wanted to want what the people wanted, so the people would want me.

Behind closed doors I ate relatively healthily and occasionally exercised, but in public I was a junk-guzzling renegade. I made sure that when I was out and about I was Stella. At lunch with a journalist I would always order pudding and chips over salad. I feigned a serious aversion to all things wellness.

'Yoga? I would never.'

'Acupuncture? Well, it's basically witchcraft, isn't it?' My natural scepticism towards alternative therapies grew into an outright dismissal of anything not based in Western science.

Instagram is designed to flatten people and is no place for nuance. You only need to google 'vegan influencer eats fish' to see what happens when an internet personality changes their mind. One YouTube video I found contained so many death threats I could only assume that it is enshrined in vegan law that any vegan caught eating meat should be released onto a grouse moor and hunted to death.

When my agent insisted that I perform my next comedy show in character as Stella it made sense. She was, after all, what I was known for, and at this point everyone thought I was her anyway. I struggled with performing as Stella. I didn't feel confident doing character comedy, having only just got the hang of stand-up. I wasn't a natural Alan Partridge or Mr Bean. Acting made me feel awkward and exposed, and I channelled this anxiety into a resentment of the character herself. Stella and I were trapped in a bad marriage, but I knew she was still my meal ticket.

I started wearing the comedy confectionery merchandise I was regularly sent.

'Yes, this is a McDonald's Christmas jumper, thanks for noticing. You're right; it is so Stella.'

My real self and the self I performed on Instagram were Russian dolls, but we weren't sure which one was supposed to go inside the other. I had created Stella, but now it felt like she'd eclipsed me. I resented her and the fake authentic life she'd attributed to me. I was tired of being the funny food girl all the time. Didn't they know I had range?

The key to being a successful influencer is consistency. Whether that's in the colour of your grid, the price point of what you're wearing, your morals, your values, your diet, your friends. A health-food blogger would never admit to an occasional McDonald's, no less than luxury lifestyle bloggers would dare set foot in a Center Parcs. Influencers I've spoken to have admitted that sometimes they feel like they've forgotten what they like, knowing only what their followers want them to like, and therefore what will perform well on Instagram.

'You just love a tea dress,' I said to a well-known fashion-blogger friend.

'Not really,' she said. 'They just perform really well on Insta so I have loads of them and now I find they're all I have to wear.'

'It's a bit like your followers have crowdfunded your dress sense.'

'I guess so. But they pay the bills, so it's the least I can do.'

The need to give the people what they want has become ever more pressing in Instagram's flooded market. More influencers means less brand money to go around, so the pressure to keep your engagement high is on. The Instagram stories 'ask me anything' feature has even got influencers asking their followers straight out:

'What kind of content do you want to see from me?'

I once DM'd an influencer to tell her I was obsessed with her dog.

'Yeah,' she replied. 'He's great content.'

The writer and influencer Tavi Gevinson wrote in *The Cut*, 'I think I came to see my shareable self as the authentic one and buried any tendencies that might threaten her likability, so deep down I forgot they even existed.'

To remain on-brand, I began a process of ritually undermining any experience that could be seen as aspirational. I went to Soho Farmhouse and mocked myself falling off a pastel-coloured bike. I went on a trip to the picture-perfect village of Rye and only posted a photo by a hazard sign. Every exciting offer or invitation had to be caveated with, 'How can I make this look a bit shit so my followers don't hate me?'

Ultimately, influencers develop their unshakeable online personas because they want to be liked. I know I did. A part of me was convinced that I was funnier than Stella, that people would love the real me if they knew me, but the part of me that was terrified of not being liked was louder.

Whether you're aware of it or not, you have created your own digestible Instagram brand that you're selling to the masses. You're leaning into the parts of you that you think that people will like. Everybody, ultimately, likes to be liked.

What happened to me, of course, was at the extreme end of the spectrum. I became a living, breathing brand and I only have myself to blame. What I was craving wasn't the opportunity to be myself on Instagram, it was the opportunity to be myself, full stop.

I know now that it is less important to be liked than to be understood. I wanted Stella and Bella to co-exist, but I couldn't help but think that for that to really happen, she'd have to be part of my past. I wanted to be seen for everything that I am, not just what I do.

# 20,000 Followers

On paper, I have almost 20,000 followers, an agent, a book deal, a new, lovely part-time job and I'm about to go on holiday. All is well in the world.

In reality, I am working four days a week while trying to kick-start a comedy career, grow my Instagram account and build a personal brand. I am also writing a book. I do not have time to go on holiday.

Having 14,000 followers didn't feel like enough to quit the day job entirely, so once Edinburgh was over I started working for Beano Studios. Flicking through *Beano* annuals all day and getting VIP access to *Bananaman* scripts was a dream. Plus it was only four days a week so I had plenty of time to keep growing my Instagram empire.

Caroline took me for lunch that first Friday. She was thrilled I'd found a day job.

'When you're starting out in comedy your income can be quite sporadic,' she warned me, 'so I'd hang on as long as you can.'

We had mutually decided that Deliciously Stella probably didn't have much left in the tank. My flirtation with Instagram success had been but a summer fling. One for the CV, but not a long-term career option. It was time to think about my next move as a proper comedian.

Almost immediately after leaving the meeting I opened my Instagram DMs. It was an editor from Penguin Random House.

In a twist of marketing genius, during my Edinburgh show my sister had gone to Hobbycraft and made sandwich boards with my show poster on the front, and my most-liked Instagram post on the back, along with my handle.

'Hello,' said the editor from Penguin. 'I saw your Instagram account on a sandwich board in Edinburgh. Have you ever thought about making Deliciously Stella into a book?' I stopped in my tracks, shaking, and immediately called my sister. When she picked up I screamed BOOOOOOOOOOOOOOOOOK like a birthing cow for as long as my breath would let me.

'What the fuck?! Bella? Are you OK? Where are you?'

'Penguin Random House saw the sandwich boards and now you have got me a book deal.'

'Have they offered you the deal?'

'No. But they will. And it's all down to you. You are my head of marketing. The Queen of Hobbycraft. A goddess.'

'Am I going to get a cut of the profits?'

'Of course not! I have to pay my agent. But I'll buy you a pint and thank you from the bottom of my heart.'

The book was to be a recipe book, written in the style of all the healthy eaters I'd been satirising, but with all of their recipes made out of sweets. Courgetti would be made out of strawberry laces, coconut bites would become bounties, and smoothies would be packed full of 'anti-oxidising' Haribo fruit.

I called Caroline and told her to brace herself.

'That. Is amazing news. Well fucking done. Now we really need to book you some gigs.'

Ugh. Gigs. Performing in front of people. I was saying I could take it or leave it with live performance but really what I wanted was to leave it behind for good. I liked that I could do stand-up because it was hard, and I knew that it was impressive that I could do it well. What I didn't like was actually doing it, because it scared me shitless.

I'd sort of hoped that I'd be able to put off performing again until Edinburgh next year. In my heart of hearts, I was hoping that I'd be famous enough by then to be able to bypass it altogether. I had an agent now. All she needed to do was get me on the telly and I'd never see the inside of a comedy club again.

Unfortunately, Caroline was good at her job and knew that the best way to get better at stand-up is to do it as often as possible. The book offer had reinstated Caroline's faith in Stella and it was decided that I should start performing as her, in character.

Other influencers don't have to deal with this nonsense, I thought. Who is stupid enough to get themselves a comedy agent when they are legitimately terrified of performing stand-up comedy?

I was being featured in a newspaper, online article or blog a couple of times a week, with each appearance gaining me a few hundred more followers. I gave an interview to anyone who asked, considering it to be part of the deal. I set up a Google alert for my name.

It was quite unusual for an Instagrammer to appear in mainstream media. There were thousands of Instagrammers with hundreds of thousands more followers than me, but something about my account had struck a chord. Both working at the *Beano* and running the evolution of Deliciously Stella meant that I had two jobs, but I carried on playing as hard as I worked.

My newfound notoriety was like pouring petrol on an already raging fire. My small talk had been elevated. I needed to tell everyone about the account. I had never been the prettiest in the room, the loudest nor the most confident, but now I had pulled my ace card. I was minorly famous and it made me feel like I dazzled.

The question 'Shall we get another bottle?' was always answered with 'Fuck it. Soon you'll be rich!'

It did feel like it was inevitable I would at some point reap some financial rewards from Stella. I had almost 20,000 followers and a book deal. My advance had only been £6,000, which was being paid in instalments, but I was certain the book would fly off the shelves.

I had started getting gifts from small brands. At first it was baked goods, soon it graduated to clothes and jewellery. Almost everything was either food-themed or emblazoned with 'Stella'. I couldn't bring myself to wear anything with Stella on it. It wasn't my name, after all. I also didn't have the heart to tell anyone I'd prefer a necklace that said 'Bella' so I could wear it. A drawer of Stella gifts piled up. Phone cases, rings, jars of peanut butter, face creams containing kale. I didn't need the stuff, but I said yes to all of it. The gifts made me feel the account was making progress; they were a stepping-stone to making money out of Stella.

'Maybe I'll be the first one of our friends to buy a house without help from their parents,' I suggested to my friends. Nobody betrayed a flicker of doubt. They were proud of me but wary that the attention might be going to my head. I was powered by the smoke being blown up my arse, and at some point the fire was going to go out.

I was at work when I heard from the *Evening Standard* again.

'Congratulations! You have been named as one of the *Evening Standard*'s Progress 1,000.' I had no idea what it meant so I forwarded the email to Caroline and went back to work. Caroline immediately called me and I slipped out into the corridor.

'Dude! They've named you as one of the 1,000 most influential people in London.'

'What? Who else is on the list?'

'It's very casual, just the Beckhams, Elton John, oh, and the Executive Director of Greenpeace.'

'What? Are you sure it's not a joke?'

'Not a joke. You need to send them a head shot. Do you have any? Or should we get one done this afternoon?'

'The only shots I have are of my Edinburgh poster and I'm swigging from a bottle of champagne in a flat cap.'

'Right. Well, they need the photo today. Looks like you might be a last-minute addition.'

'You think?'

I scanned the office for someone who looked willing. I hadn't talked about Stella much at work. I didn't want them to think I was distracted. I really needed this job. Eventually I mustered up the courage to ask the office manager if she had a camera and if she'd mind taking a couple of headshots of me at lunch.

'They have to be against a coloured background. That's all I know.'

The clock struck 12 and we walked out of the office into a maze of whitewashed corridors.

'Why don't we try the Dennis room?' she suggested, leading me into a room painted with Dennis the Menace's traditional black and red stripes.

'I think the background has to be plain.'

We took to the streets, marching up and down Fleet Street looking for a plain, coloured wall. Eventually, after a half-hour search, we settled on the only block colour we could find. My headshot was taken against a hedge, which had been topiaried in the shape of an elephant. They ended up not using a photo for my entry.

After the photoshoot, news travelled of my side hustle.

'What are you even doing here?' asked one of my bosses when I landed on the cover of the Media Eye as 'one to watch'.

I didn't mention that I'd just given an interview to the *Daily Mail*. I was there because I needed the money. Working full-time, writing a book and managing a burgeoning Instagram account were all feasible. I just needed to look after myself.

The night before my day off I went big. I ended up in an underground club in Dalston with sticky floors and abhorrent toilets before piling back to some other freelancer's house to carry on the party until dawn. When my flatmate Liv barrelled into my room the next morning my mouth was like a sandstorm.

'You're in the *Mail*!' she shouted.

'Yes,' I said. 'I know.'

'Have you read the comments yet?'

I gulped down a dusty glass of day-old water and scrolled down into the comments section.

'I promised I wouldn't do it without you. Not my first outing in the sidebar of shame.'

'You don't want to do it alone, B,' she said. 'Those people are animals.'

I opened up my laptop and braced myself. Liv sat on the edge of my bed, face a jumble of concern and gleeful anticipation.

'So. Are we laughing or are we crying?' she asked as I scrolled down into the dreaded comments section. The usual suspects were there, people calling me ugly or fat. Then they started to get more inventive.

'27?! She looks like a toothless granny is about to bust out of her.' Liv started cackling. Another person had just written 'hag'. But the winner of most creative comment must go to the man who said that I looked like 'an orc on a day trip to Earth'. For a split second, Liv looked at my face for permission to laugh. She was shaking so much I thought her towel might fall off. 'Go on,' I huffed. 'Fill your boots.'

Liv let out a rip snorting guffaw. 'You have to laugh,' Liv cackled in between attempts to draw breath. 'It wouldn't be funny if you actually looked like an orc.' She was wheezing at this point, with fat tears of mirth rolling down her cheeks.

'Fine,' I accepted. 'Everyone knows that people who comment on the *Daily Mail* are just sad incels in stained under-wear who live with their mums.'

As I've mentioned, Liv and I had bonded over our shared bouts of anxiety, and I'd been pretending for a while that mine was lying dormant. The combination of a sinful weekday hang-over and the knowledge that somebody thought I looked like an orc made for a melancholy day. I'm a people-pleaser, and although the rational part of my brain knows that I can't be for everyone and everyone isn't for me, I can't help but take criti-cism personally.

I'd been feeling a bit off for a while, but put it down to it being September, my least-favourite month. Every year around September I wonder what is up. Why am I so tearful? Do I really need to sleep twelve hours a night? Why do I not care about anything at all? The answer is that I have seasonally affective disorder. Every year I vow to myself that I will remem-ber to book winter sun, or actually suck it up and move to a hot country. Every year I wake up in the UK to find that it's September and I've got a bit sad. Usually I just ride it out. I switch on my light box and start going to therapy, but this year I was busy and I needed some extra help.

This was not my first rodeo. I'd been on and off SSRIs since I was twenty-one, usually discontinuing them because of side-effects. When your antidepressants are working, it always feels like the right time to come off them, so I was well versed in the cycle of acquisition and withdrawal.

I booked an appointment with my psychiatrist and explained what was going on. I had gone viral on Instagram and was very busy trying to get more people to follow and like me. I explained that under no circumstances was he to put me on the pills that stopped me orgasming. They also made my teeth grind and my pupils dilate so much I looked like I'd spent a weekend in Fabric.

'Have you spoken to your therapist about the "like" thing?' he asked, knowing full well that outsourcing my validation could prove troublesome.

'Sure,' I lied. I had had to part ways with my therapist because our relationship had become inappropriate. We weren't conducting an illicit affair or anything like that; it just sort of felt like she might be becoming a fan. I had started seeing her at the beginning of Deliciously Stella. She worked with a charity that supported people with PoTS, the condition that Ella had 'cured' with her diet.

I can't remember if I told her about the account, or if she brought it up, but when she told me that her friends loved it too, I knew that she'd told people that I was her patient.

We started texting at the weekends. We even came up with some posts together, which seemed as good a use of £100 an hour as any. She sent me pictures of her playing with her children, and finally, she organised the final preview of my Edinburgh show at her private members' club. I liked seeing her so much that I didn't stop to think that our relationship had become inappropriate. I was just pleased that she wanted to be my friend. I think that when I was away, she might have realised it for herself. We never spoke again.

My shrink didn't think to check that the therapist and I were still speaking, so he relented and prescribed me a drug called Mirtazapine. The only side-effect I had to worry about was weight gain, and I decided it was worth the risk. I reasoned that I didn't yet feel bad enough to take the pills, but I wanted them there just in case.

Juggling all my different commitments was harder than I'd anticipated. I never turned down an opportunity. I appeared on podcasts, wrote free articles, gave impassioned advice to people trying to make it in comedy. Between work, the book, press interviews and Instagram, I was starting to burn out. I felt myself starting to sink into old patterns. I was agreeing with my negative thoughts. Were people tiring of me being the centre of attention? Without other influencer friends or a dutiful other half, I'd had to ask whoever was in the vicinity to take a photo of me. Did they think I was silly and vacuous? I tried to ignore the creeping whisper of my low self-esteem, but soon I was unable to sleep. I staggered through my day job like a zombie, then went home to drink wine until I passed out for a couple of hours, waking with an anxious start.

We announced the book to the press. A women's magazine got in touch about me writing a column. I was living my very own version of an Instagram lie. Everybody thought I was happy, but I wasn't. I decided to take the pills.

Because I was playing a character, I felt no obligation to share my wobble with my followers. It was my job to keep up appearances, to keep everyone else laughing in the face of courgetti, not bum them out because my anxiety was a bit bad.

There is always an adjustment period when you start a new anti-depressant. Some make you a bit sleepy, some make you feel a bit on edge. This pill made me feel like I had walked out of Fire in Vauxhall at 9am after six hours in the dark room and forgotten my coat. I decided to start them at the weekend so the worst of their effects could be endured in private, but I agreed to lunch at my friend Archie's house on Sunday. My pupils were like saucers and my skin felt like things were living just beneath it. The only thing that soothed me was listening to the song 'Runnin' by Beyoncé and Naughty Boy on repeat. When I looked at myself in the mirror before lunch, I looked like the Weetos man. My hair stood on end and my jaw was clenched.

I should probably get some fresh air, I thought. I cycled to Archie's and although my memory is hazy of that day, Archie recalls he immediately knew that something wasn't right. I was slurring my words and startled by the slightest sound. The only memory I have is of repeatedly making people join me in the 'Kylie Jenner lip challenge', where you suck on a shot glass until your lips swell. I woke up the next day in a daze, sent my boss a strange email about roads and called my psychiatrist. He suggested that I stop taking the pills and see him later that week. When I stopped taking the pills, the strange feeling didn't go away. I called my psychiatrist again and asked if he could see me sooner. He told me to go to A & E.

Homerton hospital isn't exactly a comforting place to have a mental health crisis, especially when the first thing a doctor suggests is getting a blood test. I hate needles so much I had to have my wisdom teeth removed under gas. My dad ended up footing the bill and I was assured that if I got a tattoo, I would be written out of his will. At school our BCGs were performed in front of our entire year group. After the jab, you either walked away or you fainted on the mattress provided. It took me three years to work up the courage to get it done.

The doctors thought that the Mirtazapine might have caused a manic episode and they wanted to investigate the possibility of me being bipolar. I was absolutely terrified. I told them that I'd been fine a couple of weeks ago. It was just a bad reaction to the pills. My boss was unbelievably kind; he told me to take the rest of the week off and let him know how I was feeling after my upcoming holiday. When I saw my psychiatrist he told me to try to relax, and by Friday I was starting to feel like my old self. A friend was having a birthday party in a restaurant in Stoke Newington, so I dragged on some glad rags and got on the bus. When I arrived I felt anxious, but I was determined not to let my brain win. I launched into my well-rehearsed spiel about how amazing everything was now that I was big on Instagram, and yes, I did get free gifts, and yes, I had been invited to some press lunches but I was still working and hadn't been able to go.

The white wine was flowing and even I was starting to convince myself that everything was fine.

My friends and I have a complicated relationship with white wine. This is because of the white wine werewolf. It makes you practically blind, in danger of opening a tab you can't pay for, snogging exes, and waking up on the bathroom floor with little to no recollection. That night at the birthday party, I was destined to meet the werewolf. My friend owns a catering company and anyone who knows chefs knows they can drink. I drank so much I blacked out, coming to in my kitchen at 5am, having packed nothing for my holiday the next day. In my kitchen was my flatmate, our friend and a man with a broken leg who called himself notorious J.O.N. There was time for two hours' sleep.

'Fuck!' I said. 'We have got to pack and sleep.' Liv looked at her watch and groaned. 'I'll book an Addison Lee,' she said. 'Then we can sleep for three hours.' We hurled notorious J.O.N. out of the house and passed out. Liv staggered into my room in what felt like seconds later. 'The taxi's here!'

We threw as many summer clothes as we could find into a bag and ran out of the door. It was only when we arrived at Gatwick that we realised that Liv was wearing a poncho without any trousers.

My friends were waiting with nervous smiles. They had heard about my wobble.

'False alarm!' I shouted before anyone could ask me any questions. 'As you can see I am better than ever.' I was steaming drunk and dressed like a Super Mario Brother, so nothing was out of the ordinary. The party had started how it would go on.

I think it's important that I explain this group of friends, who are known as the sad blonde ravers (or SBRs), to set the scene for the holiday that lay ahead.

The SBRs are my wildest friends from university. The name was coined by a visiting friend after a night of watching us dance around our handbags with sunglasses on by a front right-hand speaker. We thought we were the coolest cats in town, told people we were born in Fabric and never, ever admitted to having gone to boarding school. We were rahvers, rahs who loved to rave, and we firmly believed that the party never dies. Our friendship was forged in the pursuit of fun, and if the SBRs have a superpower, it is that they can turn any situation into a party.

It was with the SBRs that I started a drum'n'bass rave in the car park at Goodwood races. It was with the SBRs that I was dredged, naked, from a lake at a barbecue hosted by men who had comfortably completed the 12-step programme. It was with the SBRs that my friend Kat got carpet burn on her face after we attempted 'the flying pig' at the drummer from Queen's house. It was the SBRs who realised that Gordon's would make an excellent green juice. The SBRs are mad, bad and dangerous to know.

Their motto is that bad decisions make good stories and my life would be so much less rich without them. Sure, I would have more brain cells and higher liver function, but what is liver function when you haven't had fun?

We stopped off on the way to the villa to buy supplies and I took the opportunity to stock up on my own haul of Deliciously Stella jokes. I might have been on holiday, but I wasn't going to let my followers down.

I'd noticed on the plane that at some point in the last few days I had managed to fake tan only my little toe. I had no recollection of the incident and it was clear I was unravelling, but I was about to hit the 20k mark so content planning was of the utmost importance.

My pals headed off in the direction of booze when we reached the local supermarket, while I browsed the confectionery aisle. Cheesy Wotsits for eyebrows, check. Soy sauce as tanning oil. Sugary Spanish peaches. I was all set, but I wasn't sure how my comrades would feel about playing my 'boyfriend of Instagram.' No one had said it out loud, but I had got the impression that talking about Stella too much wouldn't go down well. I didn't want to seem self-obsessed, or big-headed, but I really, really wanted to reach 20k. I tried so hard to sound nonchalant when I asked someone to take my picture that I ended up talking to my friends as if I was asking them to prom. 'It's totally fine if you don't want to, like it's not a big deal, I don't care, you can say no.'

'Bella,' someone said. 'Have you had a stroke? Just take the picture.' My friend Kat dutifully took some snaps of me pouring soy sauce all over my body. I was convinced that everybody thought I was a grade-A prick.

The villa in Spain was stunning, replete with everything you could wish for for a week-long house party. There were indoor and outdoor dining areas, a games room and an enormous pool. Just as my hangover from the night before had started to find its footing, it was announced that we were going to play drinking games.

'Let's all go around in a circle and tell the most embarrassing story you know about someone here!' I was dreading my turn. Usually this sort of game would have made me howl with laughter. I was among my best friends. We already knew everything about each other, but I couldn't take it. I was certain it was going to be something about how obsessed I was with my Instagram. I felt like my skin had been flayed off, revealing a series of buttons waiting to be pushed. Press here for anxiety and here for tears. Luckily the tears didn't come. I survived and we went upstairs to get ready.

I was sharing a room with Liv, who could see that I wasn't myself. 'Listen, B,' she said. 'I'm not surprised you're overwhelmed, but relax, you're with your mates.'

That night we walked down an A road to get to a restaurant. We were clearly the only customers they'd seen in weeks and before we knew it free shots were making their way down the table. As we stumbled back we saw there was a strip club at the roadside. We couldn't not go in. We all piled inside and everyone started swinging around the pole. Everyone apart from me. My friend Ali gave me a squeeze and asked if I was OK. 'Yeah,' I said. 'I'm just tired.' I downed another shot with tears in my eyes. I wasn't OK. I had a book to write, and I didn't have enough social media posts to last the week. I didn't dare ask for a lift to the supermarket. I felt like I was ruining everyone's holiday. I needed to go home.

The next day I tried to clear my head. I put my trainers on and filled a water bottle. A walk will make me feel better, I reasoned. A walk is all I need. When I got downstairs, everyone asked me where I was off to. With each reply my resolve weakened. Water rushed towards my tear ducts. For fuck's sake, why can't I stop fucking crying? By the time I reached the door I was in floods. I looked up and saw Archie on the other side of the glass. I'd been trying and failing to use the handle for three minutes.

From that moment I started to spiral. My stiff upper lip was wobbling and I resorted to full-blown meltdown. I called my parents, who were on an anniversary holiday in Prague, and they booked me a flight home to Scotland. Their friend Harriet offered to come and pick me up and I took a sleeping pill at 8pm so that everyone would stop talking to me. Archie drove me to the airport in silence, tears tumbled down my face while I frantically looked for a meme to plug the gaps in my Instagram grid. I reached the 20k mark in the car but I didn't utter a sound. Archie hugged me and sent me in the direction of my check-in. I tried not to make eye contact with strangers. I was disoriented and frightened and, let's face it, terrible at navigating anywhere. Once I'd made it through security, I got so lost I somehow ended up going through security again. It was at that moment that I remembered, I had to be at work on Monday.

I called my dad for the twenty-fifth time that weekend. 'Dad,' I said. 'I need you to quit my job for me.' Now my dad is a patient man, a man who shies away from confrontation, a man who wants an easy life. He is also a man who believes his children should behave like functioning adults.

'I'm sorry, darling,' he said. 'That's not a job for me, you have to let them know that you're not well.' I was hysterical now, begging in the middle of Malaga airport. 'Please, Dad,' I begged. 'I can't tell them. If you don't quit my job for me, I'll die.' I felt some gentle hands land on my shoulders. It was a man who worked at the airport.

'Excuse me, ma'am,' he said. 'It is this way to your flight.' I was lost again and someone had seen me crying. This kind man gently escorted me onto my aeroplane and I cried the whole way home. When I arrived in Scotland I was wearing a bikini and a mini skirt. Harriet came to meet me as promised and wrapped me in a huge warm hug. Her presence was so comforting, I sank into the front seat, knowing that home was only an hour away. As we pulled into my parents' drive, Harriet stiffened. 'Fuck,' she said, patting her body and rootling in seat pockets. 'Fuck, darling, I'm so sorry. I've forgotten Mum's keys. They're somewhere in my house.'

To the layman this doesn't sound so bad, but I knew that Harriet had lost my mum's keys in her castle. We pulled up outside the enormous wooden doors. 'Do you want to come in? Or would you rather wait in the car?' I imagined myself shivering in her gargantuan flag-stoned hall and resigned myself to reading *Grazia* in the Volvo. Soon I would be in my mother's chair with a heater on my feet, watching Sky TV. I would not have to sleep in a possibly haunted bedroom in a turret. The injustice would be a step too far. After about half an hour, I started to get concerned. Her husband Michael came to check on me and I tried to slap on a smile. I was so touched that my parents' friends would do this for them, for me. I felt completely non-judged. Miraculously, Harriet appeared on the front steps, triumphantly clutching the keys.

As soon as I got home I collapsed on the floor. I had a bath, changed into a dressing gown and began a *True Blood* marathon that my dad would later tell me cost him hundreds of pounds in excess download fees. I'd lost faith in my shrink in London so I found an online service for £200. I contacted the online psychiatrist from my be-dressing-gowned lair. By the afternoon, I had been diagnosed with bipolar over Skype.

Knowing how sensitive I am to new medications, my mum asked me to wait a day to start taking the antipsychotic I'd been prescribed, quetiapine, so she could be there to look after me. My mood was still erratic but my dad had granted my wish. He had called my boss and explained I wasn't well and wouldn't be coming back. They couldn't have been more wonderful. My boss sent me an email telling me not to worry about anything and told me to invoice for the week I had taken off. He was moving to LA and told me to look him up if I ever found myself there. It was kindness like this that kept me from the edge. My dad had quit my job for me and it was still OK. It reminded me that nothing is the end of the world.

Too anxious to leave the holiday WhatsApp group lest I look sassy, I soon found out that the holiday had gone from bad to worse. Pictures flooded through of my friends half naked, covered in tomato sauce. One friend managed to accidently snapchat a video of her sexily dancing half naked to a straight-laced old friend, a club promoter from university and their mum. No words. No explanation. Just vibes. Usually this would have had me in hysterics but I felt unmoved. The numbing effect of the antipsychotics was setting in.

This wasn't the only effect the antipsychotics had on me. I had started to feel extremely nauseous. This wasn't out of the ordinary when taking a new medication. My body can barely tolerate anything that helps my brain. After a week, building up my dose a quarter of a pill at a time, I was staring down the barrel of my twenty-eighth birthday. 'How do you feel, darling?' asked my mum when she woke me up.

'Well,' I answered. 'I'm twenty-eight, I'm unemployed, I live with my parents and I've had a nervous breakdown.'

And then I shat myself. I'd decided to treat myself to a whole antipsychotic to mark my day of birth, and my poor weak stomach couldn't take it. Once I'd recovered from the horror, I called my sister. I was laughing so hard she thought I was crying. When I told her what happened she erupted in fits of giggles. Mum rolled her eyes.

'Only my child could shit herself and be the happiest she's been in weeks.' I told the story of the shitting on a podcast with Bryony Gordon and it still haunts me. Every time someone says they've heard me on a podcast, I think, Do you know I shat myself? Well reader, now you know as well. Don't tell anyone.

# Parties, Events and Awkward Appearances

When I think about influencers, I always think about them standing in front of graffiti walls, kissing on big grey sofas, pretending to walk across a road at fashion week, or hanging out at parties. The thing I was most excited about when my Instagram started to grow was all of the parties I was going to be invited to. My core belief is that parties are good for the soul. I love drinking, I love chatting, I could do a masters in small talk and I am never too sober to dance. I love sequins, champagne, dancing shoes, DJs; I've even got a soft spot for that girl who always goes too far and is sick on the stairs. I love raves, discos, balls, weddings, wakes. With the right people and a bucket of booze I could raise the roof of a cardboard box. As far as I'm concerned, all parties have potential. The night is what you make it, and it's down to you to give it hell.

'Making an appearance' at an event was my Z-list holy grail, and when I eventually left my job to concentrate on having my picture taken full-time, I was ready to attend the opening of any envelope.

In spite of having tens of thousands of followers, I was apparently not yet in a position to be paid to appear anywhere. I naively thought thousands of followers meant the life of a reality TV star. I envisioned myself spraying students with champagne in regional nightclubs, before crashing parties full of people ten years younger than me and boring them to death with tales of how much of a party legend I still was even though I was pushing thirty. I had not yet reached the echelons of fame of members of *Made in Chelsea*, though, so I had to settle for events attended by adults, in London, with no financial reward.

My first ever 'appearance' in character was at a yoga studio in Hackney. I had been asked to lead a class for hotpod yoga, in the character of Deliciously Stella, and Caroline thought a bit of improv would be good practice for my show.

Before I even got to the location of the pod, there had been a disaster. One of Ella's cronies, Mind Body Bowl, had also been recruited to teach a class and although we would never cross paths, she couldn't be associated with me. I had seen her on Ella's account, doing handstands on the beach in Mustique. These influencers seemed to do nothing but handstands on the beach. I deduced that either they had private incomes or they were making some serious wedge with Instagram. Naturally the yoga studio was paying me in vouchers and exposure, with a view to paying the next time I did an event for them (which was never).

I met my friend Will at the studio. Neither of us had done hot yoga before and we agreed not to stand too close to each other to avoid getting sweated on. My friends often look to me as a sort of humidity gauge. Like a child, I have very little control over my body temperature and when mercury rises, the beads of sweat on my nose come out to say hello. I would say that my body sweats a normal amount, but my face is a different story. On family holidays in my teens, I would nip into my dad's bathroom and spray my face with Lynx Africa, convinced that men's deodorant is stronger and that although the smell of my face might be offputting to potential suitors, at least my nose sweat couldn't get there first.

A yoga instructor was taking the first part of the class so Will and I walked in and rolled out our mats at the back. The 'pod' was a pitch-black womb that smelt faintly of feet. Not a single head turned when I walked in.

'Your fans are playing it cool,' laughed Will. 'Do you think that anyone here actually knows who you are?' The instructor walked to the front and introduced me as today's special guest. Twenty blonde, lululemon-clad goddesses turned to give me a once-over. My see-through leggings and pyjama top didn't instill much faith. The next forty-five minutes were the hottest of my life. I was sliding around on the mat like a slippery walrus, gasping for breath in the hot, wet air. All I wanted was to be naked, to be free from the prison of my damp t-shirt. Eventually moving in the heat was unbearable so I put myself into child's pose and tried to breathe.

I was concentrating so hard on not sweating to death that I almost missed the instructor asking me to come to the front. I stood up and dripped my way to the head of the pod and introduced myself. Nobody laughed. I launched into my routine, encouraging people to do moves like 'the awkward mongoose' and 'the porpoise trapped in a net'. By the end everyone looked thoroughly bewildered. I slunk to the back to see Will, who was howling.

'They don't know who you are! They were expecting a yogi and instead they got you.' I lurked at the end of the class to collect my vouchers, before fleeing the scene. I never cashed them in.

As my follower number went up, so too did the calibre of event I was invited to. Beauty is in the eye of the beholder, of course, and for me, the highlight of my life was being asked to be the guest of honour at a Peperami art exhibition.

It was the eve of my thirtieth birthday, and initially I politely declined, saying that my sisters and I would be having a birthday dinner. Then they offered to pay me to turn up.

The exhibition was to celebrate the launch of the new 'beefy' Peperamis, and to enter you had to walk through 'the beef curtains', a sort-of beaded curtain stitched out of Peperami wrappers. Inside, iconic works of art had been remade using Peperamis. There was a Warhol pop-up themed Peperami animal. There was a woman wearing a Peperami dress. The *pièce de résistance* was Tracy Emin's unmade bed, covered in the horrible plastic sheath that encases the meat, known commonly as the Peperami condom.

The final part of my deal for coming that night was that I was to launch 'the beef lips challenge'. The idea was that I had to hold a Peperami between my lips and my nose for as long as possible without dropping it. A camera crew dutifully filmed my attempt, while other revellers cheered. Those were the glory days.

I wasn't only employed to turn up and take pictures. I was adamant that as a somewhat inexperienced stand-up comedian, I had a skill. The benefit of performing at events is that there was no way they could get around paying me. I was once paid so much to perform at a launch party in Soho, I begrudgingly agreed to write a fifteen-minute-long set on 'snacking', which I had to perform in its entirety, three times, in a room where guests were trying to mingle and chat. Every time I cleared my throat into the microphone, I launched into the same terrible material in front of the same faces. Toff from *Made in Chelsea* was grinning at me like a mum at sports day. Everyone else looked like they were thinking about bottling me.

I wasn't always selling out. Before I'd even started thinking about my next Edinburgh show, a friend of a friend got in touch to say she was preparing for a marathon in Sierra Leone. To raise money for her trip she was putting on a comedy night in Clapham and she asked me to headline, as Deliciously Stella. Now let it be known that one successful Edinburgh show a headliner does not make, especially when I had only performed as Deliciously Stella once.

I explained that my old material might be better as I knew it worked but she was convinced people would want Stella. They wanted to put Stella on the poster, which meant it wouldn't make sense if Bella turned up. Successful stand-up comedians always say that the best way to get good at comedy is to perform as much as you possibly can. I preferred to treat it like childbirth, leaving enough time to forget how terrifying it was before doing it again.

I was asked to come with half an hour's worth of material, which I hurriedly threw together. I recorded myself reading it and took myself on long walks around Brockwell Park trying to drum the material into my memory. My anxiety was telling me that it wasn't very good, that I wouldn't be able to remember all my lines. The rational part of my brain told me it would be fine, that everyone loved Deliciously Stella too much to care.

When I arrived at the venue, I felt sick. The room was huge, bigger than anywhere I had performed before. The organiser told me that the show would be compered by Foster's Award nominee, Ivo Graham. I would also be warmed up for by Phil Wang and Suzi Ruffell. All three of these comedians have filmed specials and appeared on *Live at the Apollo*. I tried to keep my nerves at bay with a bottle of warm prosecco, but every person who told me they were excited about my set filled me with more dread. I told my fellow comics that I was testing new material and they nodded gravely. 'I have this Instagram thing that everyone really loves,' I tried to explain, but they knew how this was going to go.

The crowd were lively and very pissed. Technical issues meant that the comics' sets were getting later and later. Looking at my watch, I could see that I was unlikely to perform before 10pm. I could have handled them as myself, but as Stella I was completely out of my comfort zone. The comedians who went before me were killing it. The crowd were going wild. I told myself to ride the wave of their laughter, that everyone would keep the same energy for me. Then, just before I thought I was going to go on, there was a change in schedule. 'I'm so sorry,' said Olivia, 'but we're going to play the video of the starving children before your set in case people need to leave.' I looked out at the braying crowd. The familiar glassy-eyed stares of people in their twenties from Clapham who had just done their first line of gear on a Thursday night. I knew then that I would be crucified.

The crowd were talking amongst themselves as the video ended. They clearly thought that the night was over. I gingerly stepped out onto the stage wearing leggings and carrying a tote bag. I realised that I was actually quite drunk. I cleared my throat and launched into my set. Nobody stopped talking. Panicking, I started racing through my material, pleading with the audience with my eyes. It was too late. The estate agents had smelled my fear. I still had twenty-five more minutes of material to get through. Blind with nerves, I decided to skip forward to a bit where I performed my made-up yoga moves. The microphone shrieked when it hit the ground. Without it, nobody could hear my instructions, and without tiered seating, the majority of the room couldn't see me on the stage. For the people in the first two rows, I was just a mad drunk woman writhing on the floor. I lay there, still for a second, before gathering myself. I stood up, picked up the microphone and said, 'I can stop now. If you want.' A weak no from someone on the front row confirmed that my torture was not over.

From the corner of my eye, I saw the professional comedians who had come before me willing me to succeed. We've all been there, I could hear them say. This was the worst gig of my life. I thought about how I'd told them I hoped to get by because of all of my Instagram followers. I limped to the finishing line and gave a shuddering bow before running off stage and back to the prosecco.

'Tough crowd,' someone said. I smiled gratefully and vowed never to be underprepared or to drink before a gig again. Then I went and got absolutely hammered. When I ask my friends about that gig they assure me it wasn't as bad as I thought, but the experience was truly scarring. If I was going to take Stella to Edinburgh I needed to get my arse in gear.

The main purpose of going to events when you're an influencer is to fill your day and get some content. It's an excuse to get a blow dry and wear something you've been #gifted. It isn't very often that you go to have a good time.

A lot of the events I was invited to were somewhat tepid. There were a lot of cookbook launches where I didn't know anyone and awkwardly latched on to journalists until it was appropriate to leave. The restaurant launches at least offered free food, but more often than not I'd been invited ironically, to celebrate the launch of a new kind of beetroot canapé that tasted like soil.

I wanted to dance on tables and rip my dress. I wanted hedonistic glamour and Andy Warhol's Studio 54. I wanted my fifteen minutes of fame to be FUN. Instead, the events I was invited to were less sex, drugs and rock and roll, more wheat-grass shots, boring speeches by CEOs and selfies. So many selfies. How more influencers are not regularly hospitalised for walking into lamp posts I will never know; they're usually staring at their phones so much because PRs are breathing down their necks to make sure they meet their 'deliverables'.

If you're a brand ambassador or are trying to build a relationship with a brand, you'd better let your followers know you're having fun at their event. One influencer I spoke to recounted having a panic attack at a jewellery launch because the PR was so intent on her posting she WhatsApped her when she was in the loo to ask if she could put up some more stories.

When the influencers weren't looking at their own phones they were looking at other people's. I became aware of a vague sort of influencer etiquette. When someone tells you their social handle it's polite to say that you've heard of them. If they follow you there and then, you must follow them back. You always offer to take a picture of them for their Instagram, and you never talk about how much you charge for sponsored content. By straddling the worlds of comedy and Instagram I got to enjoy the best of both worlds. I could make money from my account but not be tarred with the negative connotations of influencing. I sensed unease among influencer ranks that I was only there to take the piss and that I thought they were all stupid and vapid. In truth, I thought the scene was a bit stupid and vapid, but the influencers were great. They'd gamed the system to get the life they wanted and I very rarely met someone without a sense of humour.

Perhaps I thought they had senses of humour because they told me I was funny. I wasn't immune to a bit of good old-fashioned ego-stroking. My 'brand' was on the ascension and I knew it couldn't hurt to know me.

'Oh my God. Let me tell my friend I've met you,' people would say, ending our conversations before they began by disappearing into their phones. People didn't really want to meet me anyway, they were telling their friends they had met Deliciously Stella. 'Yes,' they'd confirm, 'she is really funny in real life.' People saw me coming. They knew they wanted to be my friend before I even caught their name. A selfie with me was just another gifted accessory they could show off to their followers.

I love fashion and they always looked incredible in their head-to-toe gifted outfits. I was so envious that brands helped them to look glamorous while I was well on my way to becoming 'junk food girl'. I had a collection of slogan t-shirts saying 'carbs' and 'in fries we trust', which I wore on repeat. I thought that if I made the joke early enough, nobody would think that I was there in a serious capacity. Nobody would be able to judge me for not wearing the right clothes or being able to take a good picture.

This didn't stop me trying to be on my A game at all times. I still desperately wanted them to know that Bella was funnier than Stella. That the real-life person was of more interest than the Instagram account. But to brands, PRs and other influencers that just wasn't true. Without my follower number I was as useful to them as a chocolate teapot, and people followed Stella, not Bella.

One thing I could have done with more of is good old-fashioned debauchery. Where were Tara, Victoria and Paris? In the nineties I imagine everyone was too drunk to care what they looked like. In 2017, wreckhead was not an acceptable personal brand. Unlike traditional celebrities, influencers are more clean-cut; because they're perceived as walking billboards rather than artists, a clean record and a wholesome image are imperative if they want to make money. Being dropped by Burberry for doing coke doesn't matter all that much to Kate Moss, but being messy isn't allowed to be part of an influencer's appeal.

The best influencers present themselves as the girl or boy next door. You feel like they could be your friend, like their lifestyle is attainable and that buying the stuff they're selling is probably a sound investment. Brands love associating with people like Zoella because they, a) have millions of young impressionable followers, and b) are extremely unlikely to be caught being problematic. Being surrounded by all these 'perfect' people, I felt like an absolute hound. Hardly any of them drink, they never swear, even their interiors scream squeaky clean. These holier-than-thou vloggers and bloggers have popularised an interiors trend known as the 'millennial aesthetic'. Think pink walls, velvet sofas, house plants and copper accents. In a word, the most successful influencers are usually a bit basic.

I think that's why Deliciously Stella was so popular. She was a bit basic, too. The joke was simple, clean and had mass appeal. Like a cruise-ship singer on the *X Factor*, I appealed to kids and nans alike. I was as naughty as I could be while still being commercially viable, and I knew it had to stay that way. I wasn't alone in thinking it farcical that I was considered an anarchist because I ate sweets. Standing next to the wellness witches I look like Pete Doherty. I longed to slip in some black humour, or tell some stories of real debauchery, but that wasn't the brand, so I stuck to what worked.

At times, being the only person to say yes to a drink or try to have a laugh at events was mind-numbing. I felt like a demented court jester, desperate to get the party started, when the party was in a high-street shop in the middle of the day.

I may have been obsessed with my phone when I was alone but when I had the chance to interact with someone in front of me I'd always take it. Often I'd be introduced to someone, only for them to then scroll through my Instagram in front of me, liking my posts as they went and occasionally announcing 'that's funny' without laughing. I found this excruciating. It was like performing a one-on-one stand-up set where the audience are able to skip the bits they don't get. I'd peer over their shoulders, apologising when they scrolled past a post without liking. 'Not one of my best', or 'just an ad'.

Sometimes they'd gasp, 'Oh my god! That is literally me!' and I'd blush from both the compliment and the awkwardness that I'd probably lifted the satire straight from their accounts.

Events in restaurants were pervaded with awkward silences. Every time a dish came out, I'd look up from having a mouthful and see that the rest of the table were on their feet, on top of chairs, setting up ring lights and picking lenses for their professional cameras. The PRs would eyeball me while I got out my iPhone and took a sad shot of a half-eaten arancini ball. I was damned if everything I ate had to be cold. By the time the other food bloggers were finished I would be on my third cocktail, cracking jokes and wondering if it was funny to refer to arancini as energy balls. I often found myself tipsy in the afternoon with no plans for the rest of the day. On days without events, I could spend all day in my room, waiting for a call from my agent or replying to comments. I went on long lonely walks around London, waiting for my friends to finish work.

I wondered if other influencers struggled with the solitary nature of the job, the lack of collaboration or camaraderie. The fashion influencers explained that they stayed busy by shooting their content, for which they needed a professional photographer. A lot of them said it suited their introverted nature. Some were more honest. One influencer admitted to suffering from loneliness and depression: 'It's the sad and hidden truth behind a job that can seem very glamorous and fun on surface level. In truth, it can also tear you apart emotionally.' He returned to therapy and went on to diversify his projects to work with more teams.

The most famous people I encountered at events were fellow influencers and the occasional reality star. Some events were more glamorous than others, of course, and I was terrible at working out which were worth going to. I always seemed to invite my friends to the worst of the lot.

I made my friend Camilla sit through a KitKat press dinner where every savoury dish was designed to taste like a new flavour of the biscuit. I went to a clothing launch in collaboration with SpongeBob SquarePants and I dragged my friend Olivia to a Timberland event where we watched Giggs in concert from a soundproofed penthouse where the only drinks on offer tasted like Tango Ice Blasts and the average age of every influencer there was fifteen.

I desperately tried to fill my days. I wrote scripts and treatments, poetry and prose, but I was always on my own. I doubled down on press events.

A typical day involved a press breakfast where a brand would invite you to a fancy restaurant to talk about whatever they were selling. Then I might go and meet my agent or pop into the BBC for a meeting that would amount to nothing. Fortuitously, I made a new friend at a wedding who had the most millennial of job titles. Stacy was an influencer liaison. She was in charge of the guest list for the very kinds of parties I wanted to be invited to. It was her job to make sure influencers turned up and took pictures. I wanted to be on her list.

Stacy and I were cut from the same cloth. We both loved memes and rubber-necking Z-listers at parties. She was my ticket to the fashion world, and I couldn't wait to be there.

Now as I've mentioned earlier, I consider myself to be good at parties. I am one of the few people on Earth who actually enjoys small talk, loves being somewhere early, and doesn't like to leave until they're forcibly removed. I don't believe in being fashionably late because often the best people have already gone on somewhere else, and you need to make sure you're invited. It's usually The Box – a club famed for its debaucherous cabaret, celebrity clientele and stringent door policy. I once watched someone defecate onto a pizza box on stage. If you get invited you should go to The Box at least once. I felt like my life had finally come full circle when I was invited by none other than Danny Dyer. Sure, I once went to a Young London party at the age of twenty-nine and met a man with a jacket that said 'free drinks won't pay our rent' on the back, but I later saw he had a Coutts card so I'm assuming he was OK with the set-up.

Fashion parties were where the fun was at. The champagne was better, everyone was beautiful and nobody cared that they had to be up in the morning. Finally, I could dance on a table and rip my dress without fear, because nobody there wanted to work with me anyway. Everyone is constantly looking over each other's shoulders, trying to see if someone more famous is working another part of the room. As the least famous person there, I had none of these hang-ups. I was at the bottom of a ladder I had no intention of climbing, so I and whichever friend I'd dragged along as my plus one drank free champagne to our heart's content while Z-listers pretended to DJ. You get used to feeling like a famous person quite quickly. That's what happens when people start taking your picture at parties, giving you free stuff and constantly blowing smoke up your arse. I thought I would never tire of people telling me I was hilarious, but the more people that said it, the less true it started to feel.

When you're a PR casting around for people to attend an event or a press trip, there are a lot of things to consider. Sometimes you're looking for high reach, sometimes you want press coverage or a good fit for your brand, but you're also going to take into consideration who you want to spend time with. Stacy confirmed that the people who are repeatedly booked are those who are memorable and fun to work with. While it's hard to turn down someone who shifts a lot of product, if they're awful to be around it's unlikely they'll be booked again. Apparently it's often the least well-known talent that have the biggest demands. A micro-influencer once asked Stacy for a car to an event she was one street away from.

There's a special alchemy when you cross an influencer with a party monster. When you combine notoriety, narcissism and a lack of a need to get up the next day, lube it up with free champagne and leave it in a room to stew, you've got yourself a three-day party. My rule of thumb is that as soon as you look around and realise you know nobody there, don't stop to try to make friends. It's time to leave.

Things I guarantee about these parties:

1. The drinks will be free and either lethally strong or terribly watered down.
2. Dave Benett will be taking the photos.
3. A Z-lister or child of someone famous will be the DJ.
4. Bip Ling.

It's a common trope for celebrities to claim they don't enjoy these parties, that they're full of posers and social climbers and aren't worth going to at all. But I disagree. The night is what you make it, and with enough free champagne, I could have fun in a cardboard box.

Better than a cardboard box is a box at the National Television Awards, hosted by *The Sun*. A journalist I'd befriended on my press trail invited me and I jumped at the chance. Free champagne at the O2 surrounded by the cast of the most recent *Love Island* contestants? Yes please. The potential for a selfie with our Lord and Saviour Gemma Collins? Sign me up.

I spent a day browsing iconic looks seen at the NTAs for inspiration. There was clearly a foolproof formula. Teeth on show, tits round neck and the skin colour of either a Wotsit or a walnut. More than once I had to double-take after I thought I'd spotted Melania Trump. I dug around in my cupboard and found a tuxedo – it would have to do.

I'd been asked with some other influencers to come down and take some group shots and I fancied killing some time and a free blow dry. 'Oh no,' they said, when I told them my wardrobe plan. 'You should wear something more your style, something foodie.' I looked at a dress covered in sequinned chicken drumsticks and winced. Maybe I could wear a jumpsuit, I reasoned. Something I might wear again but that's a bit more formal.

The one I found was in the AX Paris sale, had a velvet off-the-shoulder top and some slightly shiny wide-legged trousers. It was as close as I was going to get to Tulisa.

The crowd at the NTAs was everything and more. The journalist took a picture of me holding a bucket full of champagne, which I posted on Instagram as a 'grape juice cleanse'. I was in *The Sun*'s box with more than one star of *Geordie Shore*. I was in heaven.

I worked my way around the room, thrilled that everyone was polite enough to feign interest in me. Up close the reality stars all had exactly the same face. They looked like they'd just killed their ageing fourth husbands and were on their way to empty his bank account. Everyone looked ever so slightly like a sexy cat that got lost in Torture Garden. I knew the GC had to be there somewhere, I just needed to know where.

Luckily my companion was working the awards. She needed stories and it was her job to know where everyone was. I had an inside scoop on the world of the celebrity journalist. As far as I could discern, what happens at these events is that a showbiz journalist approaches a celebrity and asks them about their lives, trying to glean a story. The celebs all know they're a journalist, but it benefits them to be in the papers, so they tend to spill the beans. Upon walking into the *Daily Mail* box, Olivia from the second season of *Love Island* grabbed my hand. 'You be careful with her … don't tell her anything.' Safe in the knowledge I had nothing to tell, I followed her straight to Mecca. Gemma 'the GC' Collins was reclining on a banquette. The journalist did the introductions.

'This is Bella. She's Deliciously Stella. You'd really like her Instagram. It's so funny. We're trying to get her a TV show.'

'Please can I have a selfie,' I gushed, like a teenage Justin Bieber fan. 'Sure,' she said. As we parted, she picked up her phone and made it clear it was my time to move on.

'I'll follow you, babe,' she said, before turning off her screen and putting her phone in her bag.

Somehow, someone had managed to get me invited to the after party, where even more of ITV's finest were gathered. Holly Willoughby almost hissed as the showbiz journalist walked past. She'd clearly been stung before. Knowing the showbiz journalist had work to do, I busied myself making friends and texting blow-by-blow updates to all of my WhatsApp groups.

Yes, I had met Gemma Collins. Yes, I was at the after party. No, I hadn't managed to find Ant from Ant and Dec and remind him he'd once opened my water for me at a drum'n'bass rave. I met some other showbiz journalists, all circling drunk soap stars like sharks, waiting for someone to snap and leak a story. As the party was emptying, the showbiz journo found me and bundled me into a cab. The night wasn't over. We headed to a nearby Hilton Hotel where the cast of *Casualty* were cramming into a room. I somehow ended up on the phone to James Corden. It was time for me to leave. At around 4am, when the minibar started to look sparse, I made my excuses and fled.

The first time I got papped I was walking the red carpet for a play. Emily was producing it and it was written by and starred Matthew Perry of Chandler from *Friends* fame. I'd been told that I had to walk the carpet, but I hadn't expected anyone to know who I was. When I arrived a woman with a clipboard steered me away from my friends. I was on a red carpet, with flashbulbs everywhere. All I could think was that this would be a terrible time to have a panic attack. Everyone else on the carpet was wearing their glad rags and I was in a hoodie and jeans. People were screaming my name. I was electrified. When I finally walked into the theatre all my friends were screaming.

'You got fucking papped!' I had. I'd got papped. I couldn't believe it. I was an actual offline celebrity.

The next day, a photograph of me appeared in the *Daily Mail*. I looked like a startled mongoose. 'We need to get you some posing lessons,' said my mum. Posing lessons is the sort of thing only my mum would know about. She'd been to a sort of finishing school at Eggleston Hall where they filmed *Ladette to Lady* and was prone to putting a book on my head as I walked by to point out how bad my posture was. Within five minutes she'd located a teacher and offered to buy me a session. I quickly declined.

I was lucky in a way that I immediately had name recognition. When I went viral I made the crossover from Instagram into mainstream media. At the first few parties I attended, I was handed a watered-down cocktail and awkwardly left to make small talk with an off-duty model. By the time I'd gone viral, the champagne was flowing and everyone was desperate to meet me. I stopped having to introduce myself, because a man with a clipboard somewhere had made sure everybody knew.

'Don't forget me when you're world famous!' they said. 'I can't believe you don't have a TV show yet.' 'Mate. This is your moment. Everybody's talking about you.' It looked like praise but it felt like pressure. It was time to turn those followers into viewers.

# 100,000 Followers

I couldn't accept that I was an influencer at 10,000 followers, I couldn't accept it at 20,000 followers, but after what happened next, resistance was futile.

I was at my parents' house when Alan from BuzzFeed called. Now safely ensconced in Scotland, free from the pressures of a job, rent and the upkeep of any sort of social life, I was finally able to devote all of my time to my one true love, Instagram. I scuttled from room to room, hunched over my device like a hobgoblin. Scroll, like, comment, scroll, like, comment. The follower number going up felt like a hit. I was the sick boy of Instagram.

It had been a good day when the email from Alan came through. I had changed into fresh pyjamas and eaten breakfast. My brother was home for the school holidays so he was left to act as my ward for the day.

'I'll let you shower with the door closed,' he said. 'Nobody needs to see that.'

After I'd washed, with my phone in view on the sink, I glimpsed a notification from the corner of my eye. Press, I thought, hurriedly rinsing the shampoo from my hair.

Alan apologised for not having been in touch sooner. They'd like to do an interview, he said. I tried to impress my brother with this news, but he merely grunted and returned to playing

*Call of Duty*. I put on my best 'everything is fine' voice and prepared to speak to Alan.

I'd become a dab hand at interviews by this point. I'd worked out that the questions were always roughly the same and had rehearsed witty replies.

What made you start the account?

Why do you think it's struck such a chord?

Have you ever had any backlash?

Do you eat everything that you use on your account?

I trilled through my usual stock answers, quietly pinching myself that I was about to make it into a real-life listicle.

After the interview, Alan ended our call with a joking 'Hopefully we can help you up to 25,000.' What happened next was madness. The article went live a couple of hours after we'd had our chat. I texted my agent to tell her about it and she replied with a nonchalant 'woop'. Then I checked my Instagram.

I refreshed the page and saw that I had 2,000 new followers. When I refreshed again, I had 4,000 more. 'What the fuck is going on?' I asked my brother. 'Bells,' he said. 'You're the number one trending topic on BuzzFeed worldwide.'

I logged onto BuzzFeed and there I was. They'd created a list of my funniest moments and it had been shared thousands, no hundreds of thousands, of times. My phone crashed and I opened Twitter on my laptop. People were talking about me everywhere.

25,000, 30,000, 40,000, 70,000 …

Every time I refreshed my follower number had rocketed. When I looked down I saw that my hands were shaking. I was being love-bombed by strangers, I was both ecstatic and bewildered, flattered and bemused.

More celebrities followed me. Caroline Flack. Zoe Ball. Ashton Kutcher tweeted about me and I almost had a seizure.

I called my mum and tried to explain, but going viral is a difficult thing to translate to someone who texts with one finger and one of her eyes closed. By the time my dad had returned from work that evening I had 50,000 new followers and was planning to stay up to do interviews in the US, Canada and Moscow. I texted Caroline, 'see you on *Ellen.*'

Over the next twenty-four hours, interviews with me appeared in publications in France, Germany, New York, the Netherlands and Russia. A patissiere called Anges de Sucre announced she had designed a cake called the Deliciously Stella. The article on BuzzFeed had been shared over a million times.

Come the next day, I had gained 75,000 followers overnight. Now my biggest concern was what I was going to post. I had 75,000 new people to impress and I knew it had to be a winner. I hauled a dusty kettlebell out of a cupboard and put it on the kitchen table. I sat and stared at it until my mum turned round.

'What on earth are you doing?' she asked. 'I'm watching my weight,' I replied. Mum paused for a second, before breaking into a grin. She put some gingernuts in front of me and a ring I'd been sent by a fashion editor that said 'Stella'. The crowd went wild.

My mother was more desperate than ever to prise her adult daughter away from her smartphone. I was scrolling on dog walks, when I was watching TV, in the car, in the bath, at the table, in my bed. Eventually she tried to distract me with the prospect of new clothes, dragging me to an H & M in an industrial park nearby.

'This might be nice for work, darling?' she said, picking out a shirt.

I glanced up from my phone reluctantly.

'I don't have a job.'

'But you will have a job again shortly. You won't be feeling poorly forever.'

My parents had not yet accepted that Deliciously Stella was my job. I mean, sure, I hadn't started generating income from it yet, but I was sure that 95,000 followers was the magic number. Loads of people had started doing ads on Instagram and while I wasn't about to promote charcoal toothpaste or flat-tummy tea, I thought I'd found a pretty good niche.

'Well, you'll need some smart clothes for interviews at least,' Mum reasoned as she picked up a skirt.

I screamed and punched the air. Mum took a hard second look at the skirt.

'Do you really like it, darling?'

'No! I've just got 1,000 likes in ten minutes on today's post!'

Getting 1,000 likes was my secret milestone. Whether I hit it and how quickly helped me mentally determine how well my life was going. It was like rolling a six or pulling an ace. I was addicted to the high.

I put my phone in my pocket and looked straight through the skirt.

'Let's take these to the changing rooms, shall we? We're celebrating.'

I told myself that it wasn't really the Instagram I was obsessed with. The followers were a Trojan horse that would lead me to TV shows, magazine columns and my very own sitcom. I thought back to Faye, trying to make me take the wellness witches seriously. 'Imagine turning those followers into viewers?' I could, but I needed more of them.

Mum, quite sensibly, decided that I shouldn't be going out and about too much until the risk of a psychotic break or severe gastric distress had subsided. It's one thing to lose control of your bowels at home, but quite another to do it in ASDA in Dunbar.

She offered to go on pun runs to the supermarket, coming back with sweets she thought might make funny jokes. In between acting as my assistant, she was my carer, dosing me out quarter pills of quetiapine, which she divided with a pill cutter. I still wasn't sleeping and perpetually felt like someone was trying to punch through my chest from the inside, but I was with my parents, so I was safe.

Just because I'd had a nervy b didn't mean that Stella had. I'd decided that Stella's brand was definitely perennially cheerful. Nobody wants to laugh at a sad clown. Stella continued terrorising the world of wellness just as she always had, nobody needed to know it was from my sick bed.

I told Caroline and my editor that I'd moved home to finish working on my book, which was sort of true. It was almost like going on a writer's retreat, but my mum was there and she wouldn't let me wash with the door closed in case I tried to drown myself in the bath.

I had to invent sixty healthy 'recipes' made out of sweets for the book, but I was finding it hard to focus on anything that wasn't Instagram. I noted down the name of every celebrity that followed me, like a creep, spamming their posts with heart-eye emojis. I trawled the eat clean hashtag, liking every post. It was working. Mum followed me around, demanding that I put down my phone and change my pyjamas. The poor woman finally thought her children had all flown the nest, and here was I, a life-sapping ghoul with her head in her phone who that morning had covered her kitchen in goldfish biscuits so she could make a joke about 'seafood soup'.

I knew I was getting better when my family felt well enough to make jokes.

'What are you doing, darling?' asked my mum while I beadily waited for the croissants to rise.

'I'm thinking about sticking my head in the oven.'

'Oh, well, good luck. In case you haven't noticed, we have an Aga.'

I'd been reading countless misery memoirs, finding that languishing in others' depression somehow comforted my own. When I finished a book I'd immediately google the author to find out if they were still alive. If they were I might try to go outside or put my phone on aeroplane mode for an hour so I could shower and eat; if they had gone on to take their own lives I'd return to my room to silently scroll under the covers.

Caroline called to tell me that the phone was ringing off the hook and I needed to go back to London. Brands wanted to meet me. They wanted to pay me money to post. I was officially an influencer. I was also still living with my mum and dad. Apparently, it's crucial for influencers to build an offline brand, and that meant appearing in person. Caroline was also keen that I attempt some stand-up in character before the Edinburgh Fringe.

Weighing up my options, I realised that I didn't really have any. If I stayed in Scotland and made myself some sort of housebound Instagram enigma, I'd be stuck as an Instagrammer forever. If I went to London before I was ready, I might risk having another nervy b. I had become so good at marketing Stella, it had slipped my mind that at some point people would want to see Bella too, and it would be better for everyone if she didn't have a panic attack, start humming Beyoncé or, God forbid, shit herself.

If there was one thing I was sure of, now was not the time to be having a nervous breakdown, so I threw all of my worries into a mental trap door, slammed down the lid and slapped on a smile.

Living at home with my parents in the middle of nowhere meant that I hadn't been paying a huge amount of attention to my appearance. My hair was largely unwashed and I'd taken to wearing some tracksuit bottoms of my brother's that had lost their elastic. When I went to get my 'outside clothes' I was surprised to find that my mum had shrunk almost all of them in the wash. My mother is a notorious shrinker. She is passionate about her tumble dryer and if you don't stand in the laundry room while she's washing, your high-end threads are doomed to a life of being slightly too tight and cropped to be worn again. I stormed into the sitting room, where she was catching some well-earned rest from being my photographer.

'Mum!' I shouted. 'You have shrunk all of my clothes!'

She looked at me with deepest sympathy.

'I haven't washed any of your clothes darling. I didn't dare in case you shouted at me.'

I looked down at the newly doughy muffin top that was spilling over my jeans, screwed up my face as I spotted the first signs of cellulite on my upper arms.

'I think it's possible you might have put on a bit of weight.'

How could I have been putting on weight? I thought. I had been eating everything I usually did plus a bit more cheese, and yes, maybe a bit more afternoon toast and admittedly SOME of the sweets I bought for Stella. But all those journalists kept congratulating me for being really thin and, good God, I really don't fit into any of my jeans. I looked back through my Instagram and realised that I hadn't posted a full body shot for quite some time. Had that been a conscious decision? Confused and desperate to shift the blame, I decided to call my shrink.

'My metabolism is a hate crime and I suspect that something you've prescribed me is to blame.'

He let out a deep sigh.

'It isn't a side-effect that affects everyone.'

I was horrified. He claimed that if you maintain a normal diet you shouldn't put on more than a pound or two. I felt like Regina George post Kalteen bars, lured into a false sense of security by something that was supposed to help me and tricked into having to wear sweatpants every day of the week.

I stripped down to my pants and looked at myself in a full-length mirror. I looked like someone had shoved some bellows up my arse and blown me up. Who did I think I was? No one could live in this house and not gain weight, quetiapine or no quetiapine.

The only way Mum could think to make me feel better was to feed me. She'd been fattening me up like a foie gras goose and I'd been too busy scrolling to notice. Naturally, I wasn't willing to take any responsibility for my increased appetite. It was the drugs and Mum's fridge. It was nothing to do with my lack of willpower.

Mum pointed out that if I wanted to be a true advocate for body positivity I probably shouldn't give a shit that the pills made me fat. They were working, which was all that we could have hoped for. I insisted they were changed for a drug whose side-effects included a rash that could lead to death.

In truth, I really longed to love my body, to feel positive about my body – hell, I would have taken feeling neutral about my body – but in all honesty it was far too late. The message that thin is good and fat is bad had infiltrated my psyche. The wellness witches with their chocolate-free chocolate and their insistence that you really could make kale that tastes like crisps only served to make me feel more terrible about myself.

I truly believed that we shouldn't spend so much time thinking about our bodies, but I wasn't able to practise what I preached. I was sure I was on the right side of history, and so I pretended. I wanted future generations to feel differently. I wanted other women to find comfort in the idea that someone like me could not give a shit.

I put off my trip to London until after I'd changed my meds and Mum had taken me to Topshop to buy me some bigger jeans. She then dropped me off at the train station with a train picnic that included two chicken and avocado rolls, a packet of Wotsits, a Coca-Cola and two Tunnock's Caramel Wafers. I cursed her as I ate the whole lot.

# Self-Promotion, Swag and Sponcon

I may have fallen into influencing accidentally, but make no mistake, once I got there I was there to get the bag. Gifting truly never gets old, and at first I took to free goods like a duck to water. I would say that, in the world of the influencer there's a well-trodden path to success. The three Ss: self-promotion, which leads to swag, which leads to sponcon.

Unfortunately, brands aren't just sitting around waiting to give you stuff or throw money at you to post about them. You first need to let them know that you exist. Tagging, DMing and stalking them IRL until they take the bait and you find yourself trading #likes4gifts.

'I'm just reaching out to say thanks for the follow, I love your brand and if you're ever looking to collaborate, I'd love to get together and chat ideas.'

'Collaborate.' The polite way of saying 'give me something for free'. At first, sending these messages made me retch, but often a PR will be more than happy to take you for a coffee or a drink and sling you some brownies or a handbag. 'Reaching out' is influencer 101, and I needed to get over my fear of doing so, sharpish.

The best Instagrammers aren't necessarily the ones who take the most beautiful pictures, or even those with the most followers. They are the born hustlers.

While a lot of the time brands will come to you, if you want to be at the front of someone's mind when they're casting for campaigns, you need to make yourself known. While keeping up an online presence is important, I personally found that I was much more convincing IRL. My mother always taught me that the best way to get invited back is to help clear the table and write a thank-you letter, but I know it's better to be the funniest person in the room.

There is a finite amount of marketing budget across all brands and an ever-growing number of influencers. If you want those brand deals you have to work for them. Influencing is more than just selfies: it's setting up meetings, singling out PRs at events, building relationships, and when you do post for a brand, making sure your engagement is sky high. Engagement is likes, comments, page views, clicks through to brands. Brands keep a record of which influencers have the best conversion to sale rate and will often publish it to keep everyone on their toes. There are sharks in the boohoo-infested waters, and they're after your spon.

While I would happily tell my life story to a wall, sealing a deal is not my forte. I can make someone my best friend in the course of an evening, but I could never ask them to do something for me, let alone something that might lead to them giving me money. I told myself that was my agent's job, but really you're your own best salesperson.

I soon learned that the truth was I wasn't that good at the hustle when I was sober. When I was drunk, I was striking deals like a wine-drunk Del Boy. It's much easier to 'absolutely insist that we work together' when you're tanked up on fizzy wine and thinking about going on to a club. My drunken sales pitch wasn't even limited to networking events. I once managed to secure a deal with KFC at a house party in Dalston.

Unfortunately, I couldn't conduct all of my business affairs while under the influence, so I was lucky to operate in a very niche market. Some other bloggers would stray into promoting junk food, but if your brand had a high sugar count and a sense of humour, I was your gal.

Once I'd worked out there was money to be made by being on brands' radars, I turned my attention from stalking celebrities to emoji-bombing businesses I thought should use me as ad space. I slid into DMs, met brands for coffees and for drinks. If I'd applied the same energy to my love life that I did to seducing brands I would no doubt be married with two kids.

Of course, sometimes I was led on. If I had sealed the deal with every brand that offered me twenty grand to throw yoghurt at vegans I would be a very rich woman indeed. The yoghurt job will always be the one that got away. Twenty thousand pounds to literally stand outside a health club with a sign that read 'Dairy Free' that I could then swap around to read 'Free Dairy'.

I learnt a lot about hustling from my new friend, the clean eater, with whom I was spending more and more time. We'd been working on a web series idea that would play on our opposing attitudes to what constitutes delicious foods. We'd even got as far as a meeting with Jamie Oliver's production company. The clean eater was a born hustler, and I knew I could be pretty persuasive once you got me in a room.

We were plotting who else to approach about the show one day, when she excused herself for a minute. She told me she was having something delivered to the restaurant, and at first I thought it might be drugs. It did seem a little early, but I'm not one to judge. When she returned she was laden down with bags.

'Sorry, babe,' she said. 'I'm going on holiday next week and I need things to wear.' The bags were full of clothes she had requested from PRs. 'You just email them and ask them,' she said. As if asking for free stuff was the most natural thing in the world. 'The worst they can say is no.'

My mind was well and truly blown the first time I was invited to a gifting suite. I had heard of these – I knew that at events like the Oscars and the Grammys, they invite celebrities into a room to browse for ludicrously expensive gifts to take home, as well as putting together lavish goody bags.

When practising my Oscars speech in the mirror for my as-yet-unwritten screenplay, I often thought about gifting suites. The idea of walking about with a million dollars of swag when you're already a millionaire ten times over is revolting, but also kind of amazing.

The day I found out about regular gifting suites, it felt like my very own invitation to the Oscars. Influencer gifting suites are held by brands who are debuting new collections. They invite celebrities and influencers to a showroom, where you can have a glass of champagne and a plant-based snack, before picking out what you like from the collection and getting your nails done.

The first gifting suite I attended was being held by Converse. I'd been invited by Stacy and I took my best friend, Kat, with me.

'This is absolutely mental,' Kat said. 'What's in it for them?'

'I guess we're supposed to wear the trainers on our Instagrams. Also, it's a good networking opportunity.'

'The only person you've spoken to is me.'

'I know. I'm not very good at the hustle.'

My friendship with the clean eater was about as close as I got to camaraderie in the world of influencing. When I wasn't with her I woke up to me, attended meetings about me, made content including me and spoke to my agent about, you guessed it, me. It struck me that I needed to find some more people who shared my experience. I began to wonder, how do influencers make 'work friends'?

My own friends are amazing. They are funny, clever and supportive, but my god they didn't understand what I was going through. I had gone from being completely unknown to being a household name overnight. I went from being their mate to someone other people knew and wanted to be mates with. It was great to be able to take them out and let them exploit my freebies, but it also always felt a bit like showing off. I didn't have the language to explain that I didn't think I deserved it. I felt guilty when people gravitated towards me at parties and cringed when conversation turned to me again and again.

'I don't want to talk about my job. It's so boring! Tell me about what it's like being Instafamous!'

I'm a comedian and am therefore a narcissist with cripplingly low self-esteem, so of course I obliged. I could reel off the story of the last year of my life like a script, but I would happily have listened to someone drone on about insurance, if only to be spared from the monotony of being me.

Bored rigid by my life as a walking personal sales pitch, I'd been toying with the idea of going back to work in an office, just to keep me busy and so I could be around people. I'm an extrovert and I missed the water cooler, but everyone dismissed this as insane.

'This is your moment,' they said.

'You're living the dream.'

'You're your own boss and you're on your way to being a star.'

I missed my old boss. All I wanted was a colleague. For the sharing to go both ways.

My hunt for work friends started paying off when a fashion-forward feminist girl gang invited me to join and I started going to influencer events with them. Self-promotion and company, what could be better? Their ethos was that girls should help girls and they railed against the idea that women are all in competition.

I went to an event for Nike where we did a yoga class in an upmarket gym and were gifted their branded clothing. I was neither into yoga nor working out in only a bra in public, but the sense of community was so welcome. After our yoga class we all went for lunch and discussed what we were working on. Everyone offered to collaborate. I mean, sure, I had been co-opted into a series of humiliating group boomerangs where everyone else was able to pout and shimmy and I just rocked gently from side to side like a paralysed nugget, but I was reminded how much I'd missed feeling like a part of something.

I would argue that about 60 per cent of what is required to be a successful influencer is the art of the group boomerang. Influencers know how to make hair swishes look elegant and how to open a changing-room curtain while laughing and winking and doing the can-can all at once. They know how to position themselves in a ring light to make their skin look flawless. I just find that they make me squint. The good thing about events like these is that there is almost always free food and booze. Plus they get you out of the house and around actual people. Are the people spending most of their time looking at their phones? Yes. But then again so are you, so you can't really complain.

The leader of the girl gang assured me that she could help me do more brand partnerships. If the comedy doesn't work out, I thought, I could just be an influencer full-time. Loads of people are and they are making bank. I told her that brands had struggled with my particular brand of 'unspiration', but she dismissed this as tosh. I just needed to find the right brands.

Naturally, I started fantasising about pivoting my account into a blog that only featured five-star hotels and Birkin bags, but I knew my followers wouldn't buy it. I was the junk-food girl now. I could call in a favour for a tonne of Pillsbury dough but I couldn't justify asking for so much as a pair of socks or a mascara. My followers responded best to me looking rough. The more dilapidated the location, the better. What would I say to the PR? 'Please may I have some shoes? I won't take a picture of myself wearing them but I will make a flatlay on a bed of Peperamis.'

I became very envious of other influencers, whose experience I deemed to be far superior to mine. I watched hours of unboxing videos, seething as influencers unpacked designer clothes and skincare. When they received food I was even more jealous. That was my remit. They probably wouldn't even eat the cupcakes! At least I gave the ones I didn't eat to the homeless shelter. The people on the streets in Brixton are probably all now diabetic thanks to my good work.

Of course, I'm painting a very ugly picture of my Insta-envy, but I do so knowing that I'm not alone. A study conducted by the women's magazine *Stylist* found that 83 per cent of women feel that Instagram negatively affects their self-esteem. Everyone seems to be going on better holidays than us, have better interiors and better clothes. There's very little transparency when it comes to what is gifted, if and how it's paid for and whether everything is truly as brilliant as you say it is on social media.

A normal person can tell themselves that if they had the time and energy to get more followers, they'd have the same lifestyle, but there I was with all the time in the world, followers coming out of my ears and nothing to show for myself but a juice cleanse I'd never use and a crate of peanut butter.

I'd painted myself into a Haribo-filled corner and rather than see it for what it was, that I had built myself a brand that didn't lend itself to flogging clothes, I started wondering what was wrong with me. Was I not thin or pretty enough? Did people think being associated with me would harm their brand? I found out that influencers with far fewer followers than me were given clothing allowances for my favourite shops, when I had vouchers for Five Guys. Greed and envy were eating away at my self-esteem, and of course I told no one. How could you tell someone you didn't think you were getting the right kind of free stuff?

The gifts might not have been top end, but the money wasn't bad. I was paid intermittently, and never when it was promised, but I could charge thousands for a post so I wasn't complaining. A hundred thousand followers might seem like a lot to the layman, but in the influencer world I was small fry. I found myself absolutely ecstatic to be offered £1,000 to attend an awards ceremony for takeaways. My influencer liaison friend later told me that she had once offered someone £50k.

A common gripe for up-and-coming influencers not yet eligible for sponsored content is that parties and gifts don't pay the rent. One influencer asked Stacy for the monetary value of the gifting she was offering her in return for attending an event. The cost price was £30. She took it.

While I couldn't get anyone to go on record, it is well known in the industry that influencers sell on gifts to supplement their incomes. It's frowned upon to ask for something and then sell it on, but if it's offered to you and you photograph it, anything goes. Stacy even goes as far as to say that it's bad form to expect content in exchange for gifting. Gifting is about building a relationship with an influencer; if they post that's just a bonus.

Being a polite and anxious sort of person, I Instagrammed everything ever sent to me, whether it was a key ring or a can of beer. Now I wonder if I'd played a bit harder to get whether I would have had to Instagram so many pairs of branded socks.

It's often assumed that sponcon is the be-all and end-all when it comes to influencer's incomes, but most of us have got more than one hustle on the go. A lot of influencers have their own brands or their own range of merchandise. I personally designed a range of tote bags that read 'you can't milk an almond', which my mother and I packaged up and sent out from her basement in Scotland.

I was never at risk of collaborating on a fashion range but an influencer can sell out a collection by putting their name to it. Also, because everything I advertised cost less than a fiver, I wasn't making a huge cut through affiliate links.

Companies like rewardStyle are game-changing for fashion influencers, allowing their followers to buy everything they wear through affiliate links that give them a cut of everything they sell.

As a sponsored content virgin, I assumed that taking a picture of myself and writing a caption would be the easiest money I ever made. As far as I knew, the brand would send you the product, you'd stage a photoshoot and Bob's your uncle, you're rich.

In truth, coming to an agreement on content can be a long and arduous process. It will usually start with an NDA, to make sure you don't tell anyone about the new destroyer burger or the brand-new bubble-gum-flavoured Coca-Cola. Then they'll suggest an idea for you to run with, for which you'll pitch a few options. The brand will almost always then change their mind and you'll have to come up with three alternative, much less funny options. At this point there is still no guarantee you'll get the job. You just have to sit nicely while (insert brand name here) decide whether or not they want to pay you five grand to do yoga in a Greggs. More often than not, your deal falls through, and you must move on to butter up another PR for another brand. Occasionally, you'll succeed. Once your funny ideas have all been kiboshed, you will instead get someone to film or photograph you smiling with the product, which you send to the brand for approval. They'll then decide that the picture is too dark or it took too long or the idea isn't actually working, so you go back to square one, call your aunt again and ask her if you can film at her house because the brand isn't a fan of the colour of your kitchen.

Eventually, once you've settled on an image and a caption that doesn't align at all with your usual content, you will upload it at a strict time, including multiple embarrassing hash-tags, not forgetting #ad. Someone will then slide into your DMs to tell you you're a sell-out and you'll lose 500 followers.

'Why does that matter?' You might say. 'At least you got paid.' This is true. I did get paid, but I also cared deeply about what my followers thought of me. I was consumed with so much internalised shame about being an 'influencer' in the first place that admitting I needed a financial reward for something as 'stupid' as making jokes on the internet had tied me up in knots. I didn't look at it as a job or even as a chance to make 'easy money'. Legitimising my Instagram account by capitalis-ing on my followers felt deeply uncool, but I wasn't too cool to eat or pay rent, so I ploughed on regardless.

I lost followers every time I posted an ad and I took that loss as a direct criticism of my character and an assault on my self-worth. Lots of people choose to define themselves by their careers. Work has been described as 'the millennial religion of choice'. We live to work with even our hobbies opening up potential for more work in the form of a 'side hustle'. As far as I was concerned, comedy was my job and influencing was my side hustle. Was comedy what made me money? Was it what I spent most of my time doing? No, but it sounded better when I said it to someone in a bar.

My first lucrative deal was with ASDA, and we struggled to

come to agreement on the content. They were adamant that I could not infer that any of the sweets I was advertising were unhealthy. Fine, I said. I'll say they're healthy. That's the whole point of the account anyway. Unfortunately, they weren't happy about that idea either. What would be ideal, they suggested, would be me saying how much I love their Halloween produce, but make it funny. They weren't giving me much to work with. I also had to include two specific products: a cake in the shape of a pumpkin that could be smashed open to reveal sweets, and some creepy crawly jellies. The only problem was, they couldn't get the produce to me in time, so I'd have to go to ASDA to buy it. They assured me it would be available in all London stores, so I settled on a trip to ASDA in Leytonstone. I was recording a podcast episode with mummy blogger-turned-broadcaster Mother Pukka and was recording at her home.

ASDA in Leytonstone in the run-up to Halloween was like the seventh circle of hell. Landfill-destined plastic tat was strewn across the aisles, mothers were dragging screaming toddlers, begging them to decide what they wanted to go trick or treating as. One woman looked on the edge of a nervous breakdown as she tried to explain to her son that she was sorry, they had sold out of Spider-Man costumes and he would either have to go as a werewolf or a witch. I hurried down to the confectionery aisle, my eyes on the prize. I could see a sign pointing to smash cakes. I would be in and out in minutes. There were two pumpkin smash cakes left. Sweet relief enveloped me, but as I drew closer, devastation descended. Both of the smash cakes had already been smashed. I asked a helper to check if any others could be found in the London area. They said that they couldn't be sure, but Clapham would be my best bet. Leytonstone and Clapham are at opposite ends of London, but I needed that smash cake. My income depended on it. I clambered back onto the tube, cursing the lack of glamour that my 'influencer life' was affording me. I found two cakes in Clapham, headed over to Emily's and shot two versions of the smash. In one, I smashed the cake with my head, in the other with a rolling pin. I emailed the videos straight to ASDA HQ and by lunchtime the next day I had a reply.

'Could you do it exactly like you did, with the rolling pin, but wearing a Halloween costume from ASDA? We need the footage tomorrow morning at the latest.' I was furious. Not only did I have to go back to fucking hellish ASDA in Clapham, I now had to find another person willing to film me hammering a cake. There's a reason why so many successful influencers are in relationships, a 'boyfriend of Instagram' is almost a prerequisite for the role. Who else would take fifty different shots of you holding a latte on Portobello Road? Who, I thought, do I have to shag to get a video of me smashing a pumpkin? The only person who answered my pleas was my Aunt Jane, so I lumbered over to her house laden with the godforsaken smash cakes. This time I was clad in a 'werewolf American football player' outfit. I threw down that rolling pin like an axe, spraying Smarties everywhere. This would never have happened if I was a fashion blogger, I fumed to myself, pulling icing out of my hair. But then again, I was being paid thousands of pounds to beat up a cake. It was easy work if you could get it, and it would seem that finally now I could.

Not all brands were fans. When writing my book, I had to write to every single brand I planned on using in my 'recipes'. Unsurprisingly, lululemon wanted nothing to do with me. More surprisingly, McDonald's and Haribo wished to steer clear also, and, most surprisingly, NutriBullet were totally game and offered to send me a free food processor.

I was even quite often sent health food in the hope that I might use it ironically in a post. I passed on the juice cleanses to friends, thinking it not entirely appropriate to offer these to the homeless. Juice cleanses are, after all, just a vehicle for starvation. They're also full of sugar and cause weight loss that is impossible to maintain.

After the food came clothes. I love fashion. Getting sent free clothes played into my childhood longing to be an It Girl. Of course, the only clothes I was being sent were from Etsy designers, scribbled with slogans like 'sweat to eat' and 'cake not kale'. I readily accepted the gifts. You can never have too much loungewear, and in the comfort of your own home I see no shame in a slogan tee. I always longed for a free handbag, though.

I wanted to be photographed wearing nice clothes and have a side project in pretending to DJ at parties. At university I had even bought decks and a book called *How to DJ Properly*, but I neither looked like Alexa Chung nor had enough money to sustain a job-free existence spent flitting between nightclubs.

Not all of my collaborations were 'on brand'. Sometimes I just followed the money. I was collaborating with a beauty box subscription service on a tongue-in-cheek 'clean eating'-themed box, which I had thought would be dripping in irony. The collaboration was entirely off brand, but as far as Caroline and I were concerned, Stella's influencing days were numbered and we might as well make bank while we could. Caroline reasoned that they were paying me so much money I might as well throw in a show for the team.

Performing in a sunlit office on a Tuesday afternoon to people in desk chairs was surreal. I went straight from talking about box design to telling the CEO she had gluten face and shouting expletives into a burger phone. Part of the deal with the beauty box was that I create some original content to support the products inside. The only issue was, none of the products inside were funny.

In our meetings we had discussed my box being full of sweetie lip balms, chocolate bronzer and candy floss bath bubbles. Instead I was presented with a manuka honey face mask and a moisturiser that actually contained kale.

'Don't you think this is a bit more Deliciously Ella than Deliciously Stella?' I asked them.

'Oh no. We think it's even funnier that the clean-eating box is tied in with you. It's ironic.'

It might have looked ironic to them, but to me it looked like they wanted Deliciously Ella and I was the next best thing. My followers thought so as well. Women flooded my direct messages with questions. Why had I done it? Everyone could see it for what it was: a cash grab, and not a subtle one at that.

For me, the three Ss felt like a constant balancing act between my success and my integrity. Ironically, most of the time I felt like I hadn't mastered either.

## Objects of Desire: Sponcon Safari

We've all been chased around the internet by something we never even knew we wanted, but the best influencers are the ones who make you take out a Wonga loan to buy a velvet sofa. Here's what's currently haunting my timeline.

### The Jug that is an Arse

Hello. Hi. How are you? £400 burning a hole in your back pocket? Me too. Well, not really. I don't wear any clothes. I am the jug in the shape of an arse that you've seen all over Instagram. There's something so 'fashion' about me, isn't there? You've seen me in all the cool girls' houses. Nothing says 'I HAVE A SENSE OF HUMOUR' like putting your flowers in a butt.

Basic? Absolutely not. I'm cheeky and irreverent. I will make you feel like a fashion editor and a comedy legend. I'm just so 'witty'.

Will you look like you've copied everyone? Darling, that's what Instagram trends are for. Buy me before it's too late and they start selling knock-offs in Zara Home. You won't regret it.

### The Chonky Seal

The name's 'chonky seal' and I'm certain that if I chase you round the internet with enough urgency, you will have to buy me as 'a joke'. Online I look plush and cute but in real life my face looks cross and I smell of gasoline. My origin is ethically dubious. I'm sold from so many websites it's hard to keep track of where I come from but I'm never more than a click away.

I'm in your sponsored ads. I'm in *Vice* articles, I'm on that Instagram account you follow called 'round boys'. I'm at your friend's house. You'll buy one for your sister. I'm in your Christmas stocking and now I'm in your bed. You're not sure how I got here but you've always secretly loved the smell of petrol. The day you get me I am advertised to you on Facebook 250 times. My work is never done. Everyone needs a chonky seal.

### The Penny Lane Coat

Did you know that it's been twenty years since Kate Hudson made you want to run away to America and become a groupie? God that film was cool. Look at your Instagram. Wait. Is everyone wearing a Penny Lane coat?

They are. You saw me on Marianne in *Normal People*, too. You know you should try to buy vintage, but I'm right here in your Instagram stories. All your favourite feminists are wearing me. My fur's vegan-friendly and doesn't everything from the seventies just make you feel sexy?

If you buy me, you might find a boyfriend who looks like Billy Crudup. Think how cool I'll look with flares. Sure, you'll have to wear heels, but it will be worth it. Look how incredible I look on that TV presenter. She's posing outside Soho House. You recognise the railings. You could wear me in Soho House. Imagine how nonchalant you'll look walking past all the other girls with Penny Lane coats. You're not like them, though. No. You love the film.

# 130,000 Followers

My mental health was on a crime spree. It was a thief of joy and a murderer of hope, and worst of all, everyone thought I must be so, so happy.

I was standing on a train to Brighton at rush hour and had been held at a signal for over thirty minutes when I realised my relationship with Instagram had crossed over from problematic to deranged. I had not slept for more than a few minutes at a time for seven days. I ran through all the downers I'd taken to try to dull my zapped-out brain. Enough to tranquillise a dinosaur, and still I was awake. I'd suffered from insomnia since I was a child when I used to get up and draw. Now I sat up and scrolled. I figured there was always someone awake on Instagram. I never had to be alone with my thoughts.

I had spent three hours that day boring my sister to tears, trying to analyse why a string of recent posts hadn't performed as well as usual. She was at university, trying to live her best life, but my frantic phone calls had become incessant.

'Do you think people think it isn't funny anymore? Is the joke over? Should I just bow out gracefully before it gets embarrassing?'

She knew that she didn't need to reply. She listened to me gibbering while she boarded the bus, on her way to lectures or the pub. The only way to get me off the phone was to claim she was going to the library. Something I've since found out she hardly ever did.

'Do you think it's because I look too thin?' I'd posit, anxiously refreshing my home page in case a flood of likes had somehow been blocked from appearing. 'Maybe I had too many ads too close together. God, they probably think I'm such a sell-out.'

I'd recently hit 100,000 followers and to celebrate had taken a picture of myself in my underwear, covered in Happy Meal boxes. The number immediately slipped back down to 99.9. I'd returned to treating Instagram like Candy Crush, emoji-bombing strangers in an attempt to lure them over to my page. If I can get to 100,500 I'll be safe, I thought. My thumb was in agony. I suspected it had been repetitively strained through scrolling.

A change in algorithm had seen my engagement drop dramatically, meaning I was getting much fewer likes and comments than I had been. I'd also seen the tide turn on the clean-eating era. Wellness wasn't going anywhere but the particular food fad I'd so accurately satirised was dying out. I felt the slow creep towards irrelevance.

My posts were still getting thousands of likes, but when you've got over 100,000 followers it's hard to think about the thousand people who liked your post, and not the 99,000 people who saw it, thought nah and scrolled on past. I hadn't realised it at the time, but this was when Instagram stopped displaying posts in chronological order, and it was affecting how many people were seeing my content. I was making jokes to the equivalent of fourteen Wembley Stadiums or six O2s. The thought of bombing that many times while performing at either of those venues makes me feel sick to my stomach.

Thankfully, the show I was stuck at a red light trying to get to was not Wembley. I was heading to the Brighton Fringe, a comedy festival similar to the Edinburgh Fringe where lots of comics choose to preview early-stage shows. The frankly terrifying climate crisis was seeing to it that England was sub-Saharan and I was painfully aware that packed in my enormous suitcase were six rapidly melting mint Cornettos.

I had only been to Brighton once before, for my friend Margaret's hen, and I had hoped I might be able to take in a few sights to calm my nerves before my show. Instead, I was sweaty, cross and furious that I was going to have to do this all over again the next day.

The venue I was performing in was called the Queen Caroline of Brunswick, and I was expecting free-fringe vibes. My cab from the station drove by endless posters advertising shows from the big-hitters. I wondered if Caroline had organised for any of my posters to go up. I put a post on Instagram at the last minute, in case my fans didn't have a copy of the brochure.

I walked into the pub, banged my suitcase into everybody in the bar and took a seat. I soaked up my surroundings, noting that Slipknot was playing over the speakers and that above the bar hung a giant statue of Cerberus, the three-headed dog. I was in Brighton's premiere rock/alternative bar and I both looked and sounded like an extra from *Made in Chelsea*. Straight away, I did what I always did when I felt uncomfortable, opened my phone.

A mumble above me indicated that another show was underway, so I browsed the brochure to see who else was on. I flicked through the pages, looking for my name, but couldn't seem to find my show. I wheeled my suitcase out into the car park and called Caroline.

'Hello, do you remember that conversation we had about paying to be in the catalogue?'

'Yes,' she said. 'We decided you should be in there in case you don't have many fans in Brighton.'

'Yes. Well, I'm not in it.'

'Ah.'

I went to speak to the barman and explained my predicament.

'Not to worry,' he said. 'We'll put out a message over the speakers and ask the regulars if they want to go upstairs. We'll find you an audience.' I looked around at the regulars. Would punks like Deliciously Stella? Doesn't Brighton have an abnormally high population of vegans? I stuffed my 'you can't milk an almond' tote bag into my suitcase. This was going to be a long night. You know what, I reasoned, if nobody comes, there will nobody to perform the show to, in which case, I won't have to perform at all.

Caroline had instructed me to do as many previews as possible so I'd be in peak condition for Edinburgh, but every time I thought about Edinburgh an obscuring mist descended. My fantasy about the decimation of the city or the month-long lockdown had been replaced with an urgent desire to crack America. If America wanted me, surely that would be enough to have to turn down the Fringe. If America wanted me my life would be made. A small interview with me had been printed in *People* magazine and lots of Americans had commented that I was obese, awful and would never make it in the States. This did not deter me in the slightest; I was convinced they just didn't know what they were missing.

I'll show you, I thought. You're just a bit behind. America will come for me soon enough, then I'll never have to do stand-up again.

The muffled sound of applause and scraping chairs from upstairs let me know that the act before me had finished. I dragged my bag up the steep steps and was greeted by a friendly man with blue dreadlocks.

'Really excited to see your show,' he said, shaking my hand. 'How would you like me to introduce you? And would you like any music to play as the audience comes in?'

I asked him to introduce me as Deliciously Stella, and suggested that I come in from off stage. Of course, we weren't in a theatre, we were in a pub, but he showed me that a further seating area had been cordoned off by a curtain.

'I'll be behind the curtain,' I said, before sheepishly adding, 'I usually have the audience walking into Britney Spears, "Circus". The character's quite basic, you see.'

'Sure,' he says. 'Have you got that? Because we definitely don't.'

I opened my suitcase to see that everything inside it was covered in bright-green ice cream. I'd forgotten about the Cornettos. I begged the kitchen staff for some blue roll and frantically tried to stem the worst of the leaking mulch. I hadn't long until the show began so I started setting up my props. I had a table with a white cloth on which stood a NutriBullet. Under the table was a spiraliser, a Mars bar, a bottle of Malibu, a loaf of bread, guacamole and a tub full of Haribo eggs.

I asked him for a final favour.

'I need to hide a pain au chocolat under someone's chair so I can accuse them of smuggling gluten into a safe space. Can you make sure it's under a chair that's occupied? Otherwise the joke won't work.'

The sound of footsteps was my cue to slip behind the curtain and wait. This is always the point when my nerves peak – my heartbeat thrums in my ears, my jaw is clenched. The room behind the curtain was pitch black. I couldn't hear much but I could sense a couple of people on the other side. I hadn't got my phone with me, so I had no idea of the time. I started to feel the faint prick of pins and needles which normally precedes a panic attack. Finally, after what felt like a lifetime, I was announced and I burst through the curtain. There were three people in the crowd. One girl was sat near the front and started laughing before I'd said anything. A couple were sat at the very back, near enough to the door to make an escape in the first five minutes.

My heartbeat felt like it was pushing its way out of my skull and rather than think about the show, all my brain was saying was 'Did you remember to put a tampon in? You took a tampon out, but did you put another one in? You're wearing blue leggings. Everyone's going to see. What about when you do the yoga moves on the floor? You've clearly bled everywhere already, you are so disgusting. Everyone is going to be horrified.'

I forced down a dry swallow before looking up at my three audience members. 'Hello and welcome to my wellness work-shop – eat, body, glow!'

I'd started. I was speaking, only fifty minutes to go and then it would be over. I tried to keep my womb out of mind but the room had no windows and I was sweating like a pig in a cellar. Every fibre of my being was willing me to run off the stage, out the door and back to London, but still I soldiered on. I asked if we had any vegans in tonight. A couple at the back raised their hands and I nodded. I hadn't prepared a comeback.

About twenty minutes in, I realised that the pain au choco-lat was at least three rows from anyone. 'What's that?!' I shouted, before silently striding down the aisle between the chairs and shuffling along a row. Clattering awkwardly, I bent down and grabbed the pain au chocolat. I pointed at the couple at the back. 'Is this yours?' They didn't answer me. 'I said is this yours?!' I was pointing again. The woman let out a yawn. 'I think it is.'

Returning to my table, I felt my mind dissociating from my body. I was watching myself perform this terrible gig. I was thinking about how it would make a good story. I thanked the lord that I wasn't in the programme.

For the finale, I asked the girl in the front row to join me for some yoga. The tampon was forgotten. I was running on auto-pilot. At the end she asked for a selfie and I thanked her for coming. She said it was difficult to track down where the show was, but that she had seen I was here on Instagram. Caroline texted me to ask how it went but all I could focus on was getting back to the station. I asked to leave the suitcase there overnight and walked hurriedly uphill. I needed to be far away from that pub, far away from that performance. On the train I felt vacant and wired. When I stepped onto the platform in London I called my mum: 'I don't think I know who I am.'

Now, I don't know about you and how you talk to your mum, but for my mum, this was a pretty concerning phone call. It got further concerning when I started crying, speaking gobbledegook and hyperventilating. I still hadn't made it through the ticket barriers. She begged me to call my agent and ask her to cancel the next day's show, but I refused. 'I can't let anyone down,' I sobbed.

'For God's sake, Bella, you're not in the programme. Nobody even knows you're there.'

'You – don't – understand,' I said between ragged breaths. Mum let out an exasperated sigh. 'I'm trying to, sweetheart. Really I am. I just hate to hear you so upset.'

I composed myself and headed to the ticket barriers. After five minutes of wild pocket rustling, I conceded I'd left my ticket on the train. The panic started rising again and I went once more to call my mum. A kindly station worker saw me flapping. He helped me through the barriers and I headed back home for another sleepless night.

I wish I could tell you more about what happened that second night in Brighton, but in truth I don't really remember.

All I can tell you is that the day after that second show was one of the worst of my life. I sat up in bed after another torturous sleepless night, dragged my show notes into bed from the floor and promptly had a panic attack. The pins and needles had been raging all night. Cold electricity rushed up and down my arms and my brain felt as though it was shrinking away from my skull. I called my mum and told her that I wanted to peel my skin off. She begged me to go to A & E, but I couldn't get out of my bed.

'I think that if I get out of my bed I might die,' I told her. 'Please call the doctor,' she begged. 'I'm so far away and I feel like there's nothing I can do.' I looked at my bedside table, covered in empty blister packets from sleeping pills that didn't work. Shrapnel left behind in the war against my sleepless brain. I had tried everything at that point: Ambien, diazepam, Xanax – even Nytol for good measure. I could not rest. I was certain that I was losing my mind. Eventually I managed to focus enough to call my GP.

'Am I correct in thinking you have private health insurance?'

I did. He referred me to the Priory and after a brief phone call with a kind and patient nurse, I packed an overnight case and jumped in an Uber. I called Caroline and told her I was sorry, but I wouldn't be able to do anything for a while.

'I'm only going in for a couple of days,' I said. 'They'll probably just change my medication and then I'll be fine.'

I wanted to tell my followers that I was struggling. That my brain craved more than photo ops in restaurants. That pretending to be Deliciously Stella was eroding my sense of self. My only interactions were through a screen and my only motivation was virtual likes from strangers. My existence felt vapid and futile. I felt vapid and futile. Everywhere I went I felt like I was playing a part.

I went because I was tired. I went because my doctor told me it was the right thing to do. I went because I could not be on my damned medication for one more day. But most of all I went because I was so bloody lonely.

I had been spending my life sitting in a room, taking pictures of myself and writing a show I didn't want to perform. Everyone was telling me I must be ecstatic, but I was so jealous of them. I envied their office banter, their after-work drinks and their ability to relate to anyone beyond themselves. The illness told me that no one wanted to see me, so I'd stopped trying to make plans. I went to call Liv to tell her what was happening and realised I hadn't called her in months. My friends thought I was too busy hanging out with celebrities to want to see them anyway. The only people I regularly conferred with were my followers, and I was lying to all of them.

As I pulled up to the Priory in a taxi, shaking, crying and snotting all over my Uber rating, I was terrified. Not about being mad or about having to go to hospital. I was terrified that I wouldn't be deemed mad enough to get in. I imagined the psychiatrist I'd been sent to see as the clipboard bitch for an exclusive nightclub. I was convinced he'd see me for the chancer that I was and send me back to my incredible life where everybody thought I was hilarious and loved me. In the waiting room, I realised that I hadn't posted on Instagram that day so I dug out a meme about M&Ms and toilets. I could tell immediately that it was going to do badly, which sent me into a wild panic. When it got less than ten likes in ten minutes I dissolved.

By the time I got into the room with the psychiatrist I was hysterical. I told him all about the lack of sleep, the dissociation, the terrible gig in Brighton and the repetitive strain injury I had sustained in my thumb from scrolling. I told him about the followers and the pressure and that sometimes when I'm struggling to go to sleep I hope that when I do I won't wake up.

He asked me who my health insurer was and promptly committed me for an inpatient stay. A kindly nurse led me down a corridor with her arm around me and into what looked like a three-star hotel room. She confiscated my phone charger, my laptop charger and the drawstring from my tracksuit bottoms. On my bed were a pair of Priory-branded slippers. I signed some forms, took some pills and fell asleep for nine hours.

When I woke up it was the evening and someone was coming in to ask me if I wanted dinner. I couldn't face seeing other people so I agreed to have dinner in my room. The nurse brought in a menu and a DVD of *The Best Exotic Marigold Hotel*. I kept one eye on the film and one on my Instagram, closely monitoring how many likes I'd not got on my latest post. I was scared that if I looked away I might accidentally reveal my location. I wondered if people could tell I was mad by the emojis I use to comment on their posts. I ate one bite of my lasagne before getting back into bed.

Later that evening I was offered some pills to help me sleep, which I gladly accepted, but instead of feeling tired I felt nauseous and restless. There was a button next to my bed that called a nurse, but nobody was coming. I tried to stand up but I felt faint. My vision started to blur. Eventually a small male nurse came into my room to find me sat on the floor, sobbing, with my head between my legs.

He gently picked me up and carried me into my en suite bathroom, where I slumped on the floor with my nightshirt up around my middle, exposing my greying thong. He took my lack of dignity in his stride and listened intently while I told him that I thought the doctors had poisoned me.

'I'm so sorry,' he says. 'I don't know what they've given you. I'm going to need to check your medical sheet.' I cried and cried, begging him to make it stop. He did his best to slow down my breathing. When he came back I was still lying on the floor of the wetroom. He said that they hadn't given me anything that should make me react this way. This was just the first time in a long time I'd had permission to relax. He rubbed my back and promised that if I could make it back into my bed, he would bring me a hot chocolate.

'You can only get hot chocolate from one machine,' he said. It was on the anorexic ward and he'd be gone for about fifteen minutes. I'd stopped retching but the room was still spinning like I was half-cut. He double-checked my room, confident that there was nothing there I could use to hurt myself, then he left me on the cold hard floor. I lay there for a moment, staring at the ceiling with my ridiculous nightshirt now up by my armpits.

I feel properly mad now, I thought, as I crawled across the floor and hauled myself into bed like a sloth. The nurse came in with my hot chocolate and I sipped it gratefully.

'Please don't let them do this to me again,' I begged. And then I fell asleep. I wish I could say that I enjoyed a blissful night of uninterrupted slumber, but then I would be lying about the reality of being in a mental hospital. It's standard procedure for the first few nights for you to be checked on every fifteen minutes to make sure you've not managed to hurt yourself or escape. For some reason it also seems standard procedure to do this as loudly as possible, thus ensuring that patients like me, who have been suffering from psychosis caused by sleep deprivation, don't get any sleep at all.

In the morning a nurse came in to wake me up for breakfast, but I was comatose. My first thought was of what I was going to post on Instagram, but I couldn't lift my head from the pillow. At boarding school I was so slovenly my matron used to drag me out of bed by my feet, but thankfully this tactic appeared to be frowned upon by the medical establishment. My doctor came into my room to ask how I was feeling and suggest that I go outside. I told him I wasn't ready to leave my room yet. He told me that I had to have a blood test.

Now, as I've mentioned before, I don't like blood tests at the best of times, and as far as I am concerned, a blood test in the Priory is definitely the worst of times. When the nurse got to my room, I was unable to stand without fainting for long enough to be weighed, and as soon as I saw the needle I went into shock. One large diazepam later and I was back to where I started. Bedbound.

On my third day in the hospital, the nurses clearly decided it was time for some tough love. They refused to bring me breakfast in my room and insisted that I eat with the other patients in the dining room. Walking into the dining room felt like the first day of school. I scanned the breakfast buffet for potential jokes for Deliciously Stella. I'd already used a full English in a post, in happier times. I grabbed a tray, some juice and some toast, bypassed a group in the middle of an animated conversation and sat next to an older woman. She was shaking so much she struggled to get her fruit salad into her mouth. We didn't speak.

My dad and my sister were coming to visit me that day and I was desperate to show them that I'd made some progress. The only thing I was more embarrassed about than being an influencer was being mad.

We always used to joke that my grandmother used the Priory as a country club. Whenever it got chilly in Scotland she'd book herself in. I'd never stopped to think about why she had to go, what it felt like, how isolating it must have been in a time where the stigma around depression was so much more severe. My dad never really spoke to his mother about her mental illness. When I first showed signs of getting ill, I asked him to find out her diagnosis in case it was hereditary, but he couldn't bring himself to ask her. Instead he called her housekeeper and asked her to write down the name of the pills in her bathroom so we could make an educated guess.

When I read them out to my psychiatrist he said that they were so ancient they were no longer prescribed on label. She was so terrified of another episode she'd refused to change them.

'Maybe I'll get a discount because I'm a legacy,' I joked weakly.

My dad had never been to the Priory and was impressed with the imposing building. My sister had been before, visiting other mentally ill friends who had been to our school. A girl from the year above me was also a patient. We nodded at each other in the corridor. An acknowledgement that we were products of the same system.

'Ah,' said Dad, proffering a Sainsbury's bag, 'I almost forgot.' I'd asked him to buy me some Party Rings so that I could make a joke about 'hole foods' on Instagram. It was still easier to pretend that I was OK than admit the truth.

Beana and my dad hugged me and left, and I took my Party Rings into the communal kitchen. A tall, kind Welshman asked me if they were my parents. I made a mental note to tease my younger sister.

'You should come watch TV with us this evening,' he said. 'They're playing *P.S. I Love You* on Film4.' I nodded, took my picture and went back to my room. The hole foods post was doing really well and I started to feel more positive. Maybe a movie night and some company was just what I needed.

The living area was a sort of kitchen diner where instead of sofas, individual green-lacquered armchairs seemed to be arranged to ensure you were as uncomfortable as possible. I was reminded of seating on public transport that's designed to deter rough sleepers. The kitchen itself was sparse, with a fridge and a coffee machine without any caffeine, lest those most anxious among us overdose on Nescafé and stage a coup.

A part of me had thought that staying in the Priory might be a bit glamorous. In the early noughties a friend from school had struck up a friendship with Ronnie Wood there.

Could it be, I thought, that I am the most famous person currently in the Priory?

My moment of narcissism was quickly dashed by everyone having not only not heard of me, but also not heard of Deliciously Ella. I was completely devoid of context. Everyone wanted to know why I hadn't been coming out of my room, and why I hadn't sat with them in the dining room. The only way I could explain it to them was that whatever they were giving me to take at night made me feel like I was in a K hole until about 11am.

'OK then,' said the Welshman. 'From now on, at 11am you should come and hang out with us when you're not in group.'

'Group' was group therapy, something I had yet to attend, in spite of being handed a timetable on my first day. I couldn't think of anything worse than exploring my feelings with a load of strangers every day. All I wanted was some time out, to be alone.

'You have to go to group,' everyone said. 'Otherwise what's the point in being here?' I knew they were probably right. It was selfish to waste this opportunity sulking in my room. I had access to some of the best doctors and therapists in the world and I needed to admit that although my life looked perfect from the outside, inside I was a mess.

The first time I went to group therapy was for a 'love and relationships' class. It was in a room known as the chapel, a cavernous hall with high ceilings and a red threadbare carpet. We filed in as if for school assembly, dragging our feet as we picked up piles of leaflets. Tina Turner's 'What's Love Got to

Do With It' was playing from a tinny speaker and a woman in a kimono stood next to a projector screen covered in clip-art love hearts.

Everyone sat in a circle and took turns to give their diagnosis and reason for being in the Priory. The stories were sad and moving. People had been bereaved, divorced or lost their jobs. I couldn't believe I was really there because I had too many Instagram followers and I didn't know how to cope. When it came to my turn I burst into tears and told everyone that all I really wanted was to not have to do my Edinburgh show.

We each wrote down a list of people who love us and I was thankful to be able to fill my sheet. I hesitated and considered whether I should write 'my followers'. I hadn't posted for two days and my inbox was already flooded with messages from concerned women, asking for their daily Stella fix.

In my one-on-one session with my psychiatrist he asked me how I felt about my Instagram account and I said I didn't know. The consensus was that a short break might do me good, but that keeping up with as much work as possible was important so I didn't fall behind.

'What would happen if you didn't post for a while? If you couldn't post? Are you really so sure the world would end?'

I thought back to the only time since I'd started the account that posting seemed near impossible. The previous Christmas, my sister and I received an unexpected windfall and our cousin, Sam, had extended an open invite to visit her at her house in Kilifi, in Kenya. We booked before we'd even properly asked, knowing it would be OK. Sam had an open-door policy.

I say that Sam was our cousin but she's really a second cousin of my mum. We're close in the way that large Scottish families are. Our blood ties are diluted but we'd never have insulted each other by just using the word friend. Sam taught me that there was more than one way to be a grownup. I spent my childhood longing to see her just so I could know what colour her hair was, and which exotic destination she'd come from. Sam never lived somewhere boring like Scotland, although she maintained a lilting accent. She lived in Barcelona or Sri Lanka and her hair was always russet red or dark blue.

Sam was a true eccentric and the expat life suited her. When she settled in Kenya, with her son, Zack, she made herself part of the local community, speaking a hybrid of English and Swahili wherever she went. She taught us how to square up to monkeys who trespassed in the house. Apparently you had to bare your teeth and scream as loudly as you could. The monkeys always strolled nonchalantly past us. She had complete faith in my career ambitions and always told me to keep writing. 'Keep going,' she said. 'Keep showing up and you'll get your break.'

She also had no truck with social media. When Francesca and I visited I had been contracted by a new social networking company, called Yubl. They were paying me a thousand pounds a month to post my Instagram content on their platform, and once a month I would post about them to my followers. It was a sweet deal. It hadn't occurred to me that coastal Kenya wouldn't have 4G, and that Sam had no reason to install Wi-Fi.

I should have known from how abrupt she was over text, and how infrequently I received replies to my emails to Samwhitewitch. She was texting from a 3310 and checked her emails once a week.

'It's fine,' said Francesca. 'Think of it as a digital detox. Your followers won't even notice you're gone.' The thought of not being able to scroll through Instagram at leisure was horrifying. What was I going to do all day? Talk to people? Read a book?

'Where do you check your emails?' I asked Sam, trying to sound nonchalant.

'In the eco-hostel down the road,' she said. 'It doesn't work all the time, but it's worth popping down.'

Of course, down the road meant through the jungle. Every day I'd trek in 35-degree heat to reach the eco-lodge and desperately try to sign into Instagram. What will my followers think? I thought, sweating under a weak fan.

As I dipped in and out of service my DMs filled up.

'Where are you?' they asked.

'Are you OK?'

'I need my Stella.'

One day I thought I wouldn't be able to upload my contracted content for Yubl. I was beside myself. If I broke the contract I might not get paid. Everyone would be furious with me. How on earth did I manage to come somewhere with no Wi-Fi?!

Sam found me stressing and bought me a beer. 'It doesn't matter, honey,' she said. 'Focus on the writing, and the rest will come.'

Of course you think that, I thought. You haven't a care in the world. You have a wine fridge in your bedroom. The stress had brought me out in a flaming heat rash all over my chest which my sister referred to as 'rashwanda'.

The lack of internet at least stopped me from posting about my rashmina, plus I had bigger concerns. I was taking the mood stabiliser, whose side-effects included a rash that could cause death. Francesca found me ruminating next to the fan in our room. The rash wasn't going anywhere.

'What if this is it?' I cried, wind blowing through my hair like a Poundland Beyoncé. 'What if I'm dying of a deadly rash from the very medication that is supposed to be saving my life?!' I started hyperventilating into the fan.

'I'm sure you're not dying,' pleaded Francesca. 'You just need to calm down.' Sam heard the commotion and padded down the corridor. When she walked in she started laughing like a drain.

'You are not dying, you plonker. You have heat rash.' She went to procure some Thai cooling powder with a snake on the front. She was right. It worked. Panic attacks can be quite mortifying once you've come out the other side of one. Trying to explain to someone who doesn't get them that you genuinely thought you were dying feels ludicrous. It's a hell of a lot worse when the real source of your anguish was an inability to access your Instagram.

Sam passed away in 2019, taken far too soon at fifty-two. I'd never known someone to die who had seemed so alive. The last time I saw her I told her my sitcom had been optioned and she punched the air. She was happier for me than I was for myself. The cancer took her in four short weeks, and I didn't have a chance to say goodbye, to tell her how much her spirit had meant to me and how hard I would try to stay involved in Zack's life. I can't believe I'll never see her again. I'll never get to go back to Kenya and not give a shit about Instagram, or the internet. I'd hoped to go out there to write some of this book, but I couldn't be in that house without her voice.

Pathetically, the day she died I googled her, sure that someone who meant so much to me must have left a trace, a digital footprint that proved she'd touched others the way that she had touched me. But there was no way to find one on a 3310, and my followers wouldn't care if I told them.

On my final night in Kenya, we went to a party in the eco-lodge where I toiled for internet. Sam introduced me to some men who lived on a boat in her bay. I chatted to a white man with one long dreadlock that he had hooked over his ear to create a chin strap and I told him what I did.

'Wow. That's crazy that's a job. I don't have social media,' he said. 'There's just so much vanity, you know?'

I asked him what had brought him to Kenya.

'I'm teaching the local people to build dhows.'

'You mean the dhows that the Kenyan people have been building for hundreds of years?'

He sneered at the rash that had snaked up my chest and onto my neck, untucked his dreadlock and walked away.

My doctor deduced from my story that the most important things to do were, a) change my medication so I no longer feared the death rash; b) try to relax my use of social media, but not in a way that could harm my career; c) concentrate on not disrupting the other elements of my career by being hospitalised.

I had thought that his reaction would be to cancel all of my upcoming commitments and book me in for a month-long spa break, not medicate me to a point where I could continue at a pace that had worn my nerves to shreds.

He didn't want me to leave hospital feeling like I had catching up to do. Slipping behind on my commitments would only make the anxiety worse. I wanted to throw the commitments on a bonfire and live out the rest of my life in a cave. I didn't tell him that in case he sectioned me, but I sort of wish I had.

The consensus was that I was in the midst of the opportunity of a lifetime. I was riding the crest of a wave of success and wiping out now was the worst thing I could do. We didn't discuss whether or not I wanted this life anymore or whether it was possible to carry on without doing lasting damage. I trusted that I could get better and keep my career. After all, wasn't it all I had? If I wasn't successful, who was I? I believed success was the only thing keeping me safe.

I left the doctor's office and went to the bathroom to wash my tear-streaked face.

'Chin up,' I said to myself. 'You can't waste your fifteen minutes of fame feeling sorry for yourself.'

I called Caroline to discuss my upcoming commitments. I

was due to record an episode of my new podcast and perform two preview shows at the Pleasance Theatre in Islington.

'It's completely fine to cancel. Honestly, your health is the most important thing right now.'

I took a deep breath. 'The doctor says I don't have to.'

'Are you really, really sure? It's no big deal at all to pull the shows if you're still in the hospital.'

'I will still be in the hospital, but they've said that I can come out to do the shows and then come back. They'll let me go on day release.'

I reasoned that I was genuinely starting to feel better. My medication had stopped making me permanently shake, the K holes were less frequent and I had befriended the strange American man who ran the gym. He had an extensive DVD collection which mainly included titles like *Girl, Interrupted* and *About a Boy*, but we decided we'd rather be triggered than bored. I'd settled into the routine of hospital life; I relished the structure of set bedtimes and meal times. It reminded me of being at boarding school. Our pills were even dispensed from behind Dutch doors in a room known as 'the tuck shop'.

As I was not under section, the hospital agreed to let me Uber to the theatre and back for my comedy previews. A friend dropped off my props and I got to work trying to learn my lines. Finding alone time in the Priory was tricky. I lack discipline at the best of times and now there was always someone willing to tempt me away. I'd far rather do a jigsaw, smoke a thousand fags or help a fellow patient dislodge a vodka bottle that had been left on top of the curtains by the previous occupant in her room.

My doctor suggested I do a dress rehearsal of my show for my fellow patients to help me learn my lines. I woke up that day with a bolt, sick with nerves.

It was a day of celebration in the Priory. It was the Queen's Jubilee and we were being treated to high tea on the front lawn, complete with a cardboard cutout of Liz herself and cupcakes with edible pictures of HRH. I took a picture with one to advertise the latest episode of my podcast. It didn't reach a thousand likes and I felt like a failure.

The idea of performing my ridiculous show in front of my fellow patients made me feel sick. Performing in front of people who've bought a ticket is one thing, but to people who have absolutely no point of reference feels like lunacy. Then again, I was in a mental hospital so maybe lunacy was just what the doctor ordered. A key bit of my show involved a bottle of Malibu and the nurses agreed to let me use the prop as long as the bottle was empty and I warned the alcoholics in advance.

They guarded it under lock and key in the nurse's office, along with my laptop charger and my razor. Nothing quite beats the thrill of shaving your armpits with the door open while a nurse asks you about how you're finding the facilities. I am at least grateful not to have an eating disorder; when they use the bathroom they have to sing, to prove that they're not throwing up.

My fellow patients were in higher spirits than usual. A tea party and a show in one day had made them feel positively festive. I was reminded of the old adage that it is possible to feel happy and depressed. I ate a fourth iced bun and doubled down on my nausea.

One of my new friends, Lucy, agreed to be my prompt in case I forgot my lines, which I had written out by hand in huge capital letters on multi-coloured paper I 'borrowed' from art therapy.

More so than any pill, gossip was the drug that kept us going in the Priory. Rumours constantly abounded about a secret celebrity wing, where famous people were treated away from the riff raff. At a thousand pounds a night, it would be a stretch to suggest that anyone in there is riff raff, even if most of us were bankrolled by insurance.

The most persistent rumour going round when I was there was that Johnny Depp was on his way in. His ex-wife Amber Heard had alleged that he had attacked her in a drug- and alcohol-fuelled rage. He was filming in London. Surely this was the only place he'd be. We spent our afternoons sunbathing in the garden, looking up at the sky for helicopters. I started fantasising that he would be on my ward, we would fall in love and he'd whisk me away to Hollywood. The fact that rumours abounded he'd given his wife a black eye seemed irrelevant. At the very least if he didn't fancy me, maybe he'd play a bit part in my sitcom. If Johnny Depp comes in, I thought, I definitely won't have to do my Edinburgh show.

An hour before I was due to perform the familiar signs of panic were starting to set in. Lucy came in to see how I was. We'd been laughing earlier after she was accused of 'flaunting her scars'. It was thirty degrees outside and she was wearing a skirt. If you can't bare your self-harm scars without shame in a mental hospital, where can you?

'Bella! Have you got any tights? I'm flaunting my scars again.'

I had gone mute. I rifled through my piles of paper, swallowing down the nervous knots in my stomach.

'I've let everyone down again,' I said. 'I just can't do it.'

'I'll get a nurse,' she said.

The nurse told me I didn't have to do anything I didn't want to do. She just thought it might have been good practice before my show next week. Talk of the show sent me into full-on shock. She led me to the tuck shop and gave me a diazepam, then I went back to bed.

Lucy knocked on my door a couple of hours later to say that everyone was going to have a toga party in the sitting room. Some people with shop privileges were going to get snacks and she wanted to know if there was anything in particular I wanted. I asked her to pick up anything unhealthy and circular so I could make a joke about energy balls. And also some cigarettes. Boredom and desperation to socialise had turned me into a chain smoker.

I'd told my friends that I felt much better, and I did when I was safely ensconced within the hospital walls. I felt like I finally had a valid excuse to turn offers down. My therapist was helping me to become more assertive. She was horrified to find that I had missed a group session to write an article on day-drinking for *Vice*.

'Do you not see the irony here?' she asked.

'I know. I don't know how to say no.'

'You are writing about drinking from a rehabilitation centre.'

'But I'm not an alcoholic!' I reasoned.

She shot me a look of utter despair.

'We have got to establish you some boundaries.'

Together we wrote down some new rules for me to live by:

I will not work for free.

I will say no to favours that go over and above what is
   necessary.

I will not put content on my account that I feel uncomfortable
   with for the benefit of someone else.

I will place value on what I have created and what I do.

I will not determine my value by an arbitrary number of followers
   and likes.

It sounded easy enough. I just had to treat Instagram like a Tamagotchi – feed it enough to keep it healthy, but not take it personally when its health declined.

The head of therapy had caught wind of the fact that I was going to start going to work meetings and performing shows, so she called me into her office.

'Are you sure you're ready for this?' she asked. I told her that my doctor thought it was a good idea. That falling behind with work would only make me more stressed. She disagreed. She said that she'd been watching me in group therapy and not only did she think I shouldn't be going out, she thought I should be extending my stay.

'If you don't take this time out and truly concentrate on getting better, you will be back.'

'I can't afford to come back,' I told her. 'My insurance runs out in ten days.'

'Well, if you have to go in ten days, spend them here. You have got to learn to switch off.'

The next day I woke up early, signed myself out and headed to my meeting. Looking around at the commuters, I thought how strange it was that none of them knew how close they were to a mental patient. How the term 'mental patient' is used as an explanation for people who cause damage and hurt to others, and yet there I was on a train, on my way to a meeting with Jamie Oliver's production company. Caroline had asked to come with me to make sure I was OK and I was grateful for her presence.

The producers were brimming with ideas for me.

'Commissioners are really excited about you,' they assured me. I nodded and pretended I hadn't heard this all before. 'How's your Edinburgh show coming along? You done any previews yet?'

'A few. I've actually got one coming up.'

'I could never do stand-up. Do you get nervous before gigs?'
I think I nodded but perhaps I winced as well.

'Be careful. You don't want to end up in a mental hospital.'

They were laughing, so Caroline and I forced a chortle. My Priory slippers were in my backpack.

We shook hands enthusiastically and Caroline took me for a decaf coffee and a cake to debrief.

'I think that went well,' she said. 'You really do seem a lot better.'

I looked down at my shaking hands. 'Yeah. I'm excited about the shows.'

# Sold Out

I was not excited about the shows. In fact, I was dreading them. Everyone could see that performing stand-up was tearing strips off my mental health, but the alternative was much, much worse. I was adamant that I wasn't just an influencer.

I hadn't performed since Brighton and I was terrified about a repeat of the dissociation of doom. Thankfully I knew I would have an audience this time. I'd posted about these shows on Instagram weeks before and they had both sold out. Even Edinburgh was starting to sell out in advance. It was a lot of people to disappoint.

I was performing at the Pleasance Theatre in Islington. The last time I'd done a show there, just two months before, had been the best of my career and a huge milestone.

When I graduated university and first considered a comedy career, a friend of my dad's had put me in touch with the theatre's owner, who begrudgingly agreed to meet me so I could 'pick his brain'. I had been practising funny things to say on the train on the way down. I really wanted him to think that I had 'funny bones'. At the end of my disastrous monologue about how hilarious London escalators really are he gave me some home truths.

'I'll take a look at your blog,' he said. 'But I have to be honest, you are a woman, you are upper class, and nobody really wants to hear what you have to say.'

Tears pricked the back of my eyes.

'My advice to you is that you should try to write for other people.'

After he'd crushed my dreams, he introduced me to his team who were having a beer.

'This is Arabella,' he drawled, 'and she has a blog.'

The team tried valiantly to buoy my spirits and said they'd be in touch if they ever needed an intern in the office. The experience put me off trying stand-up for the next five years.

Flash-forward to me aged twenty-eight, and I arrived at the Pleasance with a suitcase, about to perform the first in a run of two sold-out shows. Driven by the prospect of a huge Fuck You to that man, I had never felt more ready to smash a gig.

The people who worked there were falling over themselves to tell me how much they loved my Instagram and lament the fact that they had to man reception and so couldn't slip into the back to watch. I ordered two Diet Cokes, a KitKat and a packet of Pom-Bears in a desperate bid to energise myself before the show. The man from years gone by was nowhere to be seen, but my mum was coming 'with the girls' and I knew they were having a liquid lunch.

'You won't even know we're here,' they slurred. I glanced at my godmothers, pouring ice into plastic glasses of wine.

'Sure.'

Mum, Sarah and Cilla had arrived at the theatre like they were on a hen party. They were soaked in Chardonnay and laughter. Mum came to give me a hug. She offered to help me set up and promised they would all sit at the back.

When I emerged from behind the curtain, I was greeted by a cheer. What followed remains the best gig of my life. The perfect audience. A chef's kiss of a performance. Two of my school friends were sat behind a woman who actually fell off her chair. One girl heckled 'fuck Instagram! You should do this forever!' She enjoyed it so much she fan-girled my mum.

There isn't often a rhyme or reason to why a gig goes spectacularly well. The material was the same, the demographic identical, and yet the energy was entirely different. A brilliant gig comes from a chemical reaction between audience and performer. The vinegar you pour on a volcano filled with bicarbonate of soda to make it erupt. I told my friends that that audience had cured my depression.

I could never have foreseen that only two months later, the second show in the run would be performed on day release from a mental hospital.

Thankfully, nobody I knew had seen the fiasco that was the Brighton show, so word had got out that the show was actually good. Lots of friends had texted me to tell me that they were coming and they were excited. I didn't tell anyone where I was coming from. Or that I definitely wouldn't be staying for a drink after the show.

I tried to put the drama of hospital life out of my mind and went to go and see my therapist. I hadn't really gelled with the woman I'd been assigned. I didn't think she took my stand-up career seriously.

'You know what,' she said, folding her notebook together. 'I think tonight's going to go really well.'

'Oh. Thank you. I hope so. I'm quite nervous.'

'You look very pretty today. If nobody laughs they can just look at you.'

This is not the first time she'd commented on my looks and I still can't work out if she was being predatory or trying to patch up my crumbling self-esteem.

'Actually. You know who you remind me of?'

I dreaded to think.

'The People's Princess.'

'As in Diana?'

'Yes, Diana. So serene on the surface, but under the surface, paddle, paddle.'

She mimed the legs of a paddling swan. I wondered if she shouldn't be taking some time out herself.

I couldn't face dragging my suitcase across London to the theatre so I jumped in an Uber. The driver seemed completely flummoxed by my pick-up point.

'Is this a hospital for rich people?' he asked.

'No,' I said. 'It's for nutters.'

I tried to recall the energy I felt before my last amazing show at the Pleasance. But it was hard to shake the reality that before my last show, I wasn't in a mental hospital. The show went OK, but I'd made some changes I wasn't sure about. The show now ended with the dramatic death of my spirit animal, a jelly snake. It had been a while since I bought it from an Odeon pick'n'mix, and when I went to eat it at the show's climax, I felt like I was chewing a belt. I looked out into the audience, willing them to clap, but nothing came. I spat the snake head out into my hand and shouted feebly, 'That's the end!' They erupted into applause and I felt my shoulders drop.

My friends were full of supportive words.

'It's honestly so funny,' they promised. 'Are you sure you won't stay for a drink?'

'I really can't,' I said. 'I've got to get my beauty sleep.'

Then I got in an Uber back to Roehampton and checked myself back into the Priory.

Stand-up was hard and influencing was relatively easy. But I knew nothing good came from something that was easy. Influencing was only a stepping-stone to something legitimate. I would never let it become my identity.

I'm a writer, a comedian, a social media person. Influencer is a job title I've never used outside a professional setting. I'd sooner tell someone that I was a pervert. Even that feels like it has more integrity.

Why are influencers not shouting their successes from the rooftops?

Is it because the word can seem interchangeable with blagger?

Is it because influencers are assumed to be talentless, vapid or vain?

'Nobody said there would be an influencer at the party?!' Someone once bellowed directly into my face.

I made a big show of looking around and over my shoulder. Then I started to look pained.

'Please don't call me that,' I pleaded with my eyes.

Influencing is seen to be creation devoid of art, prostitution without the sex, something for people who want to be famous but don't have the talent.

When researching this book, almost every influencer I reached out to caveated that they hoped their answers would be OK, as they didn't think of themselves as being 'very influencer-y.' They all had at least 100,000 followers.

I don't know what it is about the word that makes me wince. We all know that influencing is a job, a lucrative one, that brings you fame, attention and free stuff.

Wanting to be an influencer is like wanting to be popular: everybody wants it but nobody admits to it, because by admitting that you want to be cool, you extinguish any possibility of being so.

When I mention my Instagram without explaining its content, I've been openly laughed at, ghosted on dating apps and roundly derided. Only when I reveal that I 'sort of satirise influencers actually,' can I regain any ground. In spite of being the least-respected string to my bow, my work as an influencer quickly came to define me. It's what people knew me for, despite my best efforts, and it made up the bulk of my income.

'I'm a broadcaster,' says another friend who I know works full-time as an influencer but also has a podcast.

'Right.'

'If you tell people that you're an influencer they just treat you like you're some big-headed freak who thinks they should be a model.'

Why are we all so reluctant to admit to what we do? And why, in one of the few industries where women earn more than men, are we making them feel stupid for doing so?

It's now clear that what blighted my success was a form of internalised misogyny. It isn't a coincidence that something widely considered to be shallow, vapid and morally iffy is largely the preserve of women. Hating influencers could almost be described as a trend.

The account 'influencers in the wild' pokes fun at people posing for photos, and while it's funny, I can't help but feel it's also a little sexist. Yes, there are male influencers, but influencers are often selling you an optimised version of yourself, and the people expected to optimise are always women. Women are sold new insecurities every day, but by blaming influencers are we really just shooting the messenger?

They're easy to hate and branded content grates, but more often than not this is because brands are using the wrong influencers for the wrong job. I too was horrified to see Josh from *Love Island* employed by the British Government to promote the coronavirus lockdown. Nothing riles me more than seeing millionaires become the face of Olay when there's been a pot of Crème de la Mer in the back of their shots for the last six months.

It's tempting to think that all influencers are twats who flog snake oil, and god knows some of them are, but influencing is a job. It's hard work and the people who do it care about it deeply. I may have been too concerned with my own prejudice to see it for what it is, which is an opportunity for women to be their own boss, set their own hours and build their own brand. If somebody offered you £50k to go to a party, would you say no? Would you fuck!

Of course, we've moved on from the stereotypes of bimbos and the assumption that women who care about their appearance aren't intelligent. The question of whether you can twerk and be a feminist is thankfully dead in the water, but women profiting from selling women aspirational lifestyles is still seen as problematic.

It doesn't surprise me that the other jobs judged as ridiculous are modelling and porn, again, industries where women out-earn men. If I had a pound for every person who'd told me that what I do 'isn't really a job, though, is it?' I would be rolling around in ones like a stripper. I hate myself for biting my tongue when I should say:

'Sir, you work at an ad firm, not down a mine, and what you really mean is not that it isn't real or hard work, but that it isn't work you personally value.'

No individual has the measuring stick for what is and isn't valuable. Not liking the same influencers as your teenage niece does not mean they don't have value. The economy certainly values them. The people who follow their favourite influencers definitely do. You don't have to follow any of these people, but you're going to 'hate-follow' them anyway because sneering at influencers is fair game.

I am certain some people hate-followed me. Every time I see that someone has saved a post or sent it to a friend, I am filled with fear that they're laughing at me, not with me. If it's an ad, I'm convinced everyone's talking about how much of a sell-out I am.

Diet Prada, a hugely popular Instagram account that was

started to call out wrongdoing in the fashion industry, has now become an influencer 'digilante'.

'Can this virus please cancel influencer culture?' the authors said of COVID-19. They were rightly questioning influencer Arielle Charnas's decision to decamp to her second home after testing positive for COVID, but influencer culture isn't responsible for something so dangerous and idiotic.

The fact is, influencers are easy to hate, and in a world so full of hatred, they make an attractive scapegoat. Jameela Jamil is dragged almost daily for getting things wrong on Twitter. Granted, she makes prolific sweeping statements and appears to have a titanium hide, but we can't expect everyone we follow to be fully representative all the time, can we?

The public-shaming approach to influencing makes the internet a hostile environment for people already offering themselves up for judgement. Influencers are terrified of getting it wrong. Wouldn't a gentle DM and a request to take something down have a more effective, less devastating effect?

There's a huge amount of pressure for women in the public eye to always be on the right side of the argument. In 2020 it felt like if you blinked you would miss another natural disaster, human rights breach or protest. I tried to get involved as much as I could, but when my DMs began to flood with messages suggesting that 'if you platform Black Lives Matter it could actually be seen as racist for you not to platform this cause as well', I felt ill. Should I platform all these things? Is it helpful? Am I virtue-signalling? Do my followers want to see it?

You may find a lot of influencers annoying. Maybe they're not 'for you', but influencers provide entertainment, inspiration and advice – the sort of stuff you used to pay for from traditional media sites – and before you try to blame influencers for the decline of print media, why don't you have a word with Señor Zuckerberg and his fake news brigade.

If you don't like being sold to, blame capitalism, not the women savvy enough to carve something out for themselves in a system rigged to benefit old white men.

In the same way that models are ridiculed for being paid huge sums 'just to sit there and look pretty', I was made to feel like my earnings for Instagram were no more than money for old rope. You can have morals and get paid huge amounts of money to advertise fake tan, burgers, vibrators or Veet. If you like it and would use it, go ahead and sell it, because if you don't somebody else definitely will. It is not your moral responsibility not to get your money and live your life.

How many people sign off on these campaigns before it falls to an influencer to promote them? How much more profit will company directors take while we blame models and influencers for taking advantage of a system that does not serve them? Of course, everyone has agency and I will never condone those who promote weight-loss products or products they knowingly wouldn't use or know do not work. But I have a lot of respect for influencers, and I wish I'd levelled the same amount of respect to myself back then.

I guess what makes me so fired up is that at that time I felt exactly the same way about influencers as other people do: I thought they were shallow and pointless and just loved taking belfies, or 'bum selfies'. Then I met some and realised that I had turned other people's judgement and misogyny on myself. I had internalised a negative view of the most successful thing I'd ever done.

I joined in with my friends when they talked about my 'job'. I agreed with people when they said that 'anyone' could do it. I apologised for doing well at what I did, because my success didn't feel deserved. In spite of not having a steady income and often worrying about paying my rent on time, I felt under-worked and overpaid.

Since distancing myself from my Instagram account over the last three years, I've given a lot of thought to why I never really let myself be proud of what I had achieved, why I wouldn't let anyone call me an influencer, why I felt so desperate to legitimise it with other skills. I felt like the work I did on Instagram was flimsy and meaningless, despite it connecting with hundreds of thousands of people. I couldn't consider it a 'proper' job even when it provided the bulk of my income.

I was ashamed that the lure of a pay cheque and more traditional 'fame' appealed to me so much more than the debilitating anxiety that came from performing comedy in a lecture hall. I wanted to be one of those comedians who looks forward to Edinburgh every year, who thrives on the energy of live comedy, but the truth was I didn't really enjoy stand-up as an audience member, and as a performer it was like being plunged into the seventh circle of hell. All I wanted was to be paid to say funny stuff, but I couldn't shake my conviction that making jokes on Instagram was a joke.

Instagram was financially rewarding but I had internalised the message that nothing good was ever easy. I'd been approached by a beer company in the US to do an ad in Gawker and they'd offered me £10,000. Caroline and I planned to cancel three Edinburgh shows so I could fly to the Netherlands and do an ad for Wrangler Jeans. The Edinburgh festival is a money pit and a mental-health catastrophe waiting to happen. Caroline told me I still had to go to Edinburgh.

One thing I will say about having a lot of Instagram followers, is it opens a lot of unexpected doors. When you're officially 'the next big thing', people will let you give pretty much anything a go, regardless of whether or not you have any talent or experience.

Some things I was allowed to do with varying levels of success include:

A voiceover for a popular reality TV show – my recordings weren't used because I had absolutely no idea what I was doing.

Auditioning for a sitcom – I didn't tell anyone I'd never auditioned before, had a panic attack and spent ten minutes being consoled by the producers.

Acting in a sitcom – I played an Oompa Loompa at a festival who kept stopping people to ask for drugs. I was painted orange on the hottest day of the year and my line took fifteen takes. The show wasn't commissioned.

Writing and starring in an episode of a web sitcom – this was actually an unmitigated success. I wrote about a girl who expected to be proposed to on a weekend away and had a complete meltdown when it didn't happen. We filmed it in a yurt in Essex, next to a lake that may or may not have been full of bodies. All of the press I did to promote it only talked about Deliciously Stella, so hardly anyone saw it. It was good, though.

Motivational speaking – I tried my hand at being 'a voice of a generation', and made a joke about Beyoncé getting the shits which brought the house down.

Writing a book – I arguably secured this book deal because of my Instagram account. I told you, followers open doors.

Of course, none of these side projects scratched the surface of the success of Stella. I have made light of the intense celebrity stalking it took to get my account to where it was, but to a lot of people that would be described as strategy. I was a genius strategist, a shameless strategist. You can call me Strategor the Destroyer. If you handed me your phone and cancelled all of my plans, I could get you at least 200 followers in a week. I am extremely good at Instagram. If only I hadn't been so embarrassed to admit it, and it hadn't made me quite so sad.

# Heart-Shaped Heroin

'I'm really worried about the next generation,' my friend says, looking at her phone as we walk to the pub. 'Imagine growing up with Instagram.'

'I know,' I say, refreshing Twitter for the eighteenth time that morning. 'All I did was play outside and watch Nickelodeon.'

We sit close together so my friend can show me the guy she's dating's ex. I check yesterday's screen time. I was on social media for eight hours.

The cat is finally out of the bag. Tech giants have designed social media to be as addictive as opiates and they've put one in everyone's pockets.

I want to ask you honestly how many of these activities you usually get through, or think you could get through, without using your social media:

Can you watch a whole film?
Take a bus journey?
Sit through a meeting?
A trip to the loo?
Do you use it when in company?
Would you use it at a party?
Do you check your phone when you are already on the phone
    to someone else?

It was Meghan Markle who pointed out the significance of the language around social media; the word 'user' usually describes drug addicts. They use heroin, crack or prescription pills in the same way we use social media, and it would appear that they are similarly addictive.

The success of an app is measured by the extent to which it introduces a new habit. In Instagram's case, six in ten of its one billion users open it every day and the average person scrolls for fifty-three minutes each day.

I, of course, was using it much, much more. Addiction is a disease in which a person finds themselves unable to stop using a substance or engaging in a behaviour. Anyone who tried to have a conversation with me in 2016 will know that I could not and would not put down my phone for a second. The backlight became a security blanket, the likes a much-needed shot of dopamine.

I had always thought that dopamine was the happy hormone, but what it in fact delivers you is pleasure. Dr Robert Lustig, Professor of Paediatrics at the University of California, San Francisco, speaks of seven differences between pleasure and happiness. He finds that pleasure is short-lived while happiness is long term and that the extremes of pleasure all lead to addiction. Pleasure can be achieved with substances, while happiness cannot. By confusing pleasure and happiness we are confusing two fundamental hormones and two very different states of being.

Both serotonin and dopamine are chemicals made in the brain, which travel between neurons. Dopamine excites neurons, so to counter its effects the neurons stop making themselves so readily available. This leads to you pointlessly chasing a high that's no longer available. You can keep on scrolling but you'll never get high like you used to. Serotonin, however, inhibits its receptors, slowing them down to produce a feeling of contentment. According to Lustig, there is one thing that downregulates serotonin, and that is excessive dopamine. I'd been completely unaware that in my relentless pursuit of dopamine I had triggered what was in effect a permanent comedown. I was killing my happiness in a quest for validation.

My phone was like a bad boyfriend that I kept going back to, and nobody could get me to leave. According to app developer Peter Mezyk, 'Three criteria are required to form a habit: sufficient motivation, an action, and a trigger.' In the case of Instagram, a notification provides motivation, liking provides an action, and for me any Instagram activity at all provided a trigger.

It's clear why the apps have been designed this way. The more time spent scrolling, the more profitable they are for the companies that own them, but only now are we starting to reckon with the human cost of getting people hooked on tech.

I was addicted to the followers. I was addicted to the fame. I missed the security that came from knowing that, in that very moment, I was making the right decision. That people thought that I was doing life right. When the likes rushed in, they reinforced my value. In a world of supposed endless opportunity, where we are spoilt for choice, the satisfaction that came from knowing I'd chosen to make something that connected with people was unrivalled. And I was afraid that I'd never feel that way again. When you post something on Instagram, you roll a dice; you take a gamble on whether or not people will make you feel loved. When it goes well and the likes roll in, you win big. When it doesn't, you lose, and you are cursed to play again.

Multiple studies have revealed a link between time spent online and depression and anxiety in teenagers. Social media has facilitated comparison culture, pressure to be constantly connected and an uptick in revenge porn.

Aldous Huxley wrote: 'habit converts luxurious enjoyments into dull and daily necessities.' Likes were no longer a luxury for me. They were as important as food or breathing. The theory of the hedonic treadmill is a trap that leads you to believe that a life change will lead to lasting happiness. I believed there was a magic number of likes, press trip invitations or glamorous gifts that would make me happy.

Instead, my sense of failure was taking a pounding from what I perceived to be others' success. I spent hours scrolling Instagram, becoming increasingly envious of other people's lives. I watched other influencers' follower numbers surpass mine. Everyone I followed seemed to be on a press trip, making sponsored content or showing off their latest fabulous gifts. I pored greedily over fashion bloggers' posts, wondering what they'd got for free and whether they were being paid. The ASA were yet to impose their stringent rules on having to announce what is sponsored and gifted, and I was consumed with jealousy.

It would be so much easier if I didn't have to be funny, I thought. An idiot could take a picture of themselves in a tea dress. I wasn't just jealous of other influencers; every writer with a book deal felt like a punch to the gut, every script commission a personal attack on my failing to get one for myself. I punished myself by seeking out every creative person around my age and measuring their achievements against my own.

I was furious that someone had won an award for directing despite having no desire to direct, I was livid that I hadn't been approached to be a 'babe of Missguided' despite never having shopped there and being averse to fast fashion on ethical grounds. I was a reckless, ruthless, green-eyed monster consumed by what I did not have but also did not necessarily want. All I wanted was to feel like I was on the way up, instead of on the way nowhere fast.

Notifications lead you to experience thought processes you never would normally. They've got inside our heads, and our heads aren't ready.

A group of tech designers are in control of what information you are shown on your social media feed, as well as who is shown any content you create. The algorithm may be designed by humans, but it's intelligent enough to make decisions on its own. In essence, your work, your worth and your value are being decided by a machine. And you wonder why you feel like you've sold a tiny bit of your soul.

Talk to any influencer about the algorithm and they'll likely shake their fist, nobody knows how it works, nobody can control who sees their content, our livelihoods are at the mercy of a string of computer code, and it's unsettling to say the least.

We live in a world where our worth is directly linked to our productivity. We are our jobs. We spend most of our time doing them or thinking about them and, like it or not, they are wound up tight with our identities.

When your job satisfaction, security and achievement are already tied in with something as easily quantifiable as likes and follows, to know that no matter how perceptive, diligent and prolific you are, how well you perform isn't ultimately up to you can be maddening.

When the algorithm changed Instagram's feed in 2017 so it was no longer chronological, my following started going down and my posts started getting fewer likes. I saw it as a direct reflection of how people felt about me: washed-up, irrelevant, no longer funny. It is, in fact, highly possible that people, or maybe the right people, weren't being shown my content. Like a heroin user desperately searching for the Elysium of that first high, I wanted to feel how it felt to get more likes than I'd ever had before. I needed the feeling of going viral again.

In the Netflix documentary *The Social Dilemma*, Dr Anna

Lembke, Medical Director of Addiction Medicine at Stanford University, explained it in the simplest of terms. 'Social media is a drug,' she said. 'We have a basic, biological imperative to connect with other people that directly affects the release of dopamine in the reward pathway.'

In essence, evolution has made us happy when we feel seen and understood. Social media might be lacking in nuance, but there is no dislike button and so most of the interactions we have are rewarding and make us feel closer to the people who follow us. As someone who really likes to be liked, so much so that I will spill my guts on stage in a quest for approval, it was inevitable this was going to get to me.

The years 2010 and 2011 saw a massive spike in self-harm amongst American teenagers. Since then, in girls aged between 10 and 14 it's gone up 189 per cent. Similarly, suicide has gone up 151 per cent. It's easy to look at those figures and feel they're very distant from you and your relationship with your phone, but the spike is perfectly timed with the arrival of social media and I know what it's like to feel like your Instagram following is a matter of life and death; that it is the only thing that makes your life worth living; that it is the only thing that can give you the life that you crave.

Every single person I spoke to on this topic admitted that they have taken down and sometimes reposted a photo that didn't get as many likes as expected. I have done this, my friends who are influencers have done this, my friends with 200 followers have done this. What does this say about the effect that likes have on our self-worth? On how we think we'll be perceived by others? When my follower number started going down, I felt like everyone had noticed, that people were keeping track and were aware that I was a failure.

It's a normal part of evolution to care what other people think, no matter whether people tell you you shouldn't, or they don't. Everybody does to some extent, but we are literally not evolved to care about what thousands of people think all at the same time, let alone hundreds of thousands or millions.

For someone like me, who cries every time they hear 'Rupert The Bear' and 'The Frog Chorus' because I think I'll play it at my funeral (I'm a narcissist, I know) this is an emotional overload. It wasn't that too many people were 'liking' me, it was that I didn't feel as if I deserved it and I knew one day it would all go away.

According to Lembke: 'This fake brittle popularity leaves you vacant and empty. It forces you into a vicious cycle where you're constantly seeking that next hit of validation because you can no longer internally validate yourself.' I could see no reason within myself why all these people engaged with me, perhaps because I knew it wasn't me they were engaging with, it was Stella.

A study published in the *Canadian Journal of Psychiatry* measured how much time students spent in front of social media, television and computers: 'In terms of the relationship between screen time and depression, what we found was that social media was very robustly related to increases in depressive symptoms, as was television,' Patricia Conrod, one of the study's researchers, said. 'And there was no relationship between video gaming and depressive symptoms.'

When watching TV, kids often consume idealised lives that are different from their own experiences, Conrod also said. But social media is unique because adolescents are seeing pictures, videos and status updates from their own network of friends and peers. 'In some way, you're being exposed to a slightly biased perspective on what young people's lives are like and you compare yourself to that.'

All teenagers go through a period of insecurity. We have always been exposed to 'the ideal body' and 'aspirational lifestyles', but never before have they been in our pockets. Never before have they been presented as our peers. Would it have been so easy to accept that at fourteen I looked like a young Heath Ledger, and had chosen the colour on my train tracks 'for Halloween' and now looked diseased? Or would I be spending all my pocket money on Kylie Jenner lip kits, knowing deep down that what I really wanted was fillers?

When I was a teenager I pulled pictures of beautiful women out of magazines and ironically stuck them on the fridge. But something about the ink and paper, and the fact that I knew they were models gave me permission not to need to emulate them. I knew about airbrushing and makeup and personal trainers, but when you see someone on Instagram, who tells you to your face that they got the perfect body by giving up gluten or doing a bit of yoga, you start to wonder whether if you did those things you could be like those people. And when it doesn't work, you feel like you've failed.

'I won't let my children have social media,' say *The Social Dilemma*'s smug, slick tech bros, having cashed in the millions they made off our dope-hungry brains. I wish someone had known when I was ill that my Instagram usage was a factor. With hindsight, I wish that somebody had told me to stop.

Instagram addiction wasn't a recognised illness when I found myself welded to my smartphone, but it sure as hell is now. At the time my doctors told me it was best not to let my illness interfere with my success, and to keep up with as much work as I could manage.

When I last spoke with my psychiatrist, he mentioned that The Priory Group had opened up a new ward specifically for people struggling with technology.

'Well, at least I know where to go if this Instagram thing picks up again,' I said, last time I was in his office.

'You seem very well at the moment, which is great, so let's hope it never comes to that.'

Deep down I think I knew the damage Instagram was causing, but I couldn't fathom letting it go. I was still convinced it was my ticket to fame and fortune, and so I continued playing it like a slot machine, sure that there was still a chance of hitting the jackpot.

# 150,000 Followers

As soon as I was released from the Priory, slightly calmer but no less addicted to scrollable heroin, it was straight back to business. I put the hospital stay in my mad trapdoor and started making up for lost time. Once Edinburgh was over, I reasoned, I would have nothing to be anxious about, so all I needed to do was get through the next few weeks.

'Call everyone!' I told Caroline. 'Tell them this bitch is back!'

After a year of screaming my name around town, I was tiring of being the next big thing. I wanted to be as familiar to the British public as a favourite footstool.

The most common transition for influencers into mainstream fame is probably from influencer to presenter. Zoella and her ilk had a show on Radio 1. Maya Jama wouldn't be where she is now without social media. Amelia Dimoldenberg successfully used her YouTube show *Chicken Shop Date* as a platform to make a documentary about Meghan Markle's family and to present at the BRITs.

I started being put forward to present documentaries and for entertainment shows about wellness. Producers were nothing if not full of ideas. I was pitched for a show where influencers would live with an Amish community for a month, I auditioned to play an 'undercover intern' who causes chaos in a camera-rigged office. Surely one of these has to be commissioned, I thought. I was even pitched to replace Ruby Wax in a remake of her iconic nineties series, *Ruby Wax Meets ...*

Anyone who works in media knows that television development moves at the speed of tar. The journey from the germ of an idea to what you see on the TV can take years, and I was fresh out of patience. Once you've achieved overnight success, anything that isn't that starts to look a bit like failure. I'd become used to the instant gratification of Instagram likes and was frustrated by what I saw as the commissioner's inability to strike while the iron is hot.

Every day that went by without news of my many projects, I became more and more fraught. I completely relied on my Instagram account to convince myself that I wasn't 'over'. My follower number was still going up, but much more slowly. My hot streak was cooling. I felt that I was running out of time.

One by one, commissioners shut the ideas down. The documentaries were made with 'more mainstream talent', the entertainment shows 'wouldn't last more than one series'. I was right at the crux of the zeitgeist but nobody thought it would last. I tried to explain that I wasn't just Deliciously Stella, that I had real comedy chops, but people couldn't see me as anything else.

'Just keep going with the stand-up,' said Caroline. 'We know you're more than just Stella, everyone else will find out soon enough.'

I'd been sleeping badly for a while. Caroline knew, but we both put it down to nerves about my upcoming Edinburgh show. I threw myself into stand-up, which made me perpetually anxious and even more lonely. I stopped going to meet my new 'work friends' in favour of working on my new show, and I managed to film a sketch as Deliciously Stella for the BBC. This came about as a sort of consolation prize after I met with a producer about a show investigating wellness and clean eating. She looked apprehensive when I sat down, then disappointed as our chat went on.

Maybe it's my voice, I thought, trying to remember to drop my Ts.

'If we'd known about you earlier,' she said, 'things might have been different.' They'd already hired another influencer to present the show, and had only recently realised that I existed, and would have been perfect. This was the opportunity I'd been waiting for and I'd missed it. I was devastated.

'Where's the presenter now?' I asked.

'She's on an all-expenses-paid trip to Ibiza with Malibu. She's supposed to be eating clean for the documentary as an experiment, but keeps eating chicken wings.'

'Oh right.'

'One of our runners is going to do a nutrition course for her from Groupon over the weekend because she doesn't have time. You know what it's like, working with talent.'

They offered me the chance to make the sketch and I said yes, but felt like I was stuck, ruminating on my perceived failures. I wondered if she'd really got the job because she was better than me, because she dropped her Ts, or because she was a YouTuber.

I was convinced that performing stand-up comedy legitimised me. Stand-up was an art form. Stand-up was brave and hard. It used all my energy and was badly paid. This, I thought, is real art. Good things come to those who suffer. Unfortunately, until August, I knew I would be stuck performing as Deliciously Stella.

Performing stand-up is like exposure therapy for the terminally needy – the more you do it, the less it kills you when it doesn't go well. Eventually you get used to what it feels like when nobody laughs at your jokes and you stop caring about what other people think. That's the plan, anyway.

If stand-up is exposure therapy, Instagram is a short-term fix. It's a velvet Valium hug that keeps you from hating yourself long enough to feel that you are safe and loved. Of course it's lying. All it's providing is love lite; a proclamation declared with the tap of a finger and a millisecond of thought.

I had to work on getting my show and my Instagram into the best shape possible. The Fringe was my best chance of getting a TV show. Everyone who was anyone would be there and I was right on top of the zeitgeist. This show was my victory lap after an unbelievable year.

My publicists had been stalling any interview offers until just before my show and book came out, but I knew how overnight fame worked. Like a *Love Island* couple's dwindling fauxmance in winter, I needed to stay visible. Unable to stage a photoshoot about 'our love' on a giant grey sofa, I had to rely on being funnier than ever on Instagram.

My mum's friend filmed me rolling onto a packet of floured baps like a sunbathing walrus. I captioned it: 'on a roll with my new diet'. The crowd went wild. I felt a sweet rush of relief – 400 comments was a return to form. Maybe I was still relevant after all? I briefly considered whether I should try to incorporate the move into my show, but figured I had enough jokes that involved me lying on the ground.

The time came when I was finally allowed to do press again. I fell back into the swing of my old routine. Meeting, interview, jump in followers, meeting, interview, jump in followers. My follower number had swelled to almost 140,000 and I had established 150,000 as my new goal.

In spite of what I perceived to be repeating the same joke over and over again, the general public were still lapping up Stella. I resented her success. I knew that I owed her everything, but the more successful she became, the further away I slipped from being able to start a career as Bella. If the commissioners could see me as more than Deliciously Stella, maybe they'd be willing to give me a chance.

'Commissioners must be all over you,' suggested journalists. 'I can't believe you haven't got a TV show yet.'

My publisher had set me up with a room in the Penguin office and I met a revolving door of journalists keen to meet the woman behind Deliciously Stella.

As far as I was aware, commissioners were keeping their cards close to their chests. I thought about all the shows that got stuck in development hell. All of the reasons I'd been given for why Stella was 'a bit too faddy' or 'wouldn't stretch to more than one series'.

I wondered what would have happened if I'd done that first show without her. Would Caroline still have signed me? Would I have had the space to grow more confident as a performer at my own pace? Would I be known for being Bella, or Stella? Was my overnight success a blessing or a curse?

I quickly slipped back into bad habits, ferociously tracking engagement, anxiously waiting for Google alerts, searching for my name on Twitter.

'I could close the account after the show,' I said to myself. 'Best to go out on a high.'

Some of the interviews I was doing required photoshoots, and on one wretchedly hot day a man from the *Telegraph* was dispatched to my house to take my portrait.

I lived on a funny dead-end road that even sat-navs seemed near impossible to find. The photographer called me in a fluster.

'Can you come outside and wave, please?' he asked. 'I've been driving up and down the same road for twenty minutes.'

Panicking, I walked out of my front door without my shoes on. There was a sudden gust of wind. The door slammed shut behind me. I found the photographer, wincing as he started unpacking his equipment.

'I'm so sorry, but I've locked myself out of the house.'

His face fell. 'Oh god. I'm so sorry it's all my fault I got lost.'

'No no,' I assured him. 'It's my fault. I shouldn't have gone outside without the keys.' We stood in the glaring heat for a minute, digesting this giant fuck-up.

'Wait,' I said finally. 'I've left the back door open!' The photographer looked at the wall of Victorian terraces, then he approached my next-door neighbour's front door and started to knock.

'If we can get in through the back, then one of us can hop over the wall,' he said gamely. I paused for a second to size him up. He was in good shape but his hair was greying. Hopefully whoever answered the door would be kind and strong. That way neither I nor this photographer would risk cracking a hip.

We banged on the door together, pleading for the neighbour to be in, but nobody came to our aid. I could have sworn he was in. I had heard his radio playing over the garden wall that morning. Thwarted, we decided it was time for a different approach. After knocking on every door on the street, we got to a notorious party house on the end. I knew people on the street had complained about noise before but I hoped they'd know I was a kindred spirit. Nobody answered but I could hear them in the garden.

'Hello?!' I bellowed. The music stopped.

'Hello?' replied a confused Kiwi.

'Hello. I'm terribly sorry, but I live four doors down and I've locked myself out. Would you be able to come to the front door?'

I was greeted at the front door by a man in his twenties wearing board shorts and a lei. 'Do you want to come in for a beer?' he asked. 'All my mates have taken the day off because of the heatwave and we have a paddling pool.'

'Thanks,' I replied. 'But I've got a photographer from the *Daily Telegraph* here and we need to take some photos in my house. My back door's open. Do you think I'd be able to come in and try to scale your wall?'

'I'd never let a lady scale a wall,' said board shorts. 'The boys and I love a challenge. What number are you?' The photographer and I followed him inside and sat with his friends by the paddling pool. They offered me a beer before disappearing over the fence, and for a moment I thought we'd managed it.

That's when the shouting started. My next-door neighbour was in after all and he'd just found a bunch of Kiwis in board shorts in his back garden. I ran outside and back to his front door and rang his doorbell. He appeared in his boxer shorts, looking completely bewildered. I thought he was about to shout at me in front of a photographer from the *Telegraph* and my board-shorted Kiwi heroes, but instead he said, 'Would you like to borrow my ladder?'

He was off on holiday in twenty minutes so we needed to be quick, but it's no fun being locked out of your house in a heatwave and he recognised me from next door. It briefly flickered across my mind that the neighbour was really quite handsome and this would make a great story for how we first met, but there were Kiwis in his garden who needed ladders. Ten minutes later, the Kiwis were opening my front door and the photographer and I were inside.

Those photos in the *Telegraph* are the sweatiest pictures of me that have ever existed. And they will always exist in the pages of a national newspaper. I thank the Lord for intrepid, understanding photographers and for generous, athletic Kiwis. I went round that evening to thank them with a crate of beer and they were all still going. To the slacker Kiwi kings of Glendall Street, I hope you are all thriving.

The press drive resulted in my show being heralded as one to watch. I was staying in town this year with some university friends. I was adamant I was going to enjoy it. Caroline and my PR decided it would be best not to tell me when someone important was in the audience in case it spooked me. I was very, very spookable. People were messaging me on Instagram every day to say that they'd booked tickets to see the show. Another person to disappoint, I thought.

It's quite a step up, from unknown comedian with no expectation to 140,000 followers, reams of press coverage and the pressure to prove once and for all that I was the next big thing. Everyone wanted to see what I was made of, but I didn't feel match-fit.

In what had become tradition, Emily had come up to help oversee my first few performances, accompanied by our friend Jenny. Having Jenny and Emily there was a comfort, but I was lost in my own head. There had been no projector issues, I had an agent and a publicist to make sure I was always in the right place at the right time, but I couldn't help the feeling that it was going to be a hellish month.

The day of the first show, I woke up with a start at 4am. I turned on all the lights in my bedroom to check for intruders and hugged my knees to my chest. Nerves were tugging at me like strings on a marionette. I knew that the adrenalin would get me through. I went downstairs to the sitting room and scrolled on Instagram until my mum woke up at 6. She'd forgotten to make my granola bars and she didn't want me going into town without them.

'I feel quite anxious,' I told her, while we huddled by the Aga in our dressing gowns eating toast. 'I'm not sure that the show is very good.'

'I loved the show!' she promised. 'The girls couldn't stop talking about how good it was.'

'The girls were thundercunted,' I reminded her. Mum knows there's no use reasoning with me when I'm like this so she returned to her granola and left me to stew. Francesca was the next to find me fretting.

'You know,' she said, 'my friend gave me this pill once when I was really anxious. I think I still have some left.'

I nodded to let her know that I was listening.

'It's like a super Valium and she said it completely kills her nerves.'

I eyed up the pill. I wasn't sure that I needed a super Valium. A normal Valium maybe, but a super Valium sounded intense. I took the pill and pocketed it in case there was an emergency. Then I tried to think about anything that wasn't the show.

Emily had booked us in to see a load of shows that day to keep me distracted, but we somehow turned up on the wrong day. This meant that the first thing I did when I arrived in Edinburgh was sit in a shipping container for a 'seance', during which a group of RADA grads whispered in my ears and tickled my shoulders in the dark. Little did they know I was facing something far more scary than someone lightly blowing on my neck.

I stumbled over the cobbled streets chewing the inside of my cheek, fingering the super Valium that was gathering lint in my pocket. I was much more visible than the year before. The city was packed full of comedy fans and my face had been plastered all over the internet for a year. I stopped to take pictures with fans, cringing when they told me they'd bought tickets for the show.

I tried my best to be friendly, but these interactions felt like squeezing the last bit of toothpaste from an empty tube. The antipsychotics had rendered my personality non-existent. I couldn't give anyone a show.

Just two weeks into my run, the entire show sold out, rendering my sister obsolete as a flyerer. My mum carried on paying her so she wouldn't get another job and could still keep an eye on me. I had retreated so far into the turmoil in my head I was barely conscious.

'Is Bella even in there?' asked my sister's friend. She knew me to be gregarious and outgoing, but now all I really did was stare. Comedy is a game of highs and lows, of good and bad reviews, good and bad audiences, good and bad moods.

The medication I was on was working hard to suppress these pendulum swings, and so I felt nothing but anxiety, time and duty. How much time do I have until the next show? How much time until the end of the run? How much time until I can stop being Deliciously Stella and finally take some time to get better?

In the end I took the super Valium before the first show. I'd billed my first two nights as previews, meaning that nobody was allowed to review me and that I could get away with the shows being a bit rough. I took the pill for a test drive. Better to do it at a preview than a night when the *Guardian*'s in. I popped half of the pill onto my tongue and settled into my dressing room. It enveloped me like a weighted blanket.

'I really think tonight's gonna be great actually,' I said. Then I walked on stage and I forgot how to speak. In my mind, the first half was going swimmingly. Everyone was laughing. Someone was sat on top of the doughnut I'd planted. Then I lost my place in the script. I paused and racked my clouded brain, scanning the audience for Caroline.

I rustled under my desk for the emergency notes I'd prepared but none of them seemed to make sense.

Caroline was distracted and hadn't realised what had happened. I broke character.

'Um, can somebody grab my script?' I shouted.

Like a ninja, Emily ran into the lighting box and grabbed my tech script. She brought it down then sat in the tech box to help with direction. She'd seen the show enough before to be able to guess when I needed music.

The super Valium took the edge off this disaster.

'Worse things have happened at sea,' I said to myself as I watched Emily scuttle in and out of the lighting box.

When I spoke to my family friends about the gig they said that they thought it was part of the act. If I was relaxed enough I could ride it out. After the gig the drug finally started to wear off. The familiar gnawing feeling that I'd done something terribly wrong returned. Caroline and I sat in huge oversized deck chairs and debriefed over a cider.

'It was a car crash, wasn't it?'

'You know what, mate?' she said. 'You have written a funny, topical show that stars a character that literally everyone fucking loves. The only thing that's going to stop you having a brilliant festival is yourself. So stop worrying and enjoy it. Once you've done this show, you can do any stand-up you want. OK?'

'Everybody loves you,' was a refrain I heard over and over again, and I could never work out why those words didn't penetrate me, didn't buoy me up and give me some much-needed confidence. I think the issue was that to be loved you need to be known, and nobody really knew *me*, they just knew Stella.

As the days went by, the show got better and I felt more relaxed. As far as I was concerned, Deliciously Stella was a joke designed for Instagram, but her popularity online bought me some leeway IRL. I had thought that telling people that Ferrero Rocher are your favourite kind of energy ball wouldn't quite cut it at the biggest arts festival in the world, but most of the time it did. My publicist had masterminded a collection of reviewers so enraptured with the Instagram character that the four-star reviews rolled in, in spite of the nerves and in spite of what I had convinced myself was middling material.

I tried mentally mapping out when would be a good time to wind down Deliciously Stella.

If I do it after the show, I won't be able to promote the book.

If I do it after the book, I'll miss out on the income from winter sponcon.

There was never going to be a good time, but I knew I had to do it for my sanity.

I was convinced that the account was dying, that people didn't like it anymore and that I'd run out of good material. I was going to jump before I was pushed.

'It's embarrassing that you're still telling this joke,' I told myself. 'Everyone must be so bored with you. You should go out on a high if you want anyone to maintain any respect for you.'

I felt so isolated from my old life. All my friends were at festivals and parties, they were cycling down canals and laughing in beer gardens, and I was traipsing through soggy Edinburgh, pretending that my life was a dream come true.

I constructed a fictional barbecue, where everyone I knew was gathered, slagging me off over sausages.

'She's flogging a dead horse,' I heard them say. 'Did you see she made ANOTHER joke about avocado and eggs on toast?'

'Yep. Kinder eggs this time. Tragic.'

It didn't occur to me that they might have something to talk about other than me, that they might be worried about me, that this bout of extreme narcissism might be a sign that my mental health was far from under control.

The year before, if I thought a gig had gone badly, someone could usually convince me that it was all in my head, but this year there were almost 140,000 people waiting to tell me what they thought of the show. I was no longer waking up to thousands of new followers, and I took this as a sign that my career was over before it really began.

Most of the feedback was positive. People commented 'great show!' and quoted their favourite lines. But some people weren't so kind, and it's those comments I remember. Of course you shouldn't have to pretend to enjoy something, you are well within your rights to think it's crap, but when a girl direct-messaged me to tell me that not only did she think my show was bad, but I clearly hadn't prepared and wasn't actually funny like everyone said, I wept. I remembered her from the show, sat on the front row talking to her friend throughout. I could tell they were laughing at me and not with me. It didn't exactly help with the nerves.

I was sharing a dressing room with Iain Stirling, the Scottish voiceover on *Love Island,* who was on after me. I told him how much I was looking forward to the end of August so I could take a break.

'A break?' he guffawed. 'I'm booked every night for a gig until February.'

Caroline came to me with a question.

'The Pleasance want to know if you'd be up for adding a couple of extra shows?' she asked tentatively.

I shot the suggestion out of the sky with a look.

'OK, pal. That's what I thought.'

I was already doing twenty-seven dates. Another would surely kill me. I had told no one about my plans to kill Stella. Not even Caroline.

It's easier to remember the bad stuff than the good. When I think about that month I see the woman who fell asleep in the front row, the man in the Eagles of Death Metal t-shirt who left after five minutes. I think mostly of how sad and tired I was then, of how terrible my stage fright was, of walking through Edinburgh like a zombie, going through the anhedonic motions of my performance. I rarely think about the four-star reviews, the brilliant press the show got, the fact that I performed an Edinburgh show while suffering from severe depression and managed to further, rather than damage, my career.

Press interviews were torturous. I tried so hard to sound excited about the show, to take photos of my name on the 'sold out' board every day, but I didn't care that the show was sold out. All I cared about was that it wasn't over.

I missed my old life. I missed my friends, but most of all I missed myself. I didn't know where I'd gone. And I had absolutely no idea if I was ever coming back. I felt drab and zestless and desperate for an explanation. I read an article that claims that our personality changes with age.

Maybe this is just me now, I thought. Maybe I've outgrown being happy.

The clean eater came to stay for a few days with my family. Her list of dietary requirements read like the side-effects of my medication. No gluten, no dairy, no nightshades, no soy.

'What am I going to feed her?!' fretted my mum.

'Don't worry,' I said. 'I don't think she likes eating much anyway.'

I booked us in to see back-to-back shows, both to make sure she had a good time, and to spare me the pressure to do the entertaining myself. I longed to be lying alone in a darkened room. We went for dinner and she ordered *moules marinière* without the shallots or cream. I didn't have the strength to laugh.

Before she left to return to London we sunbathed on the lawn and daydreamed about celebrities she could date to raise her profile. I couldn't tell if we were joking or not. She stretched out her long plant-based limbs and told me that she thought she had a shot with Tinie Tempah. I felt like a baked potato with eyes.

The next I heard of her she was dating a former boy-bander. We crossed paths at a juice bar opening I had attended to fill my afternoon. Fortuitously, she had managed to get papped in the passenger seat of the boy-bander's car. She was all over the papers. We hadn't spoken in almost a year.

When a photographer approached she told him she wasn't doing photos, in spite of her having just done a twenty-minute photoshoot outside the venue. She was worried about her face, she said, as she'd just had a vampire facial. A practitioner had removed blood from her arm and injected into her face, for what reason I will never quite be sure.

'The press are absolutely hounding me,' she announced without prompting.

'Yes,' I said. 'I've seen.'

'Have you really?' she said. 'I mean, I have no idea what's going on. I'm not even reading the papers until this all blows over.'

I had just read a two-spread interview she had given to *The Times*. There had been a photoshoot. I can only assume that she had been there for that. After that day we never spoke again.

The Fringe ended with a half-hearted attempt at enjoying myself. I went to a TV party and let people congratulate me on the success of Deliciously Stella, knowing that she would be dead as soon as I could manage it.

'Have you had a good Fringe?' they asked. I nodded. While it had been far from a personal success, professionally it didn't seem to have done me any harm. 'We'd be fools not to work with you. Look us up when you get back to London.'

I wondered if they wanted to work with Bella or Stella. Would they still want to meet me after I'd killed her?

When I got back to London, I collapsed in a heap. Caroline called to congratulate me. I had sold out the whole of my Edinburgh run, a feat that is rewarded with a sticker on your poster for next year's show.

'Why,' I asked her, 'when I am still raw from the experience of this year's show, would they remind me that I have to do it all again next year?'

'Selling out the show is a good thing, mate. You should be really proud.'

I smiled a smile that only reached my mouth.

'I guess next year's show has to be about my nervous breakdown. One for the *Guardian* reviewers.'

'That's the spirit.'

Before I'd gone to Edinburgh I'd been interviewed by a wonderful woman at *The Times*, before having an excruciating photoshoot in which my hair was curled and I was wearing brown lip gloss. I picked up a copy, terrified to look at the monstrosity inside, when I noticed that staring back at me, at the top of the very front page, was my face. My face was on the front cover of *The Times*.

I called Caroline.

'You need to get a copy of *The Times*.'

Being on the front cover of *The Times* was unbelievable, but it was bittersweet. I knew enough about the press to know that fame does not equal tangible success. The fact that someone is very visible doesn't mean that they are very busy, or very rich. The writer from *The Times* finished the piece by saying that 'comedy commissioners must be salivating.' Only Caroline and I knew the truth, that the phone was far from ringing off the hook.

I was still taking occasional meetings. I was in and out of the BBC, each show I was there to discuss felt less suitable than the last. One day they asked me in to deliver a monologue about period sex, with no warning. When I told a commissioner I'd be interested in making a documentary about the effects of social media on mental health, they winced.

'What are your other USPs?' they asked. 'Apart from being Stella, what makes you interesting?'

I splurged out my life story over and over, trying to land on something that could sell, anything that made me worthy of a TV career. It wasn't enough that I was funny or clever or had worked so, so hard to get this far. They couldn't find a hook, and that was that.

Derek was beside himself when he saw *The Times*.

'Look at what posh assistant has achieved!' he wrote on Facebook. #proud.

Even my dad was impressed. His inbox was flooded with emails about his famous daughter.

'Everybody thinks you're a star!' he said. Of course they did. I had 150,000 Instagram followers. I was all over the papers. But the truth was, I was broke.

I'd burned through the first instalments of my meagre book advance on travelling back and forth to London, the Wrangler jeans job that had threatened to interrupt my Edinburgh run had fallen through, along with the £10k beer gig. I'd banked my entire income on prospective jobs and learned the hard way that nothing is certain until you've signed on the dotted line. All I'd done for the month of August was perform. I'd sold out the whole run and only made a profit of £700.

Brands were taking so long to pay me for work I'd completed, I started to think I'd been tricked. I desperately needed the money from the beauty box collaboration. It took almost six months for ASDA to pay me for the first influencing job I did. I could not wait that long again. I was calling Caroline constantly but she seemed strangely distant. She was 'away from her desk' or 'couldn't chat right now'. Something didn't seem right.

'You're lucky,' said my sister, 'because people will always think of you as being successful.'

I got talking to someone on the train who admitted she was a fan. I joked that if I didn't get paid soon I might not make my rent. She looked at me like I'd just lied to her face, brushing me off as she left with, 'You have over 100,000 Instagram followers. I'm sure you're doing alright.'

I felt like such a mug. The media was full of stories about how much money influencers were making for nothing. It was supposedly the easiest job in the world and I was working flat out. Why couldn't I turn my followers into pounds?

The truth was, I was working much harder at staying famous than I was at getting rich. Press and self-promotion were taking up all of my time and that felt like a worthwhile investment. I knew how television worked. When I worked at the BBC the papers were delivered every day so the development team could scan for up-and-coming talent. If I was in the papers, I would be that talent. The more visible I was, the better my chances at getting on the telly.

My efforts were clearly working. I had been named as one of the most influential Londoners by the *Evening Standard* again. This year, I had my own page in a specially published booklet, an interview about 'my London' in *ES* magazine and an invitation to a party at the Natural History Museum hosted by Prince Charles.

I took my oldest friend, Laura, for support. She's always impeccably glamorous and she deemed my entire wardrobe to be unfit for purpose. She hauled me up and down the King's Road trying to find an appropriate outfit. I refused to commit to heels, so I wore the pinchy gold platform trainers with a shift dress from & Other Stories.

I was nervous about the event. I'd been asked to do an interview with London Live on the red carpet and I was fearful of stage fright. I also couldn't imagine who I might know at the celebration of the great and the good. I was grateful not to be going alone.

Almost immediately after entering, I felt a panic attack rising in my chest. I was weaving down a roped-off red carpet towards the woman with the London Live microphone.

'Are you on the list?' she asked me. I nodded and tried to stutter out some sentences before scuttling inside. My face was boiling and my ears rang as if tiny bells were clattering around my head. I headed straight to the bathroom to run my wrists under the tap.

When I emerged, the Natural History Museum was dark, and I could faintly make out the silhouettes of prominent actors, architects and editors. The crowd quieted. HRH was on. Laura and I shuffled to the front of the crowd for a better look but my neck felt hot and I was struggling to breathe. I was holding a drink, a programme and a tiny bowl of curry and I couldn't mop my brow. As soon as Prince Charles started to speak I knew it was game over.

'Laura,' I whispered, 'I think I'm going to either vomit or faint.'

'What? We can't miss Prince Charles's speech!'

'I'm serious. I am going to vom. I need air. I need it now.'

Royalist that she is, Laura took my bowl food and let me run away. The pinchy trainers squeaked as I darted outside into the fresh air. I took a deep breath and gave myself a pep talk. This was the networking opportunity of a lifetime. I had to get it together, find a TV exec and dazzle them. When I got back inside Laura was eyeballing a group of men in suits.

'B,' she said. 'I think that's Nigel Farage. We should get a selfie.'

'Are you sure? Do we really want a selfie with Nigel Farage?'

'Come on,' she said. 'It'll be funny.'

And that is how I found myself with bowl food down my front and Nigel Farage's hand squeezing my waist, while he told me what a lucky man he was, to be in between two such gorgeous girls. In the picture I am making a face like a horrified duck. I will never know how I managed not to vomit.

# Fame, Cancel Culture and Staying Power

This is the bit where I say that fame wasn't all it was cracked up to be and was quite invasive actually and you wouldn't wish it on anyone – except you would because there's always a part of you that thinks it would be nice to have it back once it's gone.

I think it's safe at this point to say, without sounding like a total bellend, that I was a bit famous. I'd been assigned publicists for both my book and my show, had featured in almost every newspaper and magazine I could think of and had hit the front cover of *The Times*. People did a double-take when they saw me on the street. In London I was someone.

I had reached the lower echelons of the Z list and for the first time, I was aware of being looked at. Strangers would slow down and smile, thinking that they knew me, then clock that I was from the internet and hurry past with their heads down. I'd always wanted to be an It Girl and being recognised felt like having, if not it, then something like it.

Sometimes people would come up to me in the street and tell me they loved the account. A woman told me it had helped her to finally get over her eating disorder. Of course, I was flattered. I'd never imagined I'd actually do something good. Funny, yes, but actually useful? I gave myself a virtual pat on the back and called my mum so she could say, 'That's lovely, darling,' when she really meant, 'Can you piss off so I can watch TV? I have no idea how Instagram works.'

'You must be absolutely cleaning up now you're famous,' said a friend as she bemoaned her lack of love life.

'Have you seen my account?!' I said. 'I am professionally revolting and 98 per cent of my fanbase is female. Nobody wants to date the bird who puts barbecue sauce on her face for fun.'

'I don't know,' she said. 'I bet men think it's classic.'

I remained unconvinced. I turned over the words of my friend Archie when I showed him Stella: 'You will never get a boyfriend again.'

Maybe he was right. Maybe I was just too outwardly grotesque. I started to fear that any suitor must have ulterior motives. I stuck to one 'celebrity' dating app where Instagram models and the occasional A lister made slideshows of themselves skateboarding in black and white. It was so 'exclusive' you were pretty much shown the same seven men, over and over again, until you cracked and ended up on a date with someone who had presented a couple of shows on Radio 1 in 2002, but whose career had stalled on account of their cocaine habit.

Just you wait, I had thought during a particularly plain stage at school. One day I will emerge as a glamorous, celebrated wit and will be beating off your boyfriends with a stick. Maybe Stella might have beat someone with a stick of rock, but they wouldn't have been trying to shag her.

I had also developed a strange irrational fear that if I did pull, someone might try to shag me for the story. It's not that I think I would be anyone's fantasy shag – far from it – but I knew deep down that I would shag almost anyone famous if I thought it would make a good story. My friend Lizzie and I once spent an entire day debating who we would or would not shag for the story. I had decided that if a man came up to me in a nightclub and told me that he had played Macnair, the Hippogriff slayer in *Harry Potter*, a man who wears a hood over his head for the entire film, I would have to shag him. Lizzie said the only famouses she absolutely could not shag were Boris Johnson and Noel Edmonds.

My madness followed me into the gym changing room. When you're anonymous, it doesn't matter if someone sees you naked because you're just a naked body, but when someone knows who you are, they can go away thinking, 'That person's body is like that.' I went to an all-girls boarding school; nudity has never been something that's crossed my mind, and yet, now that I was in the public eye, I was certain that everyone wanted to know what my vagina looked like so they could talk about it later. I made a note to bring up all of these points in therapy.

I had always thought I'd find being famous easy, like slipping into a warm bath of adoration. Growing up I wanted to be a national treasure, which my therapist assures me is a result of being 'desperate to be seen'. I could tell that some of my friends were worried about my ego. They thought that I was an attention-seeker and a show-off, and in a way they were right. I liked the attention and I was showing off, but I also felt more exposed and insecure than ever. I wasn't so lacking in self-awareness that I didn't suspect they thought those things too.

Like an age-old cliché, now that I'd got what I wished for, I had buyer's remorse. Admitting to these feelings made me feel ungrateful and I was certain nobody would believe me, so I kept them inside and soldiered on. I talked about myself to distract from the way I was feeling inside, which was anxious, lonely and overwhelmed.

I frantically monitored my engagement, always looking for a reason why some posts performed better than others. I was only as good as my last output and I needed this winning streak to continue. A concerning trend I noticed was that people reacted more positively to photos in which I looked unattractive. Of course, I didn't often look attractive – it's hard when you're covered in barbecue sauce or you've strapped baguettes to your deliberately distended stomach – but the numbers were unequivocal. In posts where I was wearing makeup or looked slimmer than usual, I got fewer likes.

I confided in a friend about what was happening and they couldn't see an issue.

'Think of it like a public service. Stella makes people feel better about themselves. Everyone knows you're not really gross in real life.'

But as far as I was concerned, this was real life, that was my face and I did look like that without makeup – barbecue sauce or no barbecue sauce. Did I want to be the benchmark for everyone having a bad day? What was being the fall guy doing for my own self-confidence?

Emily interrupted the whirlwind that was my newfound fame to tell me that she had a new friend who was much more famous than I. Emily is a very successful theatre producer and was producing *Dr Faustus*, with none other than Kit Harington, star of *Game of Thrones*, in the lead role.

'I need you to be on your best behaviour.'

'Right.'

'But I'd like you to cook a roast at my house.'

'We could have a roast at mine?' I suggest.

'Well,' she says. 'It's sort of a special roast. Kit Harington, from my play, is coming, with his girlfriend. And I know you're a bit of a *Game of Thrones* fan.'

I immediately started screeching the theme tune from the top of my lungs.

'Yes, I will make a roast for Kit Harington, King in the North Jon Snow. Do you think his girlfriend will say the line?'

The conditions, Emily explained, were that I did not mention *Game of Thrones* at all. I had to pretend that I had never seen it. I accepted.

Later that week I got a call from the publicist I had been assigned by Penguin for my book. I now had two publicists, one for the book (Daisy) and one for my Edinburgh show (Charlotte), and they were having to divvy up coverage between them. Daisy had been contacted by the *Sunday Times Style*. They wanted me to answer some questions about Ella. As my team had agreed not to talk about her in the press, I declined.

'Great,' she said. 'We'll let them know not to run it.'

Sunday rolled around, bringing with it my lunch date with the King in the North. I woke up late and trotted downstairs to find my flatmate listening to Radio 2 with the *Sunday Times*.

'B!' she shouted.

'You didn't say you were going to be in *Style* again?!' She lifted up the magazine and sure enough there was a double-page spread, asking in giant neon letters: 'Are you a Deliciously Ella or a Deliciously Stella?' A picture of me took up the whole of the left page, and a picture of Ella on the right.

'Oh shit,' I said. I went upstairs to get my phone and saw that I had an answerphone message from my publicist, Charlotte. She's confused. She had no idea this was coming out and it's sort of a big deal. I rang her back and told her I didn't know either. It seemed that Daisy was also in the dark.

'Great piece, B,' said Lizzie as I made myself some toast. 'What are you going to wear later?' Lizzie was my co-chef and another attendee at an audience with Kit Harington. He was going to think that Emily invited the whole street.

'This is excellent,' she said. 'He'll be able to bond with you because you are also a famous.'

We arrived to meet Jon Snow, King of the North, with fully madeup faces and deliberately casual clothes, befitting of a normal Sunday. We noted that he is much smaller in real life, very charming and clearly desperate not to talk about *Game of Thrones*. We managed to get through the afternoon without admitting we had ever seen or heard of him before. Instead we talked about how famous I was, as if he had not just gone to a costume party as himself, because he is a pop culture icon. Emily plonked a copy of *Style* down in front of him, open on my page.

'Look, Bella's in the paper,' she said to the man who is the face of Dolce & Gabbana.

'Oh great.'

He seemed genuinely thrilled for me, so we talked about my spread in *Style* as if he is not the most famous man on Earth. I told him that I want to write sitcoms and he told me that he had a drama coming out on the BBC. I wondered if at this very moment, I could persuade Kit to get me a bit part in *Game of Thrones* and then use it as a platform to get one of my scripts made. Emily saw the cogs whirring in my head and asked for some help with tzatziki.

I somehow made it through the rest of lunch without pitching him my new food podcast idea, *Game of Scones*. The *Sunday Times* article had helped me gain 5,000 followers.

Making awkward appearances started to feel like par for the course. Even my friends started introducing me to people as Deliciously Stella. I was wheeled out at parties like show and tell. Once, I met someone on a dating app, the owner of a popular food delivery service who met me at his office and proceeded to introduce me to all of his staff, one of whom started squealing because she was a fan.

People usually don't believe me when I tell them I was a painfully shy and awkward child. Everyone who meets me assumes that I was like Honey Boo Boo, liquored up on Go-Go juice and singing and dancing in front of anyone who would listen. In reality I never left my mother alone and had to sit on my own at children's parties because I was afraid of the sound of popping balloons. The idea of being the centre of attention appalled me, and to this day I have a recurring nightmare about doing my first dance at my wedding and losing the use of my legs.

When, at age nine, I went away to school, I was forced so far out of my shell that I vowed never to be shy again. I never spoke about it, used humour to hide it, and put it beneath the same mental trapdoor as my anxiety and ignored it.

I decided to be thrilled when a stranger approached me about my Instagram account and ignore the uncomfortable feeling that I was being observed. People started stopping me to ask for selfies and on more than one occasion I caught someone trying to take a stealth photo of me on the tube. Whenever people stopped to talk to me I would feel intense pressure to perform, to impress them and to make them laugh. Stella wasn't anxious. She was a laugh. So that's what I gave them.

I am under no illusion that I was ever famous, famous. My experience of being a Z-list celebrity was that I wasn't recognised often, but when I was it was significant. Having a small-ish following secures you an intimacy not afforded to those who are loved by everyone. You're somebody's best-kept secret, and in their mind you could be their friend. I could tell you exactly where my target demographic would be at any given moment. Places I have felt the prickle of recognition include Columbia Road Flower Market, Street Feast, Pop Brixton – in fact, most of Brixton. In short, my presence had become a sort of unofficial marker of the worst of gentrification.

At Glastonbury, I dropped my driving licence in a smoking area, and after asking someone if they'd seen it, was greeted with a chorus of 'Has anyone seen Deliciously Stella's driving licence?'

I hadn't realised that anyone had noticed me. I felt suddenly paranoid that I was off my face and everybody knew it.

I remember Faye's words: 'Don't sign up to be a role model.'

The next time somebody approached me I shouted, 'I have no eyes!' Nobody asked for a photo.

We've learned from shows like *Love Island* and *The X Factor* that overnight fame is a golden ticket. That you're damned to take the rough with the smooth and that only the strong survive. I wasn't strong and I hated myself for it. I tried so hard to make the most of it, to enjoy the parts that were good, but I couldn't escape the parts that were alien, hard and lonely. I hated myself for being ungrateful.

'People would give their right arm to have this many followers,' I told my dad one day through streaming tears. 'I'm so lucky.' The prospect of influencing being my whole career absolutely terrified me. It was too risky, too quantifiable, too exposing. At least after a bad comedy gig I could comfort myself that art was subjective.

If you're wondering about the disconnect between how I perceived Stella and the way the world felt, you are of sounder mind than I was then. To the untrained eye, the account looked to be ticking along nicely. I still had heaps of followers and was still getting lots of exciting press. Only I knew that I was losing followers at the same rate I was gaining them. Only I knew that I was dangerously close to running out of content. The myth of continuous growth was untenable. I had plundered all my natural resources. There were simply no more jokes to be made.

The prospect of being somebody who 'used to be famous' was horrifying to me. I had one job, and that was to stay relevant. For me, relevance meant strong engagement and an increase in followers. As far as I could tell, my worth was a dial that either ticked up or down. It was ticking down.

I woke up in the night worrying about the decline of clean eating and the subsequent death of my relevance. I noticed the shift in algorithm that had cut the number of comments I was receiving in two. I feared that my agent would leave me because I was running out of rope.

My followers were dropping. I felt like a laughing stock. The girl who was handed fame on a plate but couldn't see it through. I was trapped in a cycle, making a variation of the same joke every day to lesser and lesser applause. I felt like a broken hologram of a clown, fading into static.

I went to see my shrink and asked if there was anything I could take for my nerves. Maybe a beta blocker or some Xanax could stop the worry? I had developed a persuasive fear that I was unknowingly problematic and that I was going to get 'cancelled'.

'I'm not fat enough. I'm too privileged. I'm taking up space I don't deserve from someone more marginalised. I wore fur at university.' I was obsessed with behaving in exactly the right way in case I tripped and Laurence Fox fell out of me and started blathering about free speech. I don't think I hold any problematic views, and I especially hope that a dormant bigot isn't lying in wait inside my body, but I sensed that I could only be the golden girl for so long. It was time for me to come off that pedestal, and again, I'd rather jump than be pushed.

I think my perfectionism was a way to positively counteract the conflicted feelings I had about Deliciously Ella. While I insisted that it wasn't a direct parody of her, just a rip-off of her name, she never engaged with me. I was desperate for her to see that it was all in good fun, but I don't think she saw it that way and I felt awful. I'm not an unkind person, I just really didn't agree with her, and for me I would have found the satire nothing if not flattering.

'Does Deliciously Ella like the account?' was a question that made me squirm. I claimed that I took her liking two of my posts as 'tacit consent,' but I knew that wasn't the truth at all. I didn't have to look far to find people to tell me the truth about how she felt about me. I was only ever a friend of a friend away.

I claimed that she'd never acknowledged the account, so probably didn't know about it. Either that or she was too busy and successful to care. I started to wonder if I would have made a good spin doctor, then I remembered the time I'd done work experience for a cabinet minister, laminated a fake driving licence in Portcullis House and been caught in the lift by William Hague. When I returned, the family friend I was shadowing was apoplectic. I'd left my dodgy Photoshop open on my computer for all to see. Before I could be properly bollocked, London won the Olympics and the office flooded with ecstatic well-wishers. He smiled at me through gritted teeth.

I thought I'd found the perfect opportunity to patch things up when my editor at Penguin admitted that she had in fact worked on Deliciously Ella's first book.

'Isn't that a conflict of interest?' I asked.

'Not if we tell her what we're doing. I'm sure she'll find it funny. Maybe we'll even get a quote for the jacket?'

I was sceptical but reassured that my editor probably knew Ella better than I did. If I wrote her a nice enough letter, surely she'd feel obligated to agree that it was a harmless joke and then we could move on?

Both my editor and I sent a message to Ella, explaining our surprise that my account had taken off the way that it had. I told her that I was writing a book but had no intention of doing anything that would hurt her feelings or her brand. I told her that I admired her as a businesswoman and offered to let her see an advance copy and veto anything she deemed to be derogatory.

Her reply contained just six words. 'My lawyers will be in touch.' I was disappointed. I had been convinced that we could both exist in harmony, that a truce could even be mutually beneficial. It wouldn't have hurt to admit to having a sense of humour.

This didn't do much to dispel my opinion that clean eaters were humourless dementors determined to sap the joy out of life one sugar cube at a time. In a way it gave me permission to lean into the joke further. I was on my own, an influencer in my own right, and I no longer felt obliged not to step on anybody's toes.

That was until Caroline called me in.

'Have you got any money?' she asked as soon as I arrived in her office.

'Errm no. I thought that was what we were trying to rectify today.'

'Yes,' she said. 'I'm sure we will. But Penguin want to know if you can afford a lawyer. Ella isn't backing down about the book.'

I paused for a second as if I had any options to consider. 'No. Unfortunately not. And even if I did have any money, it wouldn't be as much as her. Her mum's a bloody Sainsbury.'

'Right.'

'Does this mean the book is off?'

'No, no. They want you to keep writing it as if it's going to happen. I've got it written into your contract that you still get paid regardless of what happens with the lawsuit.'

Apparently the lawyers were going with an accusation of 'passing off'. Ella was worried someone's granny might see my gift-sized book in Urban Outfitters, see the picture of me eating the block of cheese on the front, and assume that it was Ella's book. Just imagine receiving my book for Christmas instead of hers? You'd be devastated. Nothing kills your motivation quite like the possibility of your work amounting to nothing, and I was still hoping that the book might make me rich. The publishers seemed to think that it might, too. Emily was hoping people would take to it like they had to the Ladybird parody books. Penguin's lawyers agreed to take the case. It was a matter of principle, they said. They weren't going to be pushed around.

A parody law brought in in 2014 to protect the satirical singer 'Weird Al' Yankovic eventually saved my bacon. My book was coming to a Christmas stocking near you.

My agent, Caroline, wanted to make sure everything was in order for my upcoming book launch. After being turned down by a number of glamorous venues, we had managed to secure a café off the Strand to host the event.

Malibu had kindly offered to sponsor the party, providing us with the ingredients for sickly sweet piña coladas. I was wearing gold platform trainers I'd been gifted that were a size too small. I liked to think that the toe-pinching helped me feel present.

Pretending to enjoy my book launch was the hardest acting job of my career. I'd already taken a Xanax to calm my nerves on my way there, but my nerves were still strumming like guitar strings. I didn't want to be there. I was tired of being on show. I didn't want people to buy the book. I didn't want them to realise how unfunny I was.

This is the final push, I told myself. The last project as Deliciously Stella then you can go back to being Bella forever. All of publishing's great and good turned up. I signed books until my wrists hurt, graciously accepting compliments, trying to avoid my real friends so nobody could see through the act.

I imagine a book launch is in some ways similar to a wedding. Everyone wants to speak to you for five minutes and you're always answering the same questions.

'How do you feel?'

'Will you sign one for me?'

'Did you ever think the account would get this far?'

I went to sit on the loo and refresh my phone.

'You're so ungrateful,' I told myself. 'You should be happy. Stop shaking. The joke's past its sell-by date and the book isn't actually funny.'

I found myself fantasising about the inside of other people's heads.

'I wouldn't be buying this if she wasn't my friend.'

'It won't sell.'

'For someone with a book coming out, she's got a face like a smacked arse.'

I slapped on a smile and made an awkward last-minute speech. The piña coladas and adrenalin curdled into nausea. All I could repeat to myself, over and over again, was: 'I am so, so lucky and yet I feel so empty.'

The book had reignited my relationship with the press, who were going over and above to make me 'happen'.

I was all too aware of the narrative arc of the female overnight success. I was sure I'd been put on this pedestal to make it all the sweeter when I was pushed off. Cancel culture wasn't yet then what it is now, but nobody is safe from tall poppy syndrome, not even a 'woman of the people' like me.

The press had torn into Deliciously Ella, who was backpedalling furiously. As the term 'clean eating' fell out of favour she appeared to dissociate herself from it completely, saying she had never used it.

She has since appeared on the podcast *How to Fail with Elizabeth Day* and complained about being compared to Donald Trump and being portrayed as 'literally the devil'. She just wanted to make lentils cool, she said. Didn't we know that our country is obese?

While I don't doubt that the media questioning was hurtful, refusing to acknowledge claims that have made you very, very rich is rightly impossible. If you play on women's insecurities to make them buy energy balls, you have to own your decisions.

She now claims never to have encouraged restriction, in spite of having declared gluten a poison and junk food to be 'gross'. A cursory sweep of the internet for 'Deliciously Ella clean eating' or 'Deliciously Ella gluten poison' will tell you that those blog posts existed but have now been removed. Unfortunately for her, the internet is littered with the ghosts of dubious claims.

The fact is, when you are as rich and as privileged as Deliciously Ella, you might feel you should operate in a space above criticism. But 'I'm just a girl who loves lentils' doesn't cut it when you're a multi-millionaire, well on your way to being a billionaire. She complained that she got more flack than male chefs who've written weight-loss books when her books weren't even about weight. To suggest that your cookbook that asks people to replace pasta with courgette, give up dairy and gluten and make cake out of sweet potatoes isn't about weight is at best unthinking and at worst ignorant and deluded.

Does she know nothing about the socio-economic factors affecting people's diets? Is she so depoliticised that she hasn't heard of poverty, austerity or any other financial barriers to eating in the way she does?

When she complained about being compared to Trump, she apologised to Trump supporters who might be offended. Trump supporters might like Deliciously Ella books, and she can't let a little controversy get in the way of profit.

It's important for us to be kinder on social media, but that doesn't mean people should stop asking questions. It isn't unkind to hold people to account. No matter what politicians would have you believe.

There is a difference between being held to account and being trolled, though. A post in which I made a joke about 'hair mayonnaise', which I'd found in Boots, was swiftly called out as racist. Hair mayonnaise is a product used by women with afro hair and a white woman joking about it was offensive and ignorant. I apologised to every person who commented, removed the post and moved on.

When I was targeted by a group of teenage competitive swimmers and called 'fat, unhealthy and jealous', I blocked them because I had nothing to learn from engaging with them.

Negativity about me was usually reserved for the comments section of newspapers. A motley crew of *Guardian* readers once laid into me for 'owning half of Scotland', producing reams of false information about who I was related to and how much money I had. I wouldn't have minded if yet more people hadn't tweeted that they were 'disappointed' to find out that my grandfather had been a Conservative MP. Apparently, I was guilty by association.

Deliciously Ella had political heritage also. Her father was a peer who had memorably crossed the chamber from Conservative to Labour. When he and her mother separated and he came out as gay, the *Daily Mail* called me and asked me to comment. I was horrified. Is this what people thought of me?

I was satirising her recipes, not trying to ruin her life. She ended the *How to Fail* podcast saying that she wished her critics had reached out to her so she could have engaged with them and defended herself. I am glad I sent that email and not at all surprised that she didn't reply.

I had one brush with cancel culture where I deserved everything I very nearly got. I was walking to the Priory for a therapy session, panicking that I hadn't posted anything for two days. A friend sent me a meme saying 'you should put this on Stella'. I gave it a cursory glance, it was a picture of an over-weight woman wearing a t-shirt that said 'I beat anorexia'. I posted it while walking, with the caption 'me too'. Within seconds the reactions poured in.

'This is disgusting.'

'Shameful.'

'Unfollowing now. I thought you were better than this.'

'Cancelled. Cancelled. Cancelled.'

By the time I arrived in my therapist's waiting room and looked at my phone my inbox was flooded with disappointed fans. I took the time to process what I'd posted. They were right. It wasn't funny. In fact, it was horrific, especially considering how many people had reached out to me about their own experiences with eating disorders.

I had made a terrible mistake, and had I left it up any longer it could have ended my career. Our capacity for forgiveness for the extremely online is dwindling, fast. We made you and we'll break you. Dems the rules.

Of course, celebrities' fear of cancel culture can be a source of amusement. Is it not, after all, fun to judge someone who sees their popularity as their life source?

During the coronavirus pandemic, Ashton Kutcher recorded a bizarre video about the Black Lives Matter movement in which he begged people not to cancel those who claim that all lives matter. It's funny to think that for a famous person, cancellation is a kind of death. What's not funny is to think about the power the media wields to perpetuate 'cancellation'. How insidious it is to have no control of your own narrative, how fruitless it is to defend yourself against the baying mob.

An online pile-on undoubtedly exacerbated the mental health issues of Caroline Flack, who tragically took her own life while awaiting a court date for allegedly assaulting her boyfriend. This was an example of cancel culture at its most extreme. Friends have revealed that she frantically scrolled through messages from trolls in between filming live scenes on TV. I can only imagine the vile abuse that filled her direct messages before her trial. A cursory scan of Twitter shows that people are still willing to condemn her, still assuming her guilt, making jokes and sneering at a tribute to her life on *Strictly Come Dancing*.

I have no idea what happened with her boyfriend, but I have some idea of what people will have said to her about it online. The words may only be spoken through a screen, you could be locked in your house, surrounded by people you love, but when people you don't know tell in their droves that you don't deserve to live, it's going to cause permanent damage. We'll never be able to get her back, and her final days must have been ones of such anguish.

I once cried because a woman wrote on my account that my face looked like a fucked-up embryo. I called her out and she later apologised.

'I'm so sorry,' she said. 'I completely forgot that you were a real person.'

Caroline Flack was a real person, with real feelings, receiving real, awful messaging about herself. While I don't doubt that Flack should have been held to account and I abhor domestic violence, I think we all wish that she could have had her day in court. People who think that a trial by media can be ignored with a stiff upper lip are extremely naive about our constantly connected world. I hope that every person who sent her an unkind private message about the situation or tagged her in a cruel tweet hangs their head in perpetual shame. Being famous does not immunise you from cruelty and pain. A nice flat and a presenting job won't stop you feeling hurt when millions of people call you a monster. And as sad and as shallow as it might seem, the prospect of your fame going away is terrifying. When your job defines you, the prospect of it all being taken away is a death in itself.

I sometimes like to compare what I went through to the cycle of *Love Island* contestants. Their social media accounts explode overnight. They're all over the papers for a year, then they're usurped by next year's gang and left to perpetually date throughout the seasons in a bid to reignite interest in their lives. Of course, they now have heaps of followers and can sell teeth-whitening strips and huge grey sofas for the rest of their days, but over time the deals will become fewer, the work less fulfilling and they, like me, will find themselves back on civvy street, wondering what the hell went wrong.

The good and bad parts of fame are so disparate and over-whelming, to have one without the other is enough to send anyone insane. The process of letting go of the fame you once held is like letting go of a guy who was the best shag of your life but who left your self-esteem in tatters. Nobody comes out the other side of it a better person. They'll always be left thinking about the one that got away.

I deleted the 'I beat anorexia' photo and apologised, but I don't know what would have happened if my misdemeanour had been allowed to gather further ire. If I had spent my ther-apy session with my phone in my pocket and news of my cancellation had reached the media. Would the end of my career have resulted in the end of me?

I read an interview with the singer Katy Perry, in which she confessed that the poor performance of her most recent album had led to her contemplating suicide. A small setback in an otherwise glittering career had been enough to push the most-followed person on Twitter to the brink. At what cost do we strive to maintain the perception that we're thriving? How much power do we give to the feeling that we are special?

I was on a family fishing holiday in Oban when the *Daily Mail* got back in touch. It was usually an annual trip I'd missed since starting Stella because I was a) at Edinburgh; b) too scared to spend prolonged amounts of time on a boat without 4G.

Not being able to refresh my phone every five seconds like a junkie meant that I had to seek dopamine elsewhere and actually talk to my family. My parents had given us walkie-talkies so we could stay in contact and insisted on us using proper military language. Telling Dad that dinner was ready and he needed to head home had now become:

'Dad. Over. Dinner is ready. Over. Do you copy?'

'Roger that. Over and out.'

We were staying in a holiday village where we'd inherited a timeshare from my grandmother. In my youth it had seemed rather grand, but it hadn't weathered well. The tennis courts were now penned in by baggy, rusted cages and the swimming pool had turned a putrid green. A forlorn plaque still hung on the wall, announcing that my grandfather had officially opened the pool in the eighties. I wasn't the only member of the Younger family with a shelf life.

Without ready access to my phone, I went crabbing and sailing; I drank gin and played board games with my siblings; I saw a sea otter.

When the *Daily Mail* called, I immediately sprang into action. How was I going to do the interview? What should I say that would make them want to run it? How could I get back in the papers? The prospect of relevance lit a fire in my belly. Maybe this could be the article that reignited my winning streak?

I tried to sound nonchalant. The *Mail* were interested in how many famous people followed me. I was 'the instacomic celebs can't get enough of.' Obviously I knew which famous people followed me – I'd made a mental note every time I saw a blue tick. I was getting on so well with the journalist I almost forgot who I was talking to. It had been a while since I'd done press and my guard was down. She asked me whether I had ever met Deliciously Ella and for the first time I said, no, but I have heard from her lawyer.

'NO WAY!' said the journalist, excitedly. 'This is great. Can I put it in the article?' Immediate regret thudded to the pit of my stomach. I took a deep breath. 'OK.'

Immediately afterwards I felt dirty. I'd sold out. I was the Kerry Katona of clean eating. I went back to meet my family feeling quiet and shifty.

'What's happened, darling?' asked my mum.

'Nothing,' I said. 'I just think I need to learn to think before I speak.'

In the weeks before the article came out, I regressed. I was back to being a nervous wreck, convinced that everyone was judging me. Why was I so desperate to stay in the papers? I was no better than those celebs who hire photographers to 'pap' them when they're in the Maldives.

My dad picked up the *Mail* when he was on a plane and texted me a picture of the article.

'I didn't know you were going to be in the papers, darling.'

I knew I never wanted to be in the papers for something other than my achievements again. Spreading gossip made me feel shallow and desperate. Fame for the sake of fame tasted a lot like shame.

My final appearance in the guise of influencer came at a protest to end period poverty. I went with the fashion-forward feminist girl gang with a jaunty pink painting of the female reproductive system. After standing in the cold for twenty minutes with the other protestors, revelling in the electric mood, the head of the girl gang tapped me on the shoulder.

'Babe, they're saying that the influencers can stand in VIP.'

'There's a VIP section at this protest?'

'Yeah, it's where the celebs are. When the speeches start you can stand on the stage for moral support.'

I looked over to see Daisy Lowe, Suki Waterhouse and Tanya Burr penned in by some metal fencing, away from the riff-raff. I thought about standing silently behind them, as if my presence meant something. As if I hadn't just turned up and put on a sticker.

'I don't think I'd feel comfortable doing that,' I said. After half of the speeches, I left.

# 140,000 Followers

Caroline had been strangely distant since Edinburgh and it was starting to concern me. She was always away from her desk when I called, and I was calling a lot.

Finally, she asked me to come into the office.

'I'm afraid I have some bad news.'

'Oh my god. You're dropping me.'

'I am not dropping you. I am retiring. I've got a job as a booker in TV.'

'So I won't have an agent anymore. Holy shit, I don't have an agent.'

'I will help you get a new agent.'

I tried to cry but I was still on antipsychotics.

'This is a nightmare.'

Caroline had been with me through my breakdown. She had helped me see off Deliciously Ella's legal team. She knew how much I hated performing.

'I'm sorry, mate, but I promise we'll find you a really amazing new agent. I'll write to them and tell them how wonderful and talented you are.'

'But you're the only person who's seen me perform as me. You're the only person who knows I do comedy that isn't Deliciously Stella. How am I going to find someone else who will have a twenty-minute conversation about whether or not people will get it if I eat an Arctic roll to "get rid of my rolls"?'

I was utterly bereft. How could she leave me? Caroline had discovered me, she knew me. She had signed me as me, not as Deliciously Stella. Caroline had talked me off the ledge when I was nervous before gigs. She knew the kind of career I wanted. She knew that I was mad. I imagined having to tell a new agent that I'd been in the Priory, or that I was nervous about appearing on TV because my performance would be permanent. What if a new agent needed to see me perform the Deliciously Stella show before signing me? What if nobody wants to sign me at all?! Within five minutes I had catastrophised so badly, I was convinced that this was the end of my career and possibly my life.

'It's not over right this second. I thought I could accompany you on a final voyage.'

I'd been invited to be a guest on *Woman's Hour*. I was hugely honoured and intimidated. Was I highbrow enough for *Woman's Hour*? Who would interview me? Jane Garvey scared me absolutely shitless, and the last time I'd been a guest on Radio 4, a presenter accused me of bullying Deliciously Ella live on air.

'I know you're not keen on doing Stella stuff, but you can't turn down *Woman's Hour*, right?'

She was right. If *Woman's Hour* wanted Stella, I would deliver her.

I didn't sleep the night before my appearance. I arrived with wild hair and tombstones under my eyes, truly a face for radio. There was a journalist from the *Evening Standard* there who I knew a bit from university and the perfumier, Jo Malone. I told Jo that my mum travelled everywhere in a cloud of lime, basil and mandarin. It turned out that her assistant had been at school with me. The small talk was soothing.

I told myself that *Woman's Hour* was no big deal. It was just a chat, after all.

A producer nipped in and asked me if I'd remembered to bring my prop. They'd asked me to arrive with a bread knife.

'Yes,' I said, pulling the blade from my handbag.

'Great. Jane would like you to make a crisp sandwich during your interview. If you could take a couple of bites as well, that would be awesome.'

The *Evening Standard* journalist was nervously flicking through page upon page of notes.

'Good luck,' she said, as the producer handed me a loaf and a packet of salt and vinegar crisps.

After a short interview, during which I decided that Jane thought me utterly moronic, I was instructed to make the sandwich. Cutting the bread and packing in the crisps seemed to take hours, and when I was done Jane asked me to take a bite. I thought of my mum listening at home to her daughter chomp through a crisp sandwich on Radio 4. Jane asked me to take another dry bite, which I choked down. Why was there no water? Why is bread so dry? Why did I not ask for butter?

I was convinced it had been a total disaster, but the reception was rapturous. I opened up my Instagram and scrolled through my account.

This bitch really does not want to die. I thought.

While I worked out my new angle, I had more pressing concerns. I was about to be without an agent, and I needed to find a new one, stat. My imposter syndrome was riding high, hurling lighter fuel onto the flaming negative thoughts inside my head.

What if nobody wants to sign you? What if they saw your show and there's a black mark against your name? What if you are an industry-wide joke due to your lack of talent and nobody will even meet you?

Maybe this is the voice of my generation? I thought. The voice that tells you to compare yourself to everyone else. That the odds are stacked against you. That you're never going to make it.

Luckily, the voice outside my head was Emily's, and she thought the only way was up. She'd asked her casting director for help in getting me in touch with agents and I had meetings set up with three of the top agents in the country.

'What you need,' she said, 'is a break. Let's go to Soho Farmhouse. We can wallow like hogs in a hot tub and plot how you're going to win over all these agents and take over the world.'

Soho Farmhouse is like Center Parcs for posh people. The 'farm' has a pool, a spa, two restaurants and bedrooms designed to look like pig pens. You can take a tour of the property in a horse and cart and it is clearly designed by nobody who has ever set foot on an actual farm. It's all log-burning fires, hot tubs and celebrities and you aren't allowed to take photos. I am in heaven.

As soon as we arrived, Emily and I set about making our destination 90 per cent less cool. We'd heard that the Beckhams were there and I delighted in shouting 'Is that Cruz?' every time a child sped past on a scooter. We got in trouble for trying to play Marco Polo in the pool and ended up retiring to the hot tub to take 'belfies'. The less flattering they were, the funnier we found ourselves. To anyone trying to have a romantic time that day, I apologise. I just take a fantastic belfie, and that's the end of that. Once we'd finished thrashing around we went for a cup of tea with Emily's friend Tom, whose job it is to know exactly who is at the farm and when.

'There's a producer here,' he said. 'From BBC comedy. He says he'd like to meet you.' I switched immediately back into work mode.

Where was he? What had he produced? Where could I find him?

'I'll introduce you over email,' said Tom, dispelling any plans I might have had to turn up at his cabin in the next ten minutes. Within a few days I was on my way to Grafton House to make my pitch.

Grafton House is where BBC Comedy is located, near the Euston Road. I had been once before, another of my failed attempts at nepotism had got me a meeting with a comedy executive when I was in my early twenties. I was interested in an assistant's job in the comedy department, and thought that my experience as Derek's PA would make me a shoe-in. Instead I was told that they weren't looking to hire any white posh girls at the moment and this was no longer the way the BBC looked for staff. Humiliated, I left the meeting in tears. While I do not condone taking meetings with naive posh women just to tell them how ridiculous they are, it gave me the wake-up call that I needed. I was not owed a career, I was going to have to work for it.

Luckily my meeting with the BBC producer went very differently. He'd read the article about me in *The Times* and was looking for someone to make a programme that satirised a particular kind of millennial. He wanted to include elements of what I was doing as Stella, but the comedy needed to reach wider touchstones. The satire couldn't begin and end with wellness.

Finally, I thought. Something new to get my teeth into.

We spent some time dissecting the faux-rustic 'farm' we'd attended the weekend before, before conceding that we had actually had a fabulous time and would probably go again. We made each other laugh and decided to write a pitch to be submitted as soon as possible.

'I think we've got a really good shot at getting this made,' he said.

I called my mum when I left. 'I think this is it.'

At a party I went to that night, I told everyone that I was 99 per cent sure I was getting a commission. There is no way they were not going to make my show.

For the next two weeks I was frantic. I needed to write the funniest treatment in the whole world, find a new agent and keep up with my rigorous Instagram schedule. I decided that good Instagram content might swing the BBC commissioners and agents in my favour. I needed to up my game.

When I went into my agent meetings it was safe in the knowledge that I had done my best. I rehearsed a speech about my achievements thus far: book deal, sold-out show, 150,000 followers, possible BBC sitcom.

I knew that I couldn't close Deliciously Stella down now. She was my calling card. Proof that I have 'funny bones'. Even with Stella, I still didn't feel certain anyone would sign me. These agents looked after comedy legends. I was just an Instagrammer with stage fright.

I met with three agents over the course of a couple of days. Everyone told me to meet as many people as possible, meet them more than once, and take my time. I didn't feel like I had the luxury of time. I wanted to nail someone down before they realised my career was on the turn. My follower number was slowly grinding to a halt and it wouldn't be long before the numbers started going down.

So, I went with the first person I met, just a day after meeting them.

I picked my new agent because she had brilliant clients, because she told me she would make me a star, and because she was a little bit terrifying.

She won't scare me, I thought to myself. It's her job to scare other people for me. Sure enough, the BBC producer called me after I signed with her.

'This is a very big deal,' he said. 'You are absolutely made.'

I anticipated a very different relationship with my new agent to the one I had with Caroline. I didn't think I'd be calling the office for a chat any time soon. I was sure, however, that they were my surest bet at success. Maybe it would do me good to toughen up. The agent would open all of the doors, I just had to walk through them.

'I'm used to quite a hands-on approach,' I said to them when we met. 'I need a bit of hand holding because it all still feels quite new.'

'That,' she assured me, 'is what we're here for. So, tell me, what do you want from your career? Did you go to drama school? Can you act? Do you want to write a sitcom? Do panel shows?'

'I want to do everything!' I said. 'I didn't go to drama school, but I think I can act. I'd love to do a panel show and my one dream in life is to write a sitcom.'

'Brilliant. Your wish is our command. Now let's talk about organising a tour.'

My stomach dropped out of my arse and I watched it writhe on the floor.

'Oh god. Not the show. Anything but the show.' I swallowed down the lump that was rising in my throat.

'Of course. A small tour would be great.'

I couldn't tell my brand-new agents that I hated my show. That the thought of performing it brought back traumatic memories of my breakdown, that performing it felt like moving backwards instead of forwards.

'I'm thinking about writing a new show,' I said. 'About all the crazy stuff that's happened to me this year.'

'That's great, but we should probably focus on this show for the moment. Everyone wants Stella, after all!'

I steeled myself. I don't want Stella. They just don't know yet, but what they really want is Bella.

I tried to look on the bright side. Her colleague had signed me as an actor without ever seeing me act. If I could just get over my fear of character comedy, it could lead to better things. My follower number still had sway. People were still lured into the assumption that someone that popular must be hiding untapped genius.

'This is so exciting. Everyone wants to see what you can do.'

Once again my followers had got me in the room, and now I had to prove I deserved to be there.

After I signed on the dotted line, she sent Emily a bottle of wine to say thank you for introducing us. Emily doesn't drink. It felt like a bad omen.

The new agent sent emails that read like she was shouting. She was always coming or going from someone important.

'Spoke to head of Soho Theatre. Interested.'

'Pitched you for *Woman's Hour* but seen you're booked.'

'Send sitcom ideas. Meetings coming up.'

The BBC producer was right: she was ferociously well-connected. The kind of person who can make anything happen for her acts.

I frantically shoehorned Stella into sitcom treatments. But as far as I was concerned, we were barking up the wrong tree. I was being railroaded into a career as a character I was desperate to drop, and I was too overwhelmed to say so.

When the agent suggested that we film one of my live shows to send to venue bookers I acted like that would be brilliant and not terrifying. When the London shows sold out, we started talking about a tour. I'd told Caroline that if I went on a tour I'd be found dead in an Ibis in Hull, but I couldn't tell my new agent that, not when she'd just signed me.

I certainly looked like I thought I was special, announcing my sold-out London shows on Instagram. People who missed out on tickets messaged me, asking when there would be more: 'It's an Edinburgh show that's transferred to London. There's talk of a tour. It must be good!'

My rise had been so quick and so fast that every move I made was high stakes. My first show was a gamble, a laugh. It was a pleasant surprise that I was talented. Everything since then had felt like a test.

On the day of the show, I woke up feeling sick. I say woke up, but what I mean is I dragged myself out of bed after a sleepless night, peppered with fretful dreams about forgetting my words, bursting into tears on stage, or having a full-blown panic attack while everyone watched. Yet again, I was faced with technical issues when I discovered that the projector I was planning to use was not compatible with my laptop. There's nothing like a couple of hours in Maplin to really make you feel like your life is over.

I hadn't performed the show for over three months. Even on its best day I wasn't completely happy with it, and now I was about to perform it in front of my new agent, a huge amount of industry people, and quite a lot of my friends. I staggered from room to room of my house, trying to find a place that quietened the worst-case scenarios careering around my head. How was it possible that I was still the next big thing? When would I just be a reliable veteran, when would a bad show just be a bad show and not evidence that I just don't have what it takes?

I arrived at the venue with an hour to kill. Ideal conditions for me to ruminate. I typed 'Adele stage fright' into Google. This was one of my favourite pre-show rituals. I read about the time Adele literally vomited before performing at the BRITs. If Adele has stage fright and she can sing like that, I could surely make it through an hour of jokes about green juice without ruining my career. The film crew arrived to discuss angles and ask me about the content of the show.

'Don't worry about the agent,' they said. 'Beneath the bravado she's a pussycat really.'

The agent also arrived early, bought me a cup of tea and told me not to worry about being nervous. 'Being nervous is good because it shows you care.'

The gig got off to a rough start. As I walked on I kicked a bucket, breaking character as I did so. I then launched into some audience participation I wasn't ready for and wasn't able to say anything clever about a woman whose spirit animal was a cat. I was rusty, but the audience were on my side. After about twenty minutes I started to warm up. This wasn't half the disaster I thought it was going to be.

At the end I felt a rush of relief. The agent told me the show had been fantastic and that lots of producers wanted to meet me. I had not only survived the show, I had thrived. The venue manager said he hoped I'd come again with my next show. Maybe a tour wouldn't be so bad after all.

The next night the agent sent her colleague, who was my acting agent, along. Emily came with him with another director, who said he'd be happy to work with me on my next show. I was relieved. Things seemed like they were on the way up again.

The agent called and asked me to come in to discuss next steps. I had another show booked for a couple of weeks' time and I expected it would be to discuss the tour.

When I got into her office, the acting agent came in to join her.

'So?' she said. 'How do you think it went?'

'Better than expected,' I replied, letting out a sigh of relief. 'I was really, really nervous and I think I'm getting back into the swing of things.'

The corners of the agent's mouth twitched downwards. 'The thing is, Bella. The show really wasn't good enough.'

I felt like I'd been sucker-punched. I looked to the acting agent, who was nodding in agreement.

'You did seem nervous, and we don't think you should be performing right now.'

I felt a lump rising in my throat while they elaborated.

'Not having a comeback to something as simple as someone having a cat as a spirit animal is not acceptable. Plus if you're going to play a clean eater, you at least need to look like one. It might have helped if you'd brushed your hair or put some makeup on. The whole thing felt very unpolished.'

I had no idea how to respond. The audience had loved it but here were two industry experts telling me it was crap. The agent drove a final nail into my coffin when she said, 'Maybe you're just really good at Instagram.'

They assured me that they still wanted to represent me. They wanted me to keep doing corporate gigs because they paid so well, but my days as an artist were done. They suggested that I focus on writing and booked me in to meet a producer who'd been to see the show. She told me that she'd never seen a comedian hold the audience in the palm of their hand like I had. It was as if my agents had seen a different show. I was in a working relationship with people who didn't believe in my talent. I should have left, but instead I became determined to prove them wrong.

The script I was working on with the BBC was finally rejected. I asked the agent if we should send it elsewhere but she said there wasn't any point. Her efforts moved into securing brand collaborations. The message was clear: keep up the Instagram, that's what you're good at. Influencing was the future of my career, and for the first time since I'd started the account, my follower number was going down.

I still had some work commitments from my time with Caroline to follow through with, which I clung onto like a dying relationship. A producer who'd come to see my show had booked me to appear on the Comedy Central show *Drunk History*.

*Drunk History* was a series in which comedians got hammered and retold historical stories. Other comedians acted out key scenes, lip-syncing along to the storyteller's words.

To prepare for my scene, I was sent a recording of Adam Buxton playing a cockney peasant.

'Remember, your face is your greatest asset,' said Caroline. I'd been texting her a lot since the disastrous show. I didn't tell her that all wasn't well with the new agent, but I needed someone professional to tell me I would nail the shoot. She was right about my face: it's as pliable as rubber. I can go from Prince Andrew's wattle to a pointy chinned witch just using my neck. My face, some might say, has range.

The *Drunk History* story was a historical classic, that of King Alfred and the burnt cakes. I was playing the peasant woman who berated him for burning said cakes and Alfred was played by the actor and *Pointless* presenter, Alexander Armstrong. I walked around London listening to my lines for days, lines that have somehow made their way onto my iTunes. Sometimes when my iPod's on shuffle, Adam Buxton's voice will interrupt a run by screaming about cakes.

A car arrived at 6am to take me to set and I was driven straight to my trailer. I'd never had my own trailer before. In it was a bottle of water, my costume and an enormous Puffa jacket which I assumed was there to keep me warm on set. I had worked on a set only twice before. Once, when working as a runner on a show starring Daniel Radcliffe, I had been pulled into the production office and interrogated. I had tweeted that I was wearing Hufflepuff socks and the head of production thought I might be a superfan there to stalk Daniel. I explained carefully that although I was a superfan and had been wearing only Harry Potter socks for a significant amount of time, I had no intention of stalking Daniel. I also promised to stop tweeting. I was pleased to see that my trailer wasn't dissimilar to Daniel's. I had snuck in there for a snoop.

My costume was more historically accurate than expected. I had imagined I'd be wearing something comically busty. Like a sort of milk wench. Instead I was presented with a brown, shapeless sack and some extraordinarily ugly leather sandals. I hadn't worn any makeup that day because I imagined the makeup artist would want a clean slate. When I sat in the chair she went outside, scooped up some mud from the ground and smeared it all over my face.

'There we go,' she said. 'You look perfect.'

Stephen Mangan, who was sitting in the chair next to me, caught my face and smirked. I looked like I'd been dug up. My final accessory was a sort of shroud, attached to my head with a rope. I sent a selfie to Caroline, who replied, 'please never change.'

The makeup ladies told me that I was the person they'd been most excited to meet because they loved my podcast. I wanted to bottle this conversation and send it to my agents, show them that Stella wasn't the only thing people wanted, and that if they gave me a chance to be Bella I could change their minds. Buoyed by their flattery, I returned to my trailer to send more selfies. I was on a professional film set and I'd be damned if I didn't make the most of it.

Because I was now a professional actor with a credit to add to my Spotlight account, I was picked up in an SUV and driven the ten-minute walk to the set. A runner made sure I wasn't cold and I was only let out of the car to walk when I absolutely had to. Another runner hovered with my coat to make sure I was warm in between takes. I felt like Leonardo DiCaprio.

Alexander Armstrong and I rehearsed our scene before going for a take. I thankfully remembered my lines and quietly started to enjoy myself. I could feel my face morphing into more and more witch-like shapes. I was playing the part I was always destined to play, I was Mad Madam Mim. The set felt like home. At the end of the scene, after I have scolded King Alfred for burning my cakes, I go to attack him with an axe. It would appear that physicality was not my strong suit. I wielded the axe once, I wielded the axe twice. My axe wielding was not working for the director.

'Could you just do it more like this,' he said, demonstrating. It would appear that I could not. In the end I think the axe was cut, but you can still find that episode of *Drunk History* on Comedy Central, and see a mad, muddy, shrouded woman auditioning for the part of Mad Madam Mim in *The Sword in the Stone*.

The agent was true to her word, and the brand deals kept rolling in. I made more and more frequent trips to my aunt's house so she could photograph me advertising rum, McDonald's, Pop Chips and the movie *Sausage Party*. For a while, it seemed like the steady flow of easy money might stave off the feeling of failure that hung over my dormant stand-up career. I spoke to a number of therapists about it. All the men said that I shouldn't let my illness get in the way of my talent. All of the women said that I shouldn't continue pursuing something that was making me so ill.

I was certain that it was Stella and not the stand-up that was getting in my way, but the account supported me financially, and I wasn't flush with other options. The agent stopped emailing me about meetings, contacts or jobs. It was as though she mentally stuffed me to the back of a drawer. My emails went unanswered. I'd fallen off my pedestal to the floor to lick her boots. I felt my presence irritating them like a fly who won't just fuck off out of the window.

Without press, auditions or meetings to keep me busy, it was just me and my Instagram, alone together all day long. My friend suggested I try temping, just to get out of the house, but that seemed ludicrous.

'My agent could need me to meet someone any minute now. Plus everyone thinks I'm successful and famous. It'll look weird.'

I still craved the company of colleagues and the camaraderie of a team, but at this stage it felt like I'd gone too far to give up a gig this easy. I didn't need the money, and I couldn't spoil the illusion. I kept grinning away on Instagram. I had to make it work.

Inevitably, sitting in my room all day and staring at Instagram was extremely detrimental to my mental health. One month later, with my follower number still dropping and no press in sight, I became suicidal.

The thing about depressed people is that they don't have a lot of get up and go. I spent hours googling the best bridge to commit suicide from in London, but ask me to put some trousers on and walk outside? No chance. I couldn't see how I could move my career on without the support of my agent. As my popularity faded online, so did my self-worth. No amount of compliments could get me to see past the people who'd chosen to unfollow me. The game was up, the emperor had lost his clothes. I wasn't a comedian anymore.

I spent hours on the phone to my parents and siblings, telling them that this was the end. That my life was no longer worth living now that everyone knew how rubbish I really was. When my parents lost the will to talk me down off the ledge, my sister Francesca stepped in.

'I need the men in white coats,' I'd say before launching into a tirade of self-pity. I judged people for being kind to me. Thinking they must be fools to love someone so intrinsically bad. I told myself that I was a burden they didn't deserve.

One day, Francesca snapped.

'If you kill yourself, I'll kill myself,' she promised. 'Next thing you know, Mum will die of a broken heart and Dad will die of starvation because he can't boil an egg. What you're threatening is a genocide.'

It was the first time I'd laughed in months.

I started to think I might need to get a new agent. I had placed so much weight on the opinion of my agent that I had let her disdain obscure the sound of every laughing audience member I'd encountered. 'They were wrong. They were idiots. My agent knew the truth. I was worthless.'

On one of my worst days, I called the Priory, begging them to 'get my bed ready', convinced I would need to be sectioned. Five minutes later, when my psychiatrist called me back, I told him that I'd just got my period, so my mood might in fact have been PMS. I was laughing.

When I called my dad to say it was in fact fine because I had just got my period, he wasn't as thrilled as I had hoped.

'You can't keep doing this to us, darling. You can't keep scaring us then making out like it's all a hilarious joke.'

My parents' patience with my condition had started to wear thin. My dad thought it could all be sorted by my giving up Instagram and going back to work. My mum told him that if I did that because of him, I'd probably never forgive him.

I plunged back into the land of cancelled plans, creating stomach bugs or imaginary deadlines that kept me away from my friends. When I did see them, I was flighty and awkward. Sometimes I imagined their thoughts hiding just behind their lips.

'Just pull your socks up, Bella. Stop feeling sorry for yourself. Get a proper job already.'

Somebody told me that to make my depression go away I just needed a boyfriend.

'You've been ill for too long now,' they said. 'You need to just try to get better.'

I dreaded being spotted by fans, convinced that everyone would ask me what I was doing next, and I'd have to admit I had no idea. I felt people's eyes on me everywhere. My most embarrassing moment on Earth remains the night I accused someone of secretly filming me in a nightclub.

'Calm down, mate. I have literally no idea who you are.' My friends laughed nervously as they dragged me away.

I decided to hire a publicist to promote me. Without any ongoing projects I had to fund her fees myself, but if she could get me back into the papers, I swore it would be worth it. It was a huge gamble, a final lunge of desperation. The fees cost more than double my rent, but if my agent didn't want to get me work, I'd get myself column inches instead.

She agreed to represent me and suggested that we could come to an affordable arrangement to raise my profile. I told her that I had been offered a column at a major magazine but that it had never come to fruition. I had loads of ideas for articles but wasn't sure how to go about pitching them.

'These are all things we can help with,' she assured me.

She suggested I start going to more awards shows and appearing on red carpets. Maybe I could get a guest spot on *Loose Women*. She sent through a brilliant pitch deck-full of information on why people should be interested in me and which brands we should approach about collaboration. She emailed the agent to introduce herself and outline her plan. My agent never replied.

I had forgotten how much I had loved the idea of being famous. How much I'd revelled in my first flush of recognition.

Now I had grown to resent it. I didn't want to be famous when I couldn't control my own narrative. I didn't want to be famous when I didn't think I deserved it.

The only thing I cared about was my career, and this imaginary point I'd reach where I was so successful my success would never be questioned. I couldn't be happy without being successful, and my definition of success was nothing if not narrow. When I imagined myself happy in the future it was smiling at an awards ceremony, accepting an award for something I'd made, making a speech about how this terrible time had been worth it.

I told myself that the pain was part of the process. I was on a journey to success, and my humility was being tested. Everyone loves an underdog.

'I think you should tell your agent,' said my mum one day while out walking the dog. 'I know she scares you but she isn't a monster. Maybe if you tell her she'll let you do the kind of comedy you like? Maybe she'll start trying to find you work again.'

The thought of telling them chilled my blood.

'They'd be even more disappointed if they knew I was mad. I lied to them. I sold them a false promise that I was a normal person.'

'I'm sure they'd rather know you were having a rough time than just think that you're a bit shit. Because you're not shit, and you know you're not. You won't feel like this forever.'

I decided that the only thing I could do was tell them the truth. I made an appointment with the agents and my stomach coiled into knots. My relationship with Caroline had been so different. I had called her almost every day, desperate to share my highs and lows and to laugh at the mysterious ways the industry worked. Going to see Caroline felt like going for a chat with my biggest champion. Going to see the agents felt like going to see the headmistress when you knew you'd been caught red-handed.

The moment I crossed the threshold of their office, I started spilling my guts. I told them about the Priory and the anxiety and the stage fright. I told them that I knew I was talented and they hadn't had the chance to see me at my best.

'I just wish you could have seen my first show,' I said with as much conviction as I could muster.

'This explains a lot,' said the agent kindly. 'We appreciate you telling us. It must have been hard.'

It had been hard. It had been so, so hard, but I was so relieved they understood.

'It will come back, you know,' she told me. 'Depression always does.'

Unsure what she meant by that I told them that I was keen to write another Edinburgh show, that I wanted acting lessons so I could get better at auditions.

'You shouldn't go to Edinburgh unless you have something to say,' they told me.

Was it not enough to say that I had accidentally become an Instagram influencer and it was the most unhappy I'd been in all my life?

I made a final attempt to get them back on board, to convince them that I still had a shot at making comedy my career.

'I've got a publicist now,' I said. 'She thinks she can get me a spot on *Loose Women*.' The agent gave me a look that said, 'I could get you on *Loose Women* in my sleep.' I sank back into my chair.

If I'm back in the papers,' I said meekly, 'maybe the offers will start coming in again.'

'Whatever you want,' they said. I left the office feeling that whatever it was that I wanted, they weren't going to help me get it.

My perspective had become so warped that my dad and I would fight over whether or not everyone is a little bit suicidal at some point in their lives. Dad insisted that he had never thought about killing himself. I was convinced he was being obtuse. To me, suicidal ideation was as inevitable a milestone as puberty or passing your driving test. Everyone gets there eventually, I thought to myself as I dragged my leaden feet around my parents' house. I just thought that some people were able to deal with it better than others.

'What you need,' he said, 'is to be around other people. And to stop listening to that horrible agent. They've completely knocked your confidence.'

'The problem with what you do,' he said, 'is that you have to do it all on your own. It's a lot of weight to carry on one set of shoulders. Why don't you go back to work at the BBC? You could work on your scripts on the side and you'd have some stability.'

I didn't know how to explain that going back to work felt like a step back. Even though it would have given me much-craved stability and company, it would make me feel like I had failed.

'Maybe I should get a writing partner?' I suggested. 'Then I wouldn't be on my own all the time.'

'Maybe,' my mum said gently, 'jobs like this are better suited to people with thicker skin.'

Everyone says to be in the public eye you need a thick skin. That you need to toughen up to withstand all that criticism, but really my thin skin was the key to my success. Giving no fucks might make you assertive and help with the dreaded hustle, but for me the best comedians and the best influencers are the ones who are soft. My thin skin makes me perceptive of how others think and feel. Caring about what other people think helps me know what they like and want. It's what helped my comedy connect. It's how I know what people will identify with. How I know what will make them smile.

Neither of my parents could get their head around why I was so committed to a lifestyle that didn't suit me. They couldn't see that my job made my life seem aspirational, that people would kill to do what I was doing, that I was winning at life. In spite of the way I felt about being an influencer, I took pride in being good at something. Nobody could say they were better at being Deliciously Stella than me.

All my parents saw was the angst that plagued me. I'd spend hours weighing up decisions with my mum, retracing my steps, questioning decisions, trying to determine why things went wrong and how it had been my fault.

'Do you think I'm making a mistake spending all this money on a publicist? Do you think I should look for a new agent who's nice to me and thinks I'm good?'

'I don't know, darling!' she'd reply, exasperated. 'I don't know anything about your world and I'm afraid I can't make these decisions for you.'

Of course, I know now that it's a myth that we're in complete control of our lives, and a harmful one at that. Illness happens, change happens, life happens. We've been missold the idea that if you never give up, eventually you'll make it. That the worst possible kind of failure comes from giving up. It was a failure I wasn't ready to accept.

# Confession as a Career Move

Influencers are such effective marketing tools because they make you feel like they're just like you, but better. They're the prettiest girl at your school with a better bikini collection. They're your friend who could have been a model if she wasn't too short, whose amazing skin could be yours if you buy all the products she uses through her affiliate links. Hearing that they had insecurities like us only served to make them more relatable.

When I first appeared on Instagram as Deliciously Stella, relatability had yet to go mainstream. The body positivity movement still belonged to fat black women, and was therefore no doubt quashed by the algorithm. Comedy on Instagram was relatively new and it was only the dawn of the much-needed transparency around mental health issues. Instagram was still a perfect place for perfect people to show off their perfect lives.

In 2015, Instagram influencers were in their infancy, and the idea of authentic or relatable content was but a twinkle in Jameela Jamil's eye. Everyone wanted us to believe that they were living their best lives and unless you had abs or a pastel-coloured house you didn't have a look-in. Instagram was a place where sincerity ruled and aspiration trumped authenticity. People's online selves were more obviously a performance, and so far this seemed to be working out pretty well.

It was this earnest tone that I originally set out to satirise when I started my account. While Ella wasn't a fan, it appeared that almost every other woman worth their cauliflower rice was. Even Madeleine Shaw, from whom I lifted the hashtag #gettheglow, was laughing along with me. People were willing to laugh at themselves, but they never suggested that they were anything other than blissfully happy, until Essena O'Neill.

Essena O'Neill was a nineteen-year-old influencer with 600,000 followers. She was slim, blonde, beautiful and making £2,000 per sponsored Instagram post. She was also, as she admitted in 2015, utterly miserable. She confessed to taking hundreds of shots before settling on one she was happy with. She said she was broke despite her Instagram suggesting otherwise. In a tearful video, she declared that Instagram 'isn't real'. Her confession propelled her from Instagram star to international news story. The confession as career move became a recognisable internet trope.

By 2017, when I made my own confession, there was a new trend in town. Instead of living their best lives, influencers were living their truth.

'You are a hurricane of fresh air,' people wrote to women who showed their stretch marks.

'Speak truth to power!' appeared under pink and gold memes about the patriarchy. Women proudly displaying their period leaks were heralded with: 'This is the authenticity we need'.

It was true, of course, we did desperately need this representation. Instagram proved to be a place that was invaluable for grass-roots activism. Young people could quickly gather interest in issues that never trouble white men. Instagram helped to end upskirting and period poverty, making the founders of their movement influencers in their own rights.

Sentiment towards traditional influencers was experiencing a sea change. A number of exposés had revealed influencers going to extraordinary lengths to construct branded content around real-life events. One woman faked a motorcycle crash, captured by a professional photographer – her hair fanned around her head, her helmet removed and a strategically placed bottle of Smartwater in her hand. The director of brand partnerships at Gwyneth Paltrow's goop was discovered to have pitched her 'surprise engagement' as an opportunity for sponsors. The pitch document was leaked with details of her fiancé's 'surprise scavenger hunt', with opportunities to provide restaurant meals, hotels and gifting opportunities.

The people wanted authenticity with their aspiration, so the influencers adapted. Influencers were queueing up to announce that their lives were less perfect than they appeared on their grids. It was as though everyone was lining up to get their honesty cookie before they could reach the next round. They knew that that cookie could only make them more powerful.

In recent years we've seen 'confessions' via documentaries from Paris Hilton, Demi Lovato and Taylor Swift. Whether it's a drug problem, an eating disorder or abuse, by approaching these topics they are both starting a conversation about difficult topics and using vulnerability to further endear them to their fans. It's a cynical viewpoint, but nobody presents a documentary, gives an interview or writes a song about their mental health just for awareness. Everybody's looking for more eyes on them, vulnerability is currency. I call it click-bleeding.

It says a lot about the way that capitalism commodifies issues that I approached writing about my mental health like an album drop.

I met up with my publicist and asked her to help me get some features in the paper.

'Maybe I could write something about how I've been feeling?'

'How you've been feeling?'

'Yeah, when my Instagram had just started I got diagnosed as bipolar over Skype and I spent a month in the Priory before Edinburgh.'

'Oh. I'm so sorry.'

'But maybe we should pitch some funny pieces first. Like about junk food and how much I hate the hashtag strong not skinny.'

'Sure thing. Whatever you feel comfortable with.'

'We have managed to get you a gig in *Heat* magazine,' they said.

'Oh?'

'Yes. They have a feature where you rate foods. They'd like you to rate five pork pies. It's a really fun feature.'

I tried to imagine the pork pie feature, sandwiched in between bikini shots of celebrities on the beach, angry red circles around their cellulite. *Heat* magazine called women whales, delighted in relationship breakdowns and bankruptcy. As a younger woman I'd revelled in tabloid gossip but my tastes had changed. I wasn't aware that *Heat* was still in circulation.

'That's great,' I said. 'I love a pork pie.'

I showed them my column ideas, floated the idea of releasing them as a blog or a newsletter. I read a half-hearted excerpt from a potential blog called 'Deliciously Stella's Diary'.

'We could do an event?' suggested the publicist. 'We could invite other people to bring their diaries and you could all read from them together. We could make it a pyjama party and host it in collaboration with a hotel.'

'Let's just run with the piece about my mental health,' I said.

'Are you sure?'

'I'm 100 per cent sure. I've built my brand around being authentic, it's high time I finally told the truth. I want to share something that's real.'

I knew that talking about my mental health would start a discussion. I knew it would mean clicks. I hoped it would mean followers. Cynically, I hoped that by demonstrating some nuance I might be able to make people see me as something other than Stella. It was a chance to be a serious writer, and to tell the truth about Instagram.

Almost immediately after giving the publicist the opportunity to shop the story, I was thrown into a wild panic.

What will my followers think? Will it upset them? Am I biting the hand that feeds by admitting to being anything but a laugh a minute?

What if people struggled to connect the jokes with the person behind them, what if I was once again going to shoot myself in the foot with one of my stupid decisions?

My publicist got back to me in record time. Would I like to write about my mental health in *The Sun*? *The Sun* had run a front page with the headline: '1,200 killed by mental patients.' *The Sun* had led the charge that bullied countless female celebrities. There was no way I was writing about my mental health for *The Sun*. She followed up with another proposition.

'No worries re *The Sun*. Had a good chat with *Loaded*, though, thought you could judge an eating competition for them.'

I burst into laughter on the street. Why would I judge an eating competition in *Loaded*? Wasn't I going to rate pork pies for *Heat*?

I replied, 'As a feminist, while I still have even the illusion of sanity, I will not judge an eating competition in *Loaded*.'

My publicist and I parted ways. I couldn't afford her and I was no longer an easy sell.

I decided to write about my mental health in the *Telegraph* and in *Vogue*. It was my story to tell. I wanted to tell it on my terms.

Of course, people without any marketable problems wanted in on the trend.

The body positivity movement was fully co-opted by thin women with rolls of skin that they delighted in showing off by bending over.

'Love yourself!' they screeched from the hilltops with their conventionally attractive body types.

'Sexy people have anxiety too!' they wrote underneath close-ups of their perfectly toned buttocks on the beach.

Fuck me, I thought. I hope I didn't contribute to this trend. And more to the point, how the hell do I parody it without being a total bitch?

Acknowledging that performing perfection on Instagram is hard is now an integral part of any influencer's journey. Instagrammers are encouraged to take digital detoxes in the name of self-care, and they are at pains to remind their follow-ers that they're real people with feelings. If you cut us we don't bleed with a crema filter.

For the most part, writing about your trauma was universally lauded as #brave, but eventually it began to wear thin. A recent essay by Emily Ratajkowski called 'Buying Myself Back' was published in *The Cut*. In it she detailed the abhorrent ways in which her image has been exploited by men throughout her modelling career, often making said men very rich.

Upon reading it, I had exactly the required reaction. I chas-tised myself for underestimating someone so beautiful. She had bravely detailed her sexual assault and I was disgusted at the men who'd exploited her. I shook my virtual fist as I read on about the people who sold her nudes without her permis-sion and the paparazzi photographer who sued her for posting his photograph of her on her Instagram. I gulped it down, mouth agape, then texted all of my friends to ask if they'd read it.

Why was she writing it now? I wondered. A quick search showed she was writing a book. It was only when I'd sat with it for five minutes that I started to wonder if this essay was really a branding exercise for Emily Ratajkowski. She was click-bleeding and it was working. In the article she goes for her honesty cookie, confessing to helping to uphold the male gaze and the patriarchal structures that her body type helps her to benefit from. But the self-interrogation stops right there. What she wanted to say was: 'I know, but I'm not going to do anything about it.'

Everyone's checking their privilege and trying to outhumble each other. When Kim Kardashian threw her fortieth birthday party on a private island, during a pandemic that had killed millions, she wanted to 'pretend things were normal, just for a brief period of time'. She caveated the picture of her wearing couture on the sand with, 'I am humbly reminded of how privileged my life is.'

When she covered the outside of her house in plastic, landfill-destined tat to celebrate Halloween, she expressed gratitude that it had helped her overcome her arachnophobia. These insidious attempts to make the billionaire queen of consumerism appear relatable are working. Authenticity is an incredibly powerful sales tool.

Authenticity is now a buzzword that has become synonymous with how we behave on social media. Beautifully filtered shots are now interspersed with people 'getting real'. Instagram models want you to know that they have bad days too, that you shouldn't be intimidated by how great their lives are and that if you buy whatever they're selling, you can be just like them.

Fitness influencers are celebrated for admitting to having eating disorders and makeup artists are praised for showing their bare, acne-marked skin. I once gave an interview on *Woman's Hour* with a woman who had pivoted her brand from her afro to justice for people with bacne. Vulnerability is an incredibly powerful personal brand.

Of course, in reality my depression stretched much further than my brand. I was living it day in, day out and I was exhausted. I had started oscillating between a depression so bleak I could barely breathe and a wild mania that made me pound the streets, desperate to expend energy. My iPhone notes were a garbled stream of ideas for books, sitcoms, documentaries and stand-up shows that I was sure would make me a star.

My shrink told me my depression was rapid-cycling. Together we were desperately trying to land on a pill combination that would put a stop to it. Rapid-cycling refers to a period where you experience multiple episodes of depression and mania within a short space of time. My mania was mild, making me incredibly productive and feeling like I'd swallowed liquid luck. My depression was ruinous.

My shrink said that he had one more medication we could try, but that if it didn't work it would be good to start thinking about alternative treatments. I scoffed and told him that I had no truck with homeopathy, that it was good old-fashioned science or the highway. He told me that was not what he'd meant. I had now become a good candidate for electroconvulsive therapy. Like most people, electroconvulsive therapy made me think about *One Flew Over the Cuckoo's Nest*, of drooling and padded cells. I knew from the actress Carrie Fisher that it had the potential to erase your memory.

'No,' I said, gripping the sides of my chair. 'Absolutely not. I'm not going to risk losing my memories. It won't be worth it.'

'It isn't what you think it is, I promise. Even lobotomies have changed. They're completely safe.'

My doctor had said lobotomy. He had said lobotomy out loud in a session, in his office. If anyone needed a lobotomy it was him. You can't say things like that in front of a mad person.

You just can't. Panic erupted from the pit of my stomach, sending molten terror coursing through my veins. On the plus side, I was pretty sure I'd be the first person commissioned to write about my lobotomy in *Vogue*.

'Take that!' I imagined saying to the pumpkin spice latte brigade. 'Sure, you had a feature on a wellness blog about porridge helping your anxiety, but I will break the internet with my lobotomy!'

'I'm not saying you need a lobotomy. Just that it's safe,' he clarified.

I stopped engaging with mental health awareness week, after I saw my 2,875th beautiful black and white photo captioned with 'It's OK not to be OK'. I seethed at brands posting mental health awareness posts when you know they work their employees to the bone. It seemed to me that awareness had become a distraction from structural, and crucially fixable, problems. People don't need to practise more self-care or talk more. Of course we should feel able to talk about our mental health. I know that getting help is especially difficult for men, but more than awareness, we need investment. The NHS needs more money. We need to fund the research of better treatment. I'm painfully aware that most accounts of mental health journeys like mine involve private treatment. A certain type of person gets to share their story, and it's almost always someone who could pay to get better.

After the articles I wrote about my breakdown were published, I felt dirty. Not because I was ashamed of my mental illness, but because I had used the exposure just like I did my social media, for clicks and retweets and words of validation. I'm ashamed to say that it made me feel relevant.

Shame dies when it's exposed to the light, and I never want to return to a time when talking about mental health was taboo, but ultimately I wanted my friends close and my followers closer. I was just another victim of the attention economy. Another woman forced to share her deepest inner turmoil for clicks.

# 135,000 Followers

'Give me the pills,' I insisted, when I next saw my shrink. 'Any pills. I'm sure these will work. I've got a really good feeling.'

We added an extra antidepressant to the antipsychotic I was already taking. This new antidepressant had only been on the market for a few months. The downside was that sometimes it could be difficult to get hold of; the upside was that it seemed to have no noticeable side-effects. Things I'd been told to watch out for were drowsiness – a blessing to this raging insomniac – and potentially compromised liver function – not such a blessing to a self-confessed hooligan.

Although the liver thing was less than ideal, I figured that I would rather die happy from cirrhosis than miserable by my own hand. Finally, I seemed to have found something that worked.

I decided it was time to catch up with the agent. I had two projects to tell her about: one was a documentary I wanted to make about social media and mental health; the other was a film script I'd been working on with a friend. I thought she'd be pleased that I was being proactive. Walking to her office, my stomach was filled with the good kind of butterflies. Butterflies of anticipation rather than fear.

I led with the film, making sure to seem cheerful and animated so she would know I wasn't depressed anymore. I told her all about all the amazing contacts my co-writer had and how excited we were about our idea. I also told her that I had set up a meeting with a production company to pitch a documentary about the links between social media and mental health. I thought I'd be a good person to present it.

She smiled. 'It's good to see you on such good form, but I have to be honest.' The knot in my stomach tightened. 'Nobody is going to make your film.' The lump moved into my throat. 'Also, there are plenty of comedians with mental health issues who are much more famous than you, don't you think?'

I was crushed. I asked if she'd thought about putting me forward for *Great British Bake Off: An Extra Slice*. She represented the talent and I thought as a foodie comedian I'd make a good fit.

'Don't you think that if anyone could get you on that show, it would be me?' she asked me.

I wasn't sure if that meant she didn't want to pitch me, or that she had but they were adamant they wouldn't have me.

'We're pitching you for things all the time,' she assured me. 'We'll let you know if anybody wants you. And remember to keep up with the Instagram.'

My currency seemed to have dropped like the pound in Brexit uncertainty. How could it have been that a few months earlier I was so in demand I left a mental hospital to take a meeting and now nobody would pick up the phone? I started to wonder if my status as an 'influencer' had tainted me. I felt like a reality star who was desperate to break into acting but could never escape the public memory of them ugly crying in a restaurant on TV.

Finally starting to feel the effects of the antidepressants and fresh out of good ideas, it seemed reasonable to hope to go viral again. I believed that every Google alert could hold the key. All I needed to do was to crack America or land my face on a front page on a TV commissioner's desk. I had to keep the account alive for just a little bit longer.

'Maybe you should become one of those people that rates snacks?' suggested one friend. 'You can take pictures of yourself eating all of the best greedy things and rate them.'

'That's a bit man vs food, isn't it? Besides, I'm trying to move away from the food thing. I never want to rate a pork pie again.'

It was late August and I was desperately trying to think of a way to pivot my account, without losing followers. Lingerie behemoth Victoria's Secret had announced that their annual 'fashion' show would be hosted in Shanghai.

'How is it still going on?' I complained to my friend Emilia. 'It's like we'll take your male gaze and raise it. Here is a fashion show designed for the appreciation of teenage boys.'

'I've heard the CEO's a perve,' she said, rolling her eyes. 'Obviously he denies it.'

'Have you seen those videos where the models cry when they find out they've been cast? Why are they called Angels? Why do they all look the same?! Even in beauty pageants women get to speak.'

We ordered a round of gin cocktails.

'Imagine if we filmed a fake audition where Stella got cast,' suggested my friend Hannah as we all laughed.

'They'd probably make me walk the catwalk covered in lard as a warning.'

'We should do it,' said Emilia. 'Let's make a spoof Victoria's Secret audition. We can call it "Stella gets her wings".'

Twelve gins later, it didn't sound like that ridiculous an idea. The wings would be chicken wings and the fantasy bra would be covered in Iced Gems. I could advertise the show using my Instagram account, and once I'd made the transition from Deliciously Stella to Deliciously Stella Victoria's Secret Angel, I'd finally have some new content. All the talk of wings was making us hungry, so we ditched our gins for a happy hour spot in Soho which promised 'as many wings as you can eat'. We plotted and giggled, fingers sticky with buffalo sauce. I uploaded a pun about thigh gaps to Instagram. The series was a chance to be Stella but not Stella. To launch Stella 2.0. It was an opportunity to prove once and for all that I was more than just an Instagrammer.

We decided to make a web series and publish it on YouTube in the week leading up to the Victoria's Secret show. Emilia would direct, Hannah would produce and I would star. Emilia and I would write the scripts and together we would do our best to cast it.

Pulling together a six-episode web series in six weeks is not an advisable thing to do. After a week of meetings where we tried to get production companies to back us, everyone said they loved the idea but they didn't think we had enough time. We each put in £500 of our own money and decided to do it ourselves.

Within a few weeks we'd managed to pull together a stellar cast, including Blake Harrison from *The Inbetweeners* as Ed Razek, Victoria's Secret's notoriously pervy CEO, and my friend Margaret, fresh off the set of ITV's *Victoria*, as a conniving former model and Victoria's Secret reject-turned-choreographer.

For the final episode, I was going to walk around London in my underwear and a skirt made out of crisp packets. The plan was that we would follow my journey to walking the runway in Shanghai, satirising the videos where models teach people to walk, talk, eat and train like an Angel.

We were so busy pulling everything together that I almost forgot I'd be acting almost exclusively in my bra and pants. The final piece of costume that had to be bought was a pair of pants big enough to cover my modesty and stop me having a full-scale mental breakdown. I decided on wearing two pairs. There was a dance, and I really didn't fancy giving the crew an eyeful during the thrusting sequence.

On the final shoot day, we were outside. There was a bitter wind and I had to walk up and down the Millennium Bridge in my Iced Gem bra and crisp-packet skirt. I stood shivering on the Embankment under a coat, staring up at the bridge as it swayed ominously.

'I don't know if I can do this,' I said. My producer, Hannah, was securing raw chicken wings to my bra straps. It was Saturday and the bridge was crawling with tourists. They were all going to point and stare at me.

'What can I do to make you feel better?' Hannah asked, beckoning over our runner. I took a deep breath.

'I am going to need a Xanax and a Wispa.'

Hannah started rummaging in my bag for my emergency Xanax. My shrink had prescribed them for times of severe panic. I don't think this is what he had in mind. I waited ten minutes for the Xanax to start moving, ascended the steps to the bridge, threw off my coat and started strutting like the world was my catwalk.

I strutted and swished my crisp-packet skirt past the London Eye, I pouted and posed outside Buckingham Palace, I jumped out of a phone box into a group of teenage tourists, and I worshipped at the altar of Emmeline Pankhurst's statue by Parliament. I was so busy trying not to get arrested or freeze to death that I didn't spare a second to think about how my body looked, or who was staring at me. Instead I had one of the funniest days of my life.

I was sure that this was a project worthy of attention. This was my difficult second album, and I was certain it was going to be a hit.

We wrapped with only a couple of weeks to edit the series, start our press drive and launch the show on my Instagram.

Emilia and our editor, Meg, were in charge of creative and I was in charge of publicity. The only problem was, we didn't have anything to show anyone. We all had different priorities. Emilia was using the show to find an agent, and therefore wanted it edited perfectly to show off her directing skills. I was using it to prove that I could write, act and make jokes about things that weren't wellness.

I wanted as many eyes on the show as possible. Endless hours were spent debating whether we should release all the episodes at once or one at a time, how important a trailer was and whether we should pay to have a screening in a cinema.

I was against the screening idea. It was too late to guarantee that anyone important would come and it was astronomically expensive. We were making a web series you could watch on the internet for free. People didn't need to come and watch it in a cinema. For once I put my foot down and refused to pay for it.

Relations were already strained when I started speaking to the press about the show. I wrote an article for the *Telegraph* where I explained that the series had been a joint effort and not my own idea, but in every interview I gave, this detail was left out. I went to pains to spell out the names of my co-collaborators, implicitly insisting that it wasn't all about me. Still the papers ran my picture and made me the centre of the story. I could tell the others were riled.

Desperate for something to come of all our efforts, I sent the first two episodes to the agent. Absolutely nothing happened.

Over all the episodes combined the series was watched 50,000 times. We had press coverage in the *Telegraph*, the *Daily Mail* and *The Independent*. June Sarpong declared it the funniest thing she had seen that year. And yet, we met with a few production companies and then it was over. It didn't change our lives, it didn't get Emilia an agent. It wasn't even a quarter as successful as Deliciously Stella had been and thus it felt like a failure.

I hadn't anticipated how hard it is to make people move from one platform to another. The kind of people who use Instagram don't use YouTube. Our concentration spans have become so short we can't even commit to a four-minute web episode.

Of course, there were other reasons why it didn't connect. Some people said that I was too slim for it to make effective commentary. Another slim, white woman telling people to accept themselves when society already deems their body acceptable.

I maintain we were on the right side of history. It was the people in control of Victoria's Secret we were looking to expose, not the models. I think it's telling that, for the first time, it was decided that there wouldn't be a runway show that year.

Everyone started playing the blame game. Hannah thought we'd released the trailer too early, I thought we hadn't put enough thought into how we advertised it on my Instagram. Emilia blamed the patriarchy.

We were devastated that all of our hard work had led to what we perceived to be a damp squib. My desperate attempt to pivot had failed and clean eating was dead in the water.

I went to breakfast with Derek, my first boss and part-time tormentor at the BBC, and who was now a great friend, to ask his advice.

'Deliciously Stella will not be your legacy,' he said. 'She's an Edinburgh show, and a part of your story, but she won't be how people remember your career.'

Stella had started to feel like a millstone around my neck. I couldn't live without her, but I couldn't move on with her. I felt like a poor man's Steve Coogan, bound to play the same character forever.

My big plans for a life on civvy street were pushed back when a production company asked to meet me to talk about a script I'd written about my time in the Priory. The agent had sent it out and after telling me that my first rejection was 'really not a good sign', it turned out that someone actually thought I was talented. I was absolutely ecstatic. Finally, someone was taking me seriously as a writer and, best of all, the script had nothing to do with Deliciously Stella.

I hadn't clicked before I went in that I had met the director of the company before, when I'd worked for the BBC many moons ago.

'I remember we had a very good runner on that show,' he said. 'That is until you started sleeping with him. He was terrible after that.' I laughed nervously.

'I remember you being funny. You were always very funny. And this is funny,' he said, glancing down at my script.

This meeting would go on to set me on the road to getting my first script option. I was officially being paid to write. I'd started writing more and more, using my Instagram account to contact the editors at my favourite magazines. I realised that pitching on my own was far more effective than going through a publicist. I also much preferred being invited to events as a journalist. Press breakfasts as a journalist felt legitimate. I felt there was worth in my writing that Instagram couldn't give me. My imposter syndrome was temporarily quieted.

# Stella Goes West

A sense of unease about my role in the influencer economy never led me to look a gift horse in the mouth, of course. I always knew which side my bread was buttered on and when I was invited on my very first influencer press trip with Universal Studios, I accepted within seconds. I may have become disillusioned with being used as a human billboard, but when the perks were good, the perks were good. Plus, I was going to Los Angeles, land of celebrity and somewhere I'd seen myself living. My dormant ambition raised its head. This could be my chance to break the US.

Going on a press trip had always been my influencer holy grail. People who went on press trips didn't get sent a bottle of free cider with a pair of socks and get blackmailed into posting on their Instagram accounts. Press trips were for a higher tier of influencer, for movers and shakers. There wouldn't be a bouquet of Peperamis in sight.

Press trips aren't a new phenomenon. They were formerly the reserve of travel journalists. All-expenses-paid trips funded by PR companies or tourist boards to showcase activities, restaurants or hotels. Experiences were and still are offered in exchange for traditional media coverage. But we are now in the age of the influencer, and press trips for likes is a booming business.

I felt a little conflicted about going – after all, my account was supposed to be super #relatable – but I had never been to LA, thought it might sort out my SAD and also, I LOVE FREE STUFF. Derek made me promise I'd go to Café Gratitude, a plant-based restaurant that 'celebrates aliveness' and asks you what you are grateful for before you get your hands on any food. Thankfully it didn't appear to be on the itinerary. I was not about to spend $17 on a bowl of vegetables called 'humble'.

As soon as the trip was confirmed, I started planning my attack. I emailed my agent telling her that I was going to postpone my flight home so I could spend some extra days there, and that I wanted to meet as many industry people as I possibly could.

'Producers in LA will literally meet anyone,' promised Emily. 'They're always on the hunt for the next big thing. Plus meetings make them look busy and important. Let me email my friend and see if I can get you a meeting at Netflix.'

My agent said she'd see what she could do. I booked an Airbnb and started compiling all of my American press clippings as ammunition.

LA was the home of wellness and I had been in *People* magazine. How could they not want to meet me?

All I have to do is dazzle them, I thought. Stella could have a completely new lease of life in the US. I'll be the British Amy Schumer in no time. They'll probably cast me in a feature film on the spot.

I decided that I was going to approach this trip like a proper influencer. I bought a swanky new wardrobe and got my highlights done. I even contacted ASOS, who offered to send me some clothes. Taking America was a logical next step. I was now sane, on the top of my game and gagging to tell anyone who'd listen about all my script ideas.

After two weeks of unanswered emails to my agent, my anticipation had curdled into panic. I had heard nothing about the producers I'd be meeting and the hosts of my Airbnb were expecting me. When I finally got in touch with my agent, our exchange was curt and brief.

'I'm sorry,' they said, 'but nobody wanted to meet you.'

Apparently nobody in the US 'got' Deliciously Stella. I was convinced they hadn't tried. Frustrated and devastated, I finally snapped. I turned to a friend. 'I think I actually need a new agent.'

An actress friend was in the process of doing the same thing.

'Do I tell them before I start looking?' I asked. 'No, no! Of course not. Reach out to some that you like, then tell them you're moving on. It's a business decision. There won't be any hard feelings.'

She gave me the email of a friend of hers who worked at an agency called Independent Talent. I knew they had wanted to sign me when Caroline retired. I imagined telling the agent I was leaving. Surely she'd be relieved?

The prospective agent emailed back almost straight away. 'I don't think I'm the right person to represent you,' he said, 'but someone else in this company will be. Let me reach out to a couple of people and we'll be in touch.'

Relief lapped at my nervous system. I was going to find an agent who supported me. Who would encourage me. I was all about the carrot not the stick and I'd been hit for the last time.

The news spread like wildfire. Before the day was up, I had an email from an agent, my agent.

'We've heard you're looking for new representation and we don't represent people who don't want to work with us.' I had been dropped, over email. My throat dropped into my stomach then out of my arse. This was not how I'd seen this playing out. I replied saying it was true and I hadn't intended for them to find out like this. Perhaps they could have called and dropped me over the phone?

'Ah. That's awkward,' said Emily. 'Is there any love lost?'

I felt more surprised and embarrassed than upset. My intention had, after all, been to leave. I sat in my agentless reality for a second, shaking. Who was I without an agent to legitimise me? How was I going to get another one? How long was it acceptable to be agentless before I was old news?

That's when I finally let myself say that I didn't really want one. This was a unique opportunity to ask myself what I wanted with no external pressure. I could get off this runaway train. I could finally get my life back.

I luxuriated for a second in my newfound freedom, convinced that it was about to be snatched away again. My mother almost cried with relief. I felt like a half-tonne lump of coal had been lifted off my chest. I didn't have to work with people who thought I was rubbish, or irritating. I was free to make my own decisions, free from my need to please, freed from my relentless quest for success, and released from the opinion of people who only valued me for what I could give them. For the first time in three years, the only person I had to answer to was myself.

I cancelled my LA Airbnb and changed my flight home. I was going to LA to live my best life, then I was going to stop being Deliciously Stella.

We were in LA to promote the film *Ingrid Goes West*, a clever satire about an unstable woman who moves to Los Angeles to stalk her favourite Instagrammer in real life. We were going to visit all the main sites of the movie, including Joshua Tree and Palm Springs.

My companions were to be a group of fashion bloggers. I stalked them voraciously before departure. Jesus, they're trendy, I thought. Their lives look so nice. Will they be funny? I wonder how much money they make? Do they get all their clothes for free? I was down a rabbit hole, moments from deep liking a post from 2015. I pulled myself out and panic-bought an over-priced skirt. I should have at least one nice thing, I reasoned, so it didn't look like they're being followed around by a tramp.

I approached the trip as an audition for my new life. I was no longer a character, I was Bella Younger, writer and influencer, and I was going to be treated and gifted like one. I had a swanky wardrobe and a swanky attitude. The airline was sending a car. It was the first day of the rest of my life.

We were flying Norwegian airlines on their 'premium econ-omy' service, which we were advertising. This felt like extremely influencer-y territory. I woke up to a text to say our flight was delayed. It was the winter of The Beast from the East and the streets of London were coated with a thick blanket of deep, crunchy snow. Unperturbed, I rebooked my taxi and went back to sleep. The second text I woke up to was to say that they'd had to change the plane and that some of the passengers who were travelling 'premium' would now be sitting in economy.

Not me, I thought, smugly. I am an influencer and a guest of the airline. I will receive VIP treatment, lounge access and endless snacks. The PR texted me. We had been downgraded. I was certain that I was the curse.

I gave myself two rules before I left: don't be a dick and never be the first to order lobster. Within minutes of arriving at the airport, I met up with one of the other influencers and got chatting about the downgrade. We both agreed that it was a bummer. 'We probably shouldn't advertise the airline,' I suggested. Five minutes in the airport and I was already the Queen of Sheba. This didn't bode well.

I had already been secretly panicking for about a week. My passport didn't have the required six months before its expiration needed to enter the US. I was just giddy I'd managed to hang onto the same passport for a whole ten years. Although the internet assured me I should be fine, I was cautioned by many that there was a chance I'd struggle to enter the US. Admin in winter is an impossibility for someone like me. As I've said, I have both crippling SAD and a fundamentally lazy disposition. So I decided I'd rather chance border control than walk to Snappy Snaps for a passport photo.

When I arrived at the airport we found the PR in a café. She was almost sick with worry about the downgrading.

'It's disappointing but we'll be OK,' I said with the haughty air of someone who has actually never travelled outside of economy. Norwegian had created a monster. And that monster wanted leg room.

'I know,' she said. 'It's a disaster. I can't get hold of the airline because it's a Sunday and the guys on the desk didn't know we were coming.'

'If it's OK,' said my new comrade, 'we won't be Instagramming about the flight.'

The PR took a deep breath. 'I've asked them to make sure we get premium meals and we've got you access to the lounge. I am so, so sorry.'

We assured her it was fine, then buggered off to buy neck pillows before hitting the lounge. I piled six miniature pastries onto my plate and ordered a full English. I was pleased to see that the PR and the fashion blogger both loved to eat as well. I don't think it's possible to put on weight when you're travelling. Likewise when you're heartbroken or grieving. Calories just cease to exist.

Eventually we boarded the plane and ordered some champagne. 'I'm sorry,' said the air stewardess, 'but only premium passengers are allowed to order alcoholic drinks.'

'We are premium passengers,' said the PR.

'Yes, but you have been downgraded.'

I sucked in my cheeks, saltily. The PR asked if she could talk to her superior. Ten minutes later the champagne arrived, replete with apology. When we landed, the air stewardess returned carrying blankets.

'These are the blankets they use in premium. If you want to take your photos in the premium seats when the passengers have disembarked that will be fine.'

The PR looked at us with pleading eyes. We shot her a look that said 'no fucking way.' I may have been gifted a free flight to LA, but it wasn't the flight I was promised.

When we disembarked I had to face the small issue that I might not be able to get into the country. I still hadn't told anyone about my passport and I was sweating like a drug mule. As soon as we hit border control, I approached a self-scanning machine and swiped my passport.

'Insufficient time on passport. See officer,' said the screen. I retched. If you're worried about getting through customs it is probably best to try to remain calm. If I had come any closer to a panic attack I would have been cavity searched. After an excruciating five minutes where the customs officer watched me squirm as I tried to explain I was an influencer, I was finally let in.

'So you're like a model?' he said, looking absolutely baffled. 'Sort of,' I replied. When I looked in the mirror I saw Worzel Gummidge.

When we arrived at the hotel I had never been so excited to see a bed. I'd barely slept on the plane and jet lag was hammering behind my eyes like a maniac. The fashion blogger looked at me pityingly. We had not come to LA to sleep.

Part of our deal was that we had to post pictures of every hotel we had stayed in as our rooms were #gifted. We were staying in a 'gram-friendly' hotel called The Kinney, which encircled a courtyard designed specifically for influencers. The walls were painted in pastel colours and neon signs and palm trees flanked a circular bar. It looked like someone had put a filter on the Tom Cruise film, *Cocktail*.

I took some ropey pictures of a hammock and posted them to my stories. We had been contracted to post at least four Instagram stories and one static post a day. I couldn't just make jokes about food. I knew my followers weren't going to like it.

True to my brand, I was at least the only person bad enough at photography to make the hotel look like a hostel. We had dinner with the tourist board to get through and we were expected to impress. By this time we'd been joined by two other influencers, one luxury fashion blogger and one twenty-two-year-old French 'comedian' with more followers than all of us put together, who spoke no English.

I was lurking in reception, waiting for my new pals, when suddenly three women bowled into the area, screaming. Before I knew it one of them had hurled her hoops on the ground and grabbed the others' weave. Ten minutes into my trip and I was involved in a brawl. Seeing the alarm on my face, the third woman shouted to me as the lift doors closed, 'Don't worry! We're sisters. We love each other really.' The receptionist called security.

The fashion bloggers emerged shortly after, looking like off-duty supermodels, and we were duly introduced to Vanessa from Discover LA. She gave us goodie bags with necklaces that read LA, sunglasses and reusable water bottles. She told us we were always welcome in California and that if we ever needed somewhere to stay when we came back, to look her up. I took a picture of her card.

We were having dinner at Gjelina's, a restaurant that featured heavily in the noughties' reality show, *The Hills*. The restaurant was lit like a sex dungeon and my flight-dry eyes had drooped to slits. Apparently, lights are foregone to protect the privacy of its diners. Still, I peered through the gloom and tried to spot Audrina or a less-famous Jenner. The fashion bloggers took some cool, sultry pictures while I pretended to climb a wine rack.

The next day the jet lag had hit even harder and I looked like I had clambered out of a coffin. We'd been asked to vlog our trip so I got up early and tried to feel normal about doing a tour of my hotel room. I 'unboxed' my goodie bag like a ghoul. Every time I caught my face in the mirror I jumped.

Glassy eyed and gangrenous was the best I could do, but I was desperate to salvage my look. I decided that today was a day for the over-priced skirt. Having been complimented by the fashion bloggers I resolved that it had been worth it and we set off to have our hair done before an afternoon of 'creating content'. Again I was asked with a quizzically raised eyebrow if I was 'really a model', again I explained that I satirised influencers but had also sort of become one. The hairdresser curled my hair into dreaded ringlets. My hair looked like wire wool.

Our itinerary that day consisted of a number of 'Instagram hotspots', which were mainly graffiti walls dotted around Los Angeles. The bloggers all packed bags of clothes and changed looks in the minibus as we travelled. Universal had hired professional photographers to document the trip and I dreaded my timeslot. After awkwardly posing on some steps while everyone watched, I turned around and lay down, pretending to fall. I just couldn't help myself. I was leaning into the role of 'court jester' – it was the only way I knew how to be.

Essentially, satirising my travel companions in front of their faces felt less awkward to me than trying to be like them. Kelly, the high-end fashion blogger, helped me to edit a photo to make the colours pop.

'You could be a normal influencer if you wanted to,' they assured me. The photographers begged me to pose for some 'cute shots' but I stood firm. I ate the first of many breakfast burritos and asked them to video me laughing at a salad.

It quickly became clear to me that not just anyone can be an 'influencer'. These girls could make anything look cool. When they posed with a pink phone in a restaurant they looked sassy. I looked like I needed to talc my thighs.

They always knew what to do with their faces, while I smiled so hard my face scrunched up and my eyes looked like tiny peas. It takes a huge amount of effort to look effortless. One of the girls had to shoot a lot of sponsored content when she was out there and she was fretting about being in LA.

'My followers don't like it when I go abroad,' she said. 'I've been setting an alarm for the middle of the night so I can wake up and reply to comments.' She told me that she'd been at a jewellery launch the week before where the PR had got quite aggressive about her posting at the event. She hounded her so hard she almost had a panic attack.

'Being an influencer is a balancing act. You have to keep the client happy and your followers happy. The last person in the pecking order is always you.'

The next day we headed off to Palm Springs via a roadside cactus farm where we were having yet another photoshoot. While the bloggers twirled near spiky vegetation, I went for a stroll near some greenhouses, before finding a cactus that looked like a penis and asking the PR to take a picture of me straddling it. This post at least broke a thousand likes.

I went back to the minibus/changing room to cool down, while the proper influencers got their shots. When the photographer got back into the bus I snooped as she edited photos.

'Maybe we could take a couple of nice ones,' I said. 'For my mum.'

I was absolutely ravenous when we arrived at what must be the world's most Instagrammable hotel. The Parker in Palm Springs is an influencer Eden, with *The Shining*-esque carpets, suits of armour and an enormous sign that read 'drugs' hanging over an open fire. It was here that my rules finally truly bit the dust. I ordered a side of lobster because I wanted to taste it. Before I knew it, I had necked three glasses of Whispering Angel and a photographer was taking pictures of me pretending to walk down some stairs. I gazed wistfully into the distance. This, I thought, must be what 'candid' feels like.

After a private tour around an Andy Warhol exhibition followed by drinks/yet another photoshoot at a hotel nestled within some picturesque mountains, we were off to our next destination. You have to cover a lot of ground when you need your four-day holiday to look like it lasted two weeks. It occurred to me that I should have packed more outfits. I'd graduated from the overpriced skirt to a denim shorts and t-shirt combo I would wear to the beach. Looking cool is hard and I was long overdue a nap. I could have stretched this content out for weeks, I thought. I was thinking like an influencer, but I still wasn't sure if I could really be one.

The minibus drove on into the night, while we sat and silently scrolled through our Instagrams, hoping that our followers didn't mind the time difference. The French girl was big on the app triller and was lip-syncing to songs and gurning at the camera. She was the kind of beautiful you have to be for your comedy to be described as 'goofy'. Her account was a blend of skits, selfies and fashion shoots. I thought about how my followers reacted when I wore makeup. It seemed she'd managed to have her cake and eat it.

When we finally stepped off the bus it was night and we were in the desert. It was cold and sandy and I couldn't stop thinking about the horror film *Wolf Creek*. My room was sparse and freezing. By the time I got into bed I had lost my phone charger and I was convinced my motel room was haunted.

A mysterious knocking on the roof and an active imagination do not a good night's sleep make. Within a couple of hours, I was sure that we were staying on an ancient Native American burial ground. I slept with one eye open, lest the ghost of Little White Feather possess me for ever more. When I woke up the fashion bloggers were already in their gladrags, posing for photos on the porch of the motel. Nobody had slept soundly. I couldn't wait to leave.

We headed off for a photoshoot in Joshua Tree National Park, where I did my best not to ruin any group shots. I had finally started getting used to having my photo taken and recovered from my jet lag. Joshua Tree is immense, a dustbowl surrounded by looming rock faces and scattered with cacti and the trees that are its namesake. Ironically, I was to be one of the last influencers to 'shoot' there that year. Influencer tourism was ravaging the national park, leading it to be closed so the trees could recover. I waited while the other influencers 'got the shot'.

To the photographer's devastation I insisted on pretending to pop a squat and piss by one of its famous trees. I opened my legs, revealing my knickers, and captioned it 'waiting for Coachella'. I think, deep down, I wished that I could feel comfortable enough to post a nice photo, but nothing makes me feel more like a twat than asking people to tell me I'm pretty. I have no issue with trying to extract laughter, but admiration doesn't come so easily. I don't think you should need external validation all of the time, or that seeking it from followers is healthy. But I had self-deprecated myself into the Californian dust. I was afraid to say that I was proud of myself, lest I be perceived as a dickhead. I wasn't ready to accept that I could be both.

By the end of the trip I was convinced that I had seen all the graffiti in Los Angeles. I'd been snapped in front of pink walls, blue walls, walls with wings on, cactus walls and rainbow stairs. My life on Instagram looked like a carefree laugh a minute and I was absolutely exhausted.

We spent our final night in lofts in the Ace Hotel in Downtown LA. I took a picture of me drinking a Sprite in my room and made a joke about green juice that fell entirely flat. I couldn't be both funny and aspirational. I couldn't have my cake and eat it too.

We hit the bar and nursed the next day's hangover in The Ivy. Within minutes I spotted three Real Housewives and almost crashed into Isabella Rossellini on my way to the bathroom. I ordered champagne, lobster ravioli and Key lime pie. I felt like a Kardashian, in a good way I thought. Sometimes pretending to be glamorous can feel glamorous all the same. We ate in spurts of silence while we Instagrammed our food, posting with the hashtag #ingridgoeswest. Somebody wondered whether it would be appropriate to stand on their chair to get a good shot of their main course. I looked around, 'I don't see why not.'

We left with bags of warm, freshly baked cookies which were more moreish to me than crack. Then we headed to Reformation on Melrose to millennialise our wardrobes. I bought clothes to wear in my real life. The others bought clothes to wear on their Instagram.

I was intrigued by how often they bought their own clothes when they got so much stuff for free. How much is worn once and discarded? Is there a charity shop somewhere filled with rails of #sponcon overspill?

One of the girls was given a clothing allowance by all major high-street fashion brands. Another was gifted a designer hand-bag from every seasonal drop. Some people, they say, buy things, photograph them with the tags in, then send them back.

'Do you ever worry,' I asked, 'that the content you make isn't what you actually like, but what other people want from you?'

'All the time.'

'Everything I do has to be luxurious or I tarnish my brand,' said one.

'I have posted a tea dress almost every day for six months,' said the other.

'But you're being yourselves, aren't you? You feel like you're authentic?'

'Of course!' they all answered. 'It wouldn't work if we weren't being ourselves.'

'The problem with what I do,' I said, 'is that people only care that I'm funny. And they only know I'm funny about one thing. I want to share more about myself. I want to really connect.'

They nodded in agreement.

'I think I like Bella more than Stella,' says Kelly when we part. Staring out of the window on my taxi ride home, I found myself hoping that the rest of the world would feel the same.

I sat in bed, scrolling through my posts from my trip to LA, and counted how many followers I'd lost since Deliciously Stella's peak: 15,000. Best to go out on a high, I told myself, you don't want to flog a dead horse.

People will like Bella as much as they like Stella, I told myself. And then I committed a murder.

I'm frowning in the picture, my mouth curled into a down-turned smile. I apply a sombre black and white filter, and I finally do that murder. I kill Deliciously Stella.

Immediately grief started pouring in from all corners of the internet. Everyone wanted to know why. What had I done? Didn't I know they needed me?

I worried I'd made a mistake. That I'd terminated my only hope for success. Nobody else had noticed how infrequently I'd been posting, that my engagement had dropped, that I'd lost almost 15,000 followers since my peak. The only person who cared about that was me, and that's why I had to stop.

Almost immediately Kelly called me. 'What's going on?' she asked. 'Are you OK? Why didn't you tell us you were going to kill her?'

'I'm going to have a go at being myself online,' I said.

'You're gonna smash it!' She promised.

I let the feeling of freedom and hope for the future wash over me. Finally, I was living my truth. Like all women, I am inconsistent, filled with conflict, funny, mean, stylish, loud, ambitious, anxious, a good friend, a poor friend, sexy, pretty, grotesque, kind.

My problem was that I didn't just want validation for being funny. I wanted validation for all of the parts of myself. I wanted my followers to confirm that I was good, that I was right, that I was somebody worth being.

Of course, this didn't happen. I was commissioned to write think pieces about my decision. I wrote that I wanted to post pictures of jumpers I like and of dogs. I wrote about my longing to be a bit more basic and a bit less cynical. I think what I really wanted was to be a bit more like everyone else. I wrote about my ambition to stop being a brand, my desire to express myself freely, to live my life online as a nuanced, multi-faceted person. What I hadn't realised in all my time of playing a character is that being yourself on Instagram just isn't possible.

Since Deliciously Stella's peak, I have lost 50,000 followers. For two years I told people I didn't care when every post caused people to defect in their droves. I was still partially financially dependent on the account, so I couldn't divorce myself from it completely. If I'm totally honest with myself, it's taken writing this book, living through a global pandemic, and learning who my friends really are for me to stop caring what the strangers who follow me think.

What I know now is that the people who follow you on Instagram can never know you. They only know the parts of you that you choose to present. You cannot make yourself appeal to all people all the time, and the pursuit of doing so will drive you mad.

I was desperately searching for my authentic self, but on Instagram I wasn't sure who that really was. In real life I am so many things to so many people. How do you distil yourself into a caption and a photo, and engage and connect with people who don't yet know who you are?

My first few posts as Bella felt strained. People were confused and the posts performed badly. My followers thought I was gone for good and yet here I was, trying to pull off an arty shot in my friend's kitchen. Without being able to corral the opinion of my followers, I wasn't sure who I was when I was online. I lost thousands of followers in only a few days.

The more I tentatively posted as myself, the further my following plummeted. I told myself it would level out, that people would start following Bella instead of Stella. All I needed to do was find out who Bella was as a brand. It didn't take long to figure out there was no way to do that and stay well. I knew I couldn't carry on as an influencer. I needed to get offline and be myself. I needed to get a job.

'What are you going to do for money?' asked my parents, when I told them I'd decided to quit both Instagram and my attempts to get a new agent.

'I'm thinking about writing a book,' I said.

My dad put his head in his hands.

'But I'll get a normal, reliable job first, so I'm solvent and leaving the house.'

He breathed a sigh of relief. The thought of me sitting at home all day watching my career swirl down the toilet was too much to bear.

'I'm not sure your insurance will cover another Priory stint, is all.'

'Dad. Are you ready to joke about it now?'

'Sort of,' he said, before wrapping me in a hug.

I'd been mulling over what I might be good at apart from comedy for some time. I didn't want to go back to working in TV, it felt like a step back, and while I was making a bit from freelance journalism, it wouldn't be enough to fill the hole that influencing would leave in my salary. There was one other thing that I had become very good at, and that was social media.

I'd been moonlighting as a community manager for Channel 4 for a few months when I killed Stella. I was live-tweeting episodes of *First Dates*, relying on my ability to pull a witty gif under pressure.

I'd heard from Emily about a company that hired comedians to be funny on Twitter. I looked them up, emailed the CEO and asked him if I could give it a go. As luck would have it, he was the comedian David Schneider and he was a Deliciously Stella fan. My trial was to live-tweet an episode of *Hollyoaks*, using a brief story outline sent to me in advance. A lot happens in the unlucky village of *Hollyoaks*. A typical episode outline would be: 'Tony steals Jackie's nan's wheelchair. Runs into Warren who is having an orgy. Warren sets everyone on fire.'

I took to it like a duck to water and started consulting businesses on their social media strategies. I designed a personality for the Mr. Men character Little Miss Sunshine, I briefly worked for *Dave*, 'The Home of Witty Banter'. Unfortunately my style of humour wasn't quite bantery enough and I left after being reprimanded for tweeting that strippers would be flying at half-mast the day that Peter Stringfellow died.

I only had two rules: 1) That I had at least one day off a week to write whatever novel/script/sketch/treatment I was currently working on; 2) I wouldn't work from home. At first being recognised from my Instagram in the office was embarrassing, but I'd finally accepted that life's too short to do something because other people think it should make you happy. It seems absurd that a breakthrough in my happiness came from having a desk job, but what I'd been lacking had been structure and security. I'm an extrovert, a people person, an office jester. I suffer alone and I thrive amongst others, that's why I love being on set so much. It's why I like making things with other people. Of course, I hate commuting, I hate meetings that should have been emails, I hate Studio 54-themed office parties, but I love camaraderie. I love hearing about people's weekends, I love trying to make my colleagues laugh. Most of all I love interacting with people in real life. I no longer live my life through a screen.

Deliciously Stella was a once-roaring fire that had finally reduced to just embers. I was damned if I was going to hang around to poke it with a stick. The final Google alert I received was to notify me that somebody was selling my book on Gumtree for a pound. Instead of making me feel sick, this made me laugh. Nobody could take away what I'd achieved with my Instagram. And I wasn't any less of a person for walking away from it. I didn't have to be special. I could just be free.

# Conclusion

I really want to be able to tie this story in a neat little bow. To say that I've deleted all my social media accounts, that I no longer outsource my validation, that what people think of me doesn't affect me anymore. But I can't. Those apps have become so embedded in our culture and for me in my career that it would be extremely difficult for me to do so. For now I have accepted that I must find the healthiest way possible to work within this system. I need social media to promote my work, I still occasionally post sponsored content, but I don't rely on it entirely for my income. I'm quick to notice I'm scrolling more when I'm anxious or tired. I do have a much more healthy relationship with social media. My follower number is still going down and I can finally honestly say it doesn't make me feel a pang of sorrow when people leave. I've accepted that there isn't a magic level of success. There is no magic follower number I can reach that will make me happy. No accolade that can give me the invincibility that I craved. It's been said that it's impossible to be both happy and ambitious. Every time I achieved a goal the goal posts moved further away.

When the pandemic hit, I moved to Mallorca, an island relatively untroubled by the virus, where my parents have a house. Nobody there knew or cared who I was. Nobody even spoke enough English for me to explain. For the first time in years, I was on my own with only myself to rely on. I started deleting Instagram from my phone for days at a time. I walked in the mountains and swam in the sea. I revelled in making new friends as Bella. I found pleasure in things outside of my phone and my career. In a way the pandemic gave me permission to finally let go of my life as an influencer. I posted freely and without consistency. I posted what I felt like sharing. I was definitely no longer a brand.

For a lot of people, the pandemic made it clear who their real friends were. It was the people you rang for a chat or met up with for a socially distanced walk. The people you offered to do a shop for and the ones who threw chocolate fingers through your window when you had the virus. The best relationships you have are the ones that go both ways. They aren't performed or filtered. They are intimate and mutually rewarding.

When Tim Kreider wrote that, 'If we want the full rewards of being loved, we have to submit to the mortifying ordeal of being known,' he can't have foreseen how many of us would try to obscure ourselves through our screens. You can feel like you're loved on Instagram, but you'll never truly be known. I'm looking for more than digital hearts. Likes and follows have finally stopped serving me. They thud dully into my timeline and I rejoice, for I am finally free.

# Acknowledgements

Thanks must firstly go to my agent, Laura, who persuaded me that the world is not yet tired of mental health memoirs and that I might be able to write a good one. To my editor, Katya. Thanks for being an epic cheerleader and for teaching me the power of editing. To all of the people who helped to shape the book: Zoe, Holly and Amandeep. Amandeep, your wise counsel got me to the finish line. I am so grateful. Faye Stewart, boss turned pal and all-round hilarious human, without you Stella and this book would not exist. Thanks for making it all happen. I'd like to thank my family, who have endured me the longest. Mum, Dad, Beana, Francesca and Geordie. Sorry for the things I said when I was mad. Thanks for having such brilliant senses of humour. A special mention must go to my pig, Emily Vaughan Barratt, who stayed in with me on New Year's Eve, fixed my broken projector and never stopped telling me I was talented. You are a brilliant friend, and not just because you introduced me to The King in the North. My therapist, Alice, and my psychiatrist, Dr Hopley, you got me through writing a book in a pandemic with less tears than I thought possible. And finally, thanks must go to my health insurers, AXA PPP healthcare. I'm sure you're sorry you took me on, and I know I've cost a bomb, but I really, really couldn't have done it without you.